Management and managed

Management and managed

Fifty years of crisis at Chrysler

STEVE JEFFERYS

Department of Economics and Economic History,
Manchester Polytechnic

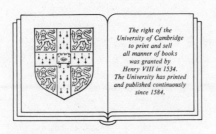

The right of the
University of Cambridge
to print and sell
all manner of books
was granted by
Henry VIII in 1534.
The University has printed
and published continuously
since 1584.

CAMBRIDGE UNIVERSITY PRESS

Cambridge
London   New York   New Rochelle
Melbourne   Sydney

Published by the Press Syndicate of the University of Cambridge
The Pitt Building, Trumpington Street, Cambridge CB2 1RP
32 East 57th Street, New York, NY 10022, USA
10 Stamford Road, Oakleigh, Melbourne 3166, Australia

First published 1986

Printed in Great Britain at the University Press, Cambridge

British Library cataloguing in publication data

Jefferys, Steve
Management and managed: fifty years of crisis
at Chrysler.
1. Chrysler Corporation – History   2. Industrial
relations – United States – History – 20th century
I. Title
331'.04292'0973   HD6976.A82U5

Library of Congress cataloguing in publication data

Jefferys, Steve.
Management and managed.
Bibliography.
Includes index.
1. Strikes and lockouts – Automobile industry – United
States.   2. Chrysler Corporation.   I. Title.
HD5325.A8J44 1986   331'.04292'097385-30910

ISBN 0 521 30441 5

For Joan and Kerry

Contents

Figures

Tables

Preface

> Someone manages and someone is managed, and this is an eternal
> opposition of interest, which may be made bearable but can never be
> eliminated in a complex, industrial society.
>   Clark Kerr, *American Journal of Sociology*, November 1954

Chrysler Corporation has been the most strike-torn of the big three
American automobile manufacturers. Between 1937 and 1958 it had
more big strikes involving over 10,000 workers than its rivals Ford and
General Motors, while from 1940 to 1980 it had ten times as many strikes
per workers as GM. An even more important difference between
Chrysler and GM during those forty years was in strikes that occurred
without official sanction from the international UAW: for every hour a
GM worker lost on unauthorized strikes, a Chrysler worker lost 8.2
hours; and at GM just 4% of all striker-hours were unauthorized
while at Chrysler the figure was 29%.[1]

Much can be learned about the American working class, the labor
process and managerial control by examining why huge firms operating
similar technology in the same market should experience such different
strike profiles. This book places the changing pattern of conflict at the
point of production in the context of a changing political world within
which managers and managed co-exist. To fully explain the underlying
trends requires detailed analysis of the workplace politics of the companies. The main focus of this study is on Chrysler and its flagship Dodge
Main plant, a company and a workplace with a high level of visible
conflict from the first trace of mass unionism in 1933 to the economic
recession of 1979–82.

The history of industrial relations at Chrysler shows important worker
restraints on management's freedoms being regularly exercised until the

late 1950s. It also reveals considerable local union independence from the international union machine – at least until the early 1960s. Similar worker restraints and local union independence had been lost anything between ten and fifteen years earlier at GM, and between five and ten years earlier at Ford. This different history developed unintentionally out of the interaction of Chrysler management's autocratic and anti-labor management with an increasingly 'rights' conscious labor force in the 1930s and 1940s. Despite Chrysler's generally successful recovery of control in the three years from 1957 to 1959 (a watershed in Chrysler labor relations), traces of this earlier tradition survived to fuse with the new assertiveness of the black workers' movement of the late 1960s and early 1970s. In the mid 1970s, a second significant shift in the balance of forces between management and labor in Chrysler occurred. This eliminated what was left of the 1960s' fusion and prepared the way for Chrysler workers' precedent-setting acceptance of concessions between 1979 and 1981.

This study, by showing that the balance of power between management and managed was in contention *throughout* the last fifty years in a core US company, challenges a rigid tripartite periodization of recent American working class history. The scenario of the 'militant' 1930s, of a passive continuity from World War II to the late 1960s, and of a new 'militancy' in the late 1960s and 1970s, doesn't fit Chrysler.[2] Kerr's 'eternal opposition of interest' is a better description of the Chrysler experience. This study also challenges assumptions about the greater passivity of the American labor movement and suggests fewer divergences between the American and British workplace experience than has usually been assumed.[3] It supports the conclusion that the American working class is not peculiarly backward and helps explain why workers' responses to the late 1970s recession have been remarkably similar in both countries.

In the course of the narrative three key industrial relations questions are also confronted: First, how does management exert its control over the labor process? Second, how are changes in managerial control legitimized in workers' own beliefs? Third, how are particular traditions of workplace behavior and worker organization created? To answer it is important to understand the process of simultaneous consent and resistance in the workplace, the change in balance between both, and their different degrees of intensity over time. This is more problematic than a simple counterposing of 'managerial control' to 'workers' ... strong unilateral control'.[4] Management, the study argues, is a highly complex, contradictory and as political a process as is the collective organization of workers.

The early chapters introduce the reader to current theories of the development of the labor process and managerial control and outlines an alternative perspective. Rather than assume the dominance of any one control system, or of a rigid periodization, the evidence of an historical survey of one major auto company suggests the continuing presence of both worker resistance and worker accommodation (Chapter 1). The following chapter challenges certain interpretations of recent American labor history and locates the development of the Union of Automobile Workers (UAW) against the major political changes that affected labor relations between 1928 and 1983 (Chapter 2).

The Chrysler narrative begins by showing how weak management and weak unionism at Dodge Main in the 1930s interacted to produce a particularly powerful shopfloor unionism (Chapters 3–4). It demonstrates how the frontier of managerial control at Dodge Main was continuously struggled over as management attempted to re-establish its autonomy in the 1940s and 1950s (Chapters 5–7). In the 1960s and 1970s it examines the way Chrysler adapted its managerial control system to undermine the new challenge of the black movement (Chapters 8–9). The narrative ends in the early 1980s when Chrysler workers voted to accept pace-setting contract concessions (Chapter 10). The final chapter summarizes this historical micro-study, concluding that Chrysler's relatively high levels of open conflict were the product not of a super-militant labor force but of management failure under conditions of considerable market pressure. Elsewhere in the US auto industry managements were able to suppress open conflict more effectively, while Chrysler management performed similarly in many ways to the ineffective management of the UK car industry (Chapter 11).

I owe much to Warwick University for help in writing this book. Its industrial relations department gave me a doctoral studentship and encouragement to research into the origins of shopfloor unionism, while its Industrial Relations Research Unit gave me a room and a stimulating atmosphere in which to work. To all staff and fellow postgraduates, my thanks. The Social Science Research Council funded my initial research at Warwick and did not blink an eyelid when I turned from Birmingham and Glasgow to Detroit. In the United States the Walter Reuther Library of Wayne State University, Detroit, was my home for several months in 1981 and 1982, and I'd like to thank the staff there too.

Several individuals played key parts by reading various drafts of the book and making extremely helpful and encouraging suggestions as to how to develop its argument. Willy Brown, now at Cambridge University, and Paul Edwards of the Warwick Industrial Relations Research Unit are the two whose encouragement and criticism on various drafts went far beyond the call of duty. Richard Hyman, also of Warwick, Nelson Lichtenstein of the Catholic University, Washington DC, Craig Zabala of the US Department of Commerce, Howell Harris of Durham University, Steve Wood of the London School of Economics, Chris Smith of Aston University and Joan Smith of North Staffordshire Polytechnic have read all or part of various drafts and all made very useful criticisms. Finally, I would like to thank Dave Lyddon, a fellow Warwick postgraduate and old friend, who, like myself, worked for several years in the British motor industry. He gave freely of his enormous knowledge in the area and with Mary Issitt actually made the whole endeavor humane.

Of course, while acknowledging their assistance, I must add that I remain wholly responsible for the book's arguments and its inevitable shortcomings, two of which I feel I should point out here. One arose from my failure to gain access to Chrysler's own archives, which had been closed in the company's economy drive. The result is that this book cannot do what I would have liked, that is to interweave a full business history of Chrysler based on original source material into the texture of its labor relations. The second obvious shortcoming, the absence of a systematic treatment of women workers in Dodge Main, stemmed quite simply from a lack of research time in Detroit. Those issues which were not conveniently accessible had to be left on one side, and Dodge Main's women workers were certainly hidden from history in the Walter Reuther archives. I believe, however, that the book's narrative still stands. It would have been richer if these omissions had not been present, but there was nothing in what I did uncover that makes me feel its argument would have been significantly different.

Part I
Introduction

1   Management, managed and control

This chapter outlines the general line of enquiry taken in the book. It first argues for detailed historical examinations of changes in the labor process and managerial control systems before rushing to generalize (section I). It then sketches the high-strike profile of Chrysler Corporation (section II). Finally it introduces an approach to management and the collectivity of workers that sees them as complex and changing processes rather than as finished actors on the stage of history (section III).

I. The need for dynamic history

Investigations of the historical dynamic of company-level labor relations are rare in the US.[1] A recent study of American labor in World War II commented on the 'vacuum in historical understanding' of shopfloor experience.[2] And an American sociologist with four years' personal experience of work in the auto industry is more strident still: 'The industrial relations literature is devoid of rigorous studies of the behavioral underpinnings of micro collective bargaining or of the impact of trade unionism on the formation and consciousness of American workers.'[3]

Why has there been this neglect? In part the presence of deceptively similar formal institutionalized bargaining procedures has fostered a narrow focus. This is encouraged by a reliance on the US Bureau of Labor Statistics strike data which under-reports workplace stoppages, and is not particularly sensitive to important inter-firm differences.[4] But the most important reason for the neglect has been political. Managerial welfarism in the 1910s and 1920s spawned industrial relations experts in the 1930s and 1940s who saw themselves as advisors to management on the control of labor. In 1941 Slichter's influential study *Union Policies and Industrial Management* made this clear:

Protecting the status of management and preserving its essential prerogatives have not been a sufficiently definite objective of either union or employers policy in building up our system of industrial jurisprudence ...
The workers, though they have an interest in preventing arbitrary decisions by management, also need to have the management able to maintain reasonable efficiency.[5]

Twenty years later he made these managerial aims still more explicit, writing that 'in case of conflict' between the needs of management and the workers, the book's 'orientation is provided by the goals of management'.[6] Most social scientists who examined American industrial relations in the 1950s and 1960s assumed that open conflict was bad or unnecessary or both, and that the tendency of union organizations to emulate the oligarchic structure of business was either unavoidable or a positive good.[7] Research tended to focus on the strengths of pluralistic institutions rather than on their limitations.

Meanwhile, outside the academic milieu, the post-war isolation of the US Communist Party and the dominance of Maoism and neo-Maoist ideas within the American New Left reinforced assumptions about the impotence of the American working class.[8] Coming from this background, Braverman and his critics appear to take management for granted. They credit management with the capacity to conceive, develop and execute a universally effective labor control strategy.[9] There is no sense of the interaction of management and managed in Braverman, whose important work *Labor and Monopoly Capital* initiated the current debate about the relationship of capital, the labor process and labor beliefs. His endeavor to draw 'a picture of the working class as it exists, as the shape given to the working population by capital accumulation',[10] however powerful and illuminating, is ultimately flawed by the assumption that it is possible to draw such a picture without building in the political and organizational experience of the working class at the outset. A critique made of Marx's neglect of 'supervisory requirements and existing managerial structures' in the nineteenth-century cotton industry bears powerfully on Braverman: 'Marx derived his conclusion of the omnipotence of technology in the subjection of labour to capital from an uncritical acceptance of capitalist ideology, instead of using his theoretical framework for an empirical investigation of the *interaction of the relations and forces of production* in cotton spinning.' [my italic][11]

Managerial control systems do *not* always correspond with the dominant managerial ideology of the moment.[12] The interaction of workers with management impacts back on management's response to technological change. The contradictory views workers hold about technological

change reflect a sense of workplace legitimacy which is also shaped by full
employment or unemployment, and by the dominant political identity of
the day.[13] Workers must be seen as workers in a particular historical
context who both accept and reject the beliefs of the time according to
their own experience of life, organization and struggle.

A lack of awareness of the historical interaction between living forces
in the capital–labor relationship also overwhelms those who have criticized Braverman from a dual labor market approach. The failure to
capture the presence of both shopfloor resistance and accommodation in
working class history is the principal defect of *Segmented work, Divided
Workers*. Gordon *et al.* explain working class behavior in terms of major
shifts in managerial control strategies related to long-term business
cycles. They see the years from World War I to World War II as
volatile years of transition from the earlier phase of the 'homogenization of labor' and 'drive' control to the period when 'the segmentation
of labor forged and reproduced materially based divisions among US
workers that inhibited the growth of a unified working-class movement'.[14]

This analysis brushes aside evidence of continuing shopfloor conflict in
the post-war period – designated as a 'labor truce' – in the same way it
ignores evidence that the 1930s 'labor upsurge' was much less widespread
than has generally been assumed. Labor relations are viewed as a
residual element left over after managers have finished managing.
Workers are either quiescent or in rebellion. Evidence that both
moments coexisted throughout the last fifty years is ignored because it
means that shopfloor conflict has to be brought back to the center of a
theory of industrial relations from which their structural labor market
determinism and long-swing capitalist cycles theory has just pushed it.
The 'segmented-privileged' argument and its corollary, the assumption
of pure working-class consciousness somewhere else, do not tackle the
problem of changing levels and forms of struggle. Indeed, since they tend
to dismiss all post-war American working class activity as inherently
divisive or as utterly determined by outside economic forces,[15] their
generalizations ultimately fail to come to grips with the dynamic of
change that has taken place.

While it is necessary to generalize about the consequences of change it
is crucial to first understand the process of change. Another of Braverman's critics, Michael Burawoy, has filled out our knowledge about how
the organization of work can help control and shape workers' consciousness. But his argument that the 'manufacturing of consent' to the
subordination of labor to capital takes place primarily in the workplace at
the point of production is an overstatement.[16] His study recognizes that

accommodation and resistance are intertwined, but dissent and the possibility of it being mobilized through plant committeemen or union stewards does not appear.[17] It is not difficult to demonstrate that workers experience 'inhibitions against class consciousness in everyday industrial relations'.[18] But to look *only* at the 'inhibitions' in the immediate work environment is to fall into a classic error of the 'human relations' school.[19] The Chrysler experience shows how important the outside world was in shaping and reshaping the limits of workplace legitimacy. The Roosevelt 'rights' explosion', leftism, anti-communism and Black Power all impacted massively on the workers and managers to give a distinctive shape to the 'factory regime'.[20]

The examination of the impact of political change on workers and managers and of how the process of change affects the shopfloor is a necessary complementary approach to an exclusive focus on the nature of work and the organization of the labor process. Factory and office environments do provide a degree of autonomy from exogenous influences. The range of consciousness, organization and activity within the *same* industry among workers and managements facing the same technology, work organization and payment system illustrates this point. But this does still not deny the significance of social and political attitudes that the actors take into the different environments.

By focusing on the frontier of interaction between management and managed this study is able to demonstrate a highly complex pattern of internally- and externally-shaped determinants that defy gross generalization but still permit some theorization. The challenge is to present the historical dynamic of American working class experience in such a way as to embrace both consent within resistance and resistance within conformity – without idealizing workers by viewing these components of consciousness as incompatible. Section II argues that a longitudinal profile of one important company raises questions that can only be answered through a detailed examination of the historical dynamic of the labor relations of its major plant.

II. Chrysler: profile of conflict

Chrysler was America's tenth largest corporation for most of the last fifty years and was a key core firm in the post-war economy before it made America's biggest-ever loss of more than $1 billion in 1979. Its size and strength make possible effective inter-firm comparisons with the other major automakers, General Motors and Ford, whose technology and markets were very similar. MacDonald's twenty-year-old study of collective bargaining in the US auto industry had already

Table 1 *Work stoppages at Chrysler's US locations, 1940–80*

Five yearly averages	Annual average number of strikes		Annual average manhours lost in strikes	
	Unauthorized	Authorized	Unauthorized	Authorized
1940–44	110	0	485,882	0
1945–49	120	(a)	1,118,437	(a)
1950–54	128	(b)	1,644,510	(b)
1955–59	289	1.2	2,471,528	1,458,212
1960–64	14	2.2	81,349	284,891
1965–69	46	1.6	359,975	514,749
1970–74	62	4.6	308,813	1,174,001
1975–79	33	6	215,179	120,532
1980	3	0	39,269	0
Total 1940–80	4,009	(c)81	33,467,861	80,964,399

Source: Company data.
(a) One authorized strike in 1948 with 9,572,968 manhours lost.
(b) Two authorized strikes: a 104 day strike in 1950 with 53,614,805 manhours lost (two thirds of the total manhours lost in authorized stoppages over the whole 41 years), and one in 1952 with 14,700 manhours lost.
(c) There were only three authorized strikes [see notes (a) and (b)] from 1940 to 1956. From 1957 to 1980 there were authorized strikes in every year except 1965, 1972, 1975 and 1980.

observed that 'under collective bargaining ... differences in labor practices were in large part attributable to the differences in the judgment, skill and foresight exercised by respective managements'.[21] These differences are clearly highlighted by the contrasting strike rate of Chrysler and the other major automakers.

The statistics Chrysler kept itself reveal, in table 1, that all but 2% of Chrysler's recorded strikes between 1940 and 1980 were unauthorized. Unauthorized strikes predominated during the 1940s and 1950s, with a dramatic drop in 1959 following a small but distinct recovery from 1966 providing four lesser peaks of strike activity – in 1968, 1970, 1973 and 1977. The sharp break in strike trend in 1959 is repeated for manhours lost.[22] The year 1959 was also a turning point in the UAW's willingness to sanction official action against Chrysler outside of the national contract negotiations, and two-thirds of all authorized strikes against Chrysler from 1940 to 1980 occurred in the ten years after 1967.[23]

Chrysler had both more large and more unauthorized strikes per employee than General Motors or Ford from 1937 to 1958. These two decades of high strike frequency contrast with a much reduced strike rate during the 1960s and 1970s, but even then Chrysler workers were on strike more often than GM or Ford workers. Over the years from 1937 to

Table 2 *Chrysler and General Motors, strike frequency rates per 1,000 hourly paid workers, 1940–79*

Five yearly averages	Chrysler		General Motors[a]	
	Unauthorized strikes/1000	All strikes frequency	Unauthorized strikes/1000	All strikes frequency
1940–44	1.57	1.57	0.24	0.24
1945–49	1.74	1.75	0.13	0.13
1950–54	1.47	1.47	0.11	0.11
1955–59	3.50	3.52	0.10	0.11
1960–64	0.23	0.26	0.09	0.10
1965–69	0.48	0.50	0.09	0.21
1970–74	0.62	0.66	0.07	0.11
1975–79	0.35	0.41	0.02	0.06

Source: Company data.
[a] GM data not available for 1940, 1941 and 1975. The averages for 1940–44 and 1975–79 are therefore calculated on less than the full five year spans.

1978 Chrysler experienced over twice as many big strikes – involving over 10,000 workers – as Ford, and slightly more than GM – despite having a smaller workforce.[24] Chrysler's large strikes were concentrated before 1959 and its large strike frequency rate dropped to the industry 'norm' after 1959.[25]

Chrysler's strike frequency rate (the frequency with which strikes occurred per 1,000 Chrysler manual employees), shown in table 2, contrasts the dramatic change in Chrysler's strike pattern after 1959 with a barely perceptible movement at GM. The average annual unauthorized strike frequency was five times higher in the twenty years from 1940 than in the twenty years after 1959. From 1941 to 1958 Chrysler's all-strike frequency only fell below one per 1,000 hourly paid workers in two years (1953 and 1954); while after 1958 it only reached 0.9 per 1,000 twice (in 1968 and 1977). At GM, by contrast, the average unauthorized frequency started at a much lower level and only slipped significantly in the 1970s. Why there should have been a strike hiatus at Chrysler in the late 1950s is a central part of the narrative.

Two graphs illustrate the divergent strike rates between Chrysler and GM since 1940. Figure 1 graphs the unauthorized Chrysler and GM strike frequencies on an annual basis and shows a major divergence between the two companies from 1955 to 1960. Figure 2 (p.10) shows the contrasting record of hours lost per worker between Chrysler and GM and highlights Chrysler's late 1950s hiatus. Its unauthorized loss rate only fell below ten hours a year twice between 1941 and 1958, and only once

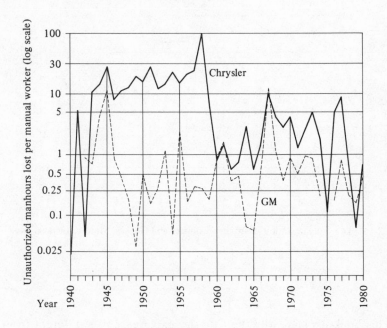

Fig. 1   Unauthorized strike loss ratio, Chrysler and General Motors, 1940–80

reached ten hours in the years that followed. The narrative part of the book explains the movement of the pattern of conflict at Chrysler from unauthorized strikes, and then to virtually no strikes, against the background of changes in management and union organization in a single, key plant, Dodge Main.

One company has been chosen for the study so that the way in which management exercises control over the labor process can be tested in a specific historical context. The approach adopted here is an historical reconstruction of the industrial relations pattern in a single plant. Detailed surveys of the industrial relations systems in single plants are a recognized research method,[26] but this study is trying to understand the dynamics of change, so it has taken one further step. It presents a factory micro historical account over a fifty-year period and so tries to overcome the weakness of most industrial relations studies, which are too close to one particular situation, and of most broad historical studies, which are not close enough.

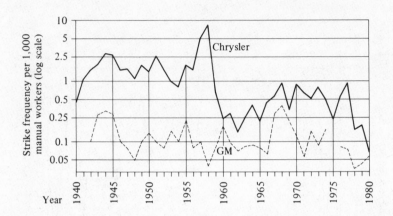

Fig. 2   Strike frequency ratio (all strikes), Chrysler and General Motors, 1940–80

This book explains why the Chrysler experience was different from GM's and suggests that an historical approach to workplace struggle offers significant insights for the understanding of industrial relations. It recognizes that conditions outside the workplace crucially influence managerial control. These include the supply of labor (including its political, ethnic and religious dimensions); labor legislation; and the form and extent of union organization and activity.[27] The study also stresses a critical fourth condition: the form and history of management organization and activity. A recent study of the Brazilian auto industry points out:

> When these influences are taken into account, the factory is no longer seen as a subsystem largely independent of the wider society. Rather, it becomes a site at which the relations between labor and capital, as a whole are brought to bear on the particular terrain of concrete labor processes and concrete managerial practices.[28]

A factory study that stresses the impact of external influences can become the basis of generalizations about capital–labor relations in society as a whole.

Why choose Dodge Main for such a study? A longitudinal historical section of Dodge Main has several advantages. First, three generations of autoworkers and their managers worked in the plant during the period covered. Perhaps over 200,000 different men and women had significant parts of their working lives shaped within Dodge Main's factory walls. By taking the long view and narrowing the focus to one plant over such a long period of time detailed consideration can be given to the process of change in their lives. Second, the selection of a plant as central to Chrysler's business activities as Dodge Main, which consistently employed between 15% and 50% of its entire workforce, allows top management's company-wide policy to be closely monitored.

Finally, the historical study of 'processes at the micro level'[29] also tests the relevance of the conceptual categories introduced in the next section: the concepts of managerial control, power and authority, of worker-imposed, operational and societal restraints on managerial authority, of a sense of workplace legitimacy and of organizational 'independence'. As another plant-level study argues, the method allows 'a concreteness' lacking in both institutional and populist/syndicalist approaches.[30]

III. Management restrained

What is management? A pioneering study of British management suggested it could be viewed as an 'elite social grouping', as an 'economic resource performing a series of technical functions', and as a 'system of authority through which policy is translated into the execution of tasks'.[31] Each perspective reveals management as a process rather than a fixed and permanent entity. At Chrysler, management was at times a totally closed family while at others the elite was more open to new blood and new ideas. It performed technical functions efficiently on some occasions and inefficiently on others. At one moment it would choose one authority system, then abandon it for another soon after. So this study of the interaction of management and managed will have to examine how management is moulded.

Workers' independent activity, for example, tended to be more assertive in those spaces left for it by management, while managerial authority was most assertive when working class resistance was weakest. But how were spaces left by management at some times and not at others? Sometimes the answer lies in the leeway, or managerial discretion, allowed to individual managers in policy execution.[32] But discretion afforded top managers included a limited, but definite, choice in policy formation. The breadth of 'strategic choice' as to which policy to formulate and implement depended on the specific circumstances, on the quality of individual top managers, and on an effective decision-making managerial structure. The combination meant that when strategic choices were made, managers' politics and prejudices ensured that the decisions were not 'neutral', taken rationally purely in terms of non-competing organizational objectives.[33] Managerial discretion and managerial strategic choice make the history of the managerial elite, and of the structural and market constraints influencing it, crucial for understanding labor relations conflict.

The concept of 'managerial control' will be used to embrace the 'power' wielded by capital over workers in the labor market and the subsequent 'authority' system management uses to ensure particular work tasks are completed.[34] In broad terms then, management has two kinds of relations with its employees: economic 'market relations' lay down the terms and conditions on which labor is hired, and 'managerial relations' arise out of what management seeks to do with its labor having hired it.[35] While no Chinese wall divides the external from the internal labor market, or managerial power from authority, it is useful to remember that since both are flexible they do not always keep in step. Different aspects of managerial control can change at different times.[36] At Chrysler, managerial economic power increased significantly in the 1930s but was accompanied by the erosion of managerial authority. Only after the recession of 1979–82 did Chrysler's economic power and its workplace authority begin to move together in the same direction.

Managerial economic power is not a fixed historical given. The power resources of different units of capital vary enormously in size, use and degree of capital mobility and ease of access. Habit, mismanagement, conscious self-restraint and changes in managerial ideology can all check the maximizing of profit. State legislation, or other forms of political pressure, workers' collective pressure and changes in the product and product technology can also check economic power.

Managerial authority determines how work is organized and executed in the workplace. Management's prevailing politics and discipline secures adherence to the effort bargain – what is promised by workers in return for their wages. At its core the concept of managerial authority is about what Goodrich described as 'How the worker is treated – what sort of authority he is under, how much freedom he is allowed'.[37] Its flexibility lies in the fact that what workers 'promise' they do not necessarily deliver, and that what managers initially ask for they do not always want.

The 'frontier of control' between managerial authority and workers' self-organization is often very difficult to locate.[38] Some restraints over managerial authority owe little to positive worker resistance and a great deal to management. As Goodrich found: 'There is a significant psychological difference between "admission" and "invasion", between control presented to and control seized by a trade union.'[39] Since management's influence extends also to the shaping of shopfloor union organization, the difficulties in establishing the limits of management's unilateral shopfloor authority are clearly considerable.[40]

In this study a distinction is drawn between 'worker-imposed' restraints, which were brought about and maintained by collective industrial action, and 'operational' and 'societal' restraints. Worker-imposed restraints arise from contests between managerial authority and worker resistance. The achievement of a struggled-for concession, and its maintenance through continual ideological and industrial mobilization of workers against their employer, has different implications for labor relations than a restraint introduced by management to improve the plant's operational efficiency or in response to legislation.

The scope and level of formal collective bargaining clearly influenced the opportunities available for workers to codify these restraints, and codification itself changed their character. At Chrysler, over the last forty years, the proportion of worker-imposed restraints over managerial authority has fallen as some have been permanently lost and others (such as seniority) codified. By comparison, 'operational' restraints (such as management being obliged to provide efficient elevators so workers can arrive and leave quickly) or 'societal' or social restraints (such as non-discriminatory hiring established by legislation or other forms of external political pressure) have come to dominate formal bargaining. This development was much less the result of conscious managerial control strategies than of a continuing labor–management conflict in which the accumulation of serious organizational and political defeats eventually eroded labor's ability to maintain its worker-imposed restraints.

The shift in the *source* of restraints on management does not mean operational and social restraints do not impede managerial authority. Indeed, the possibility of political or industrial mobilization by workers in defense of these restraints is a key factor in constraining management from acting consistently in its own short-term profit-maximizing interest. A restraint remains a limitation for management regardless of its origins.[41] The argument here is that the presence or absence of worker-imposed restraints is one measure of the strength and strategizing capacity of shopfloor unionism as an independent factor influencing managerial response.

The body of restraints on managerial autonomy exercised by workers is often confused with 'job control'. One reason for this confusion is that the term 'craft control', which is a special form of job restriction exercised by those who possess skill and knowledge that the employers lack, is often used indiscriminately.[42] Clearly a *fair* seniority system for lay-offs is not in the same league as the insistence on a special apprenticeship before a worker is allowed to do a particular job. 'Control' should also not be confused with fair practices conceded by management. To isolate one restraint on managerial authority and to elevate its significance as a 'control' over management, is to idealize that moment of workplace organization. Such an idealization deprives the observer of the language and the understanding to describe accurately historical periods in which the social relations or production are actually being challenged.

The term 'job control' is loaded: it carries the assumptions of pre-mass production 'craft control'[43] or of post-mass production 'workers' control'.[44] Although both of these ideologies were present in Chrysler plants, neither dominated workers' collective consciousness. Instead, workers' actions took place in the context of underlying commonsense beliefs about what they could 'legitimately' do. What was believed legitimate was composed of strands of craftism and workers' control, but also of changing political views on workers' rights and of observations of what management allowed. All of these strands create what I have called a sense of 'workplace legitimacy'.

The workers' sense of how far they are justified in taking action to restrain managerial authority is established by the interaction of three key elements: tradition, recent experiences of workplace struggle and workers' politics (ideology and organization).[45] The concept of workplace legitimacy has an important implication for changing levels of labor combativity. For if workers' responses to management actions and to movements in the labor market depend crucially on their understanding of what is 'legitimate', then the ability of the employers' world view to shape workers' views of legitimacy becomes a major factor determining worker combativity.[46]

Workplace legitimacy is not, of course, the exclusive product of the employer's world view.[47] Although it is influenced by a short-term commonsense pragmatism on which management has a direct effect, it is also moulded by a deeper awareness of workers' rights. This awareness has two sources. First, the dominant nineteenth- and twentieth-century philosophy of political democracy provided a strong political source for the legitimization of industrial action when workplace democracy was denied in the early 1930s and again for black workers in the 1960s. Second, an awareness of workers' rights arises out of the contradictory character of the capital–labor relationship itself. Within capitalist employment relations, workers are held to be 'free'; but they must sell their labor to live and surrender their 'freedom' in order to find a buyer for their labor.[48] They have the theoretical 'freedom' to move around and to tell the foremen where to get off, while they are simultaneously forced by the exercise of sanctions to attend one workplace punctually and regularly and to obey that foreman. The uneasy balance between these two ultimately contradictory elements, the rights that rest on an absolute 'freedom' and the immediate requirements of subordination in the workplace, gives rise to a framework of legitimate action. This concept is neither total subordination nor total freedom. Instead it suggests a changing and often contradictory pattern of workers' rights against managerial authority. Rights are respected and defended *within* the overall acceptance of management power – in what has been called the 'strange world of intricately mixed, highly organized, and yet morally compulsive expectations'.[49] As the author of *Wildcat Strike* found thirty years ago: 'workers usually defined the strike in ethical terms, holding it to be morally justified'.[50]

The concept of workplace legitimacy provides a two-sided view of the labor process by stressing the ways in which management and labor constantly and conflictually remake workplace rules and then penalize the other side for transgressing them.[51] Workplace legitimacy is seen here as highly malleable, reflecting the mediating influence of tradition and workers' current political experience (in society and in the work-place) and the traditions and political experiences of management.[52] Workers may therefore believe their own actions are legitimate even though – in wildcatting – they defy the law. And managers may also act in ways that defy the law in the belief that all laws that interfere with managerial authority are illegitimate.[53] The limits of workplace legitimacy result from a two-way exchange between the way workers try to maximize their rights and freedoms and the way managers try to exercise control.[54] So workplace legitimacy customarily reflects ambivalent consciousness: worker resistance and subordination share the same moment. The aspect which appears to dominate this mixed conscious-ness is strongly influenced by workers' collective self-confidence, and that is a function of history, economics, politics and their experience of organization.

Workplace organization is first constructed and then maintained by a layer of key individuals.[55] Subsequently, its degree of autonomy from domination either by the international union, or by management, or both, largely explains its relative sensitivity to rank and file concerns and demands. But several factors interact to influence that autonomy: the specific plant organizational tradition, the political composition and strength of the international union leadership and the intervention of management. Organizational 'independence' is a changing set of ideological positions and actions rather than a fixed constitution. It is an important concept because it suggests that labor's capacity to develop distinct strategies to represent workers' interests is not simply an ideological question: there is a symmetry between shopfloor participation in union organization and that organization's representation of workers' distinctive interests. Managements did not simply have things all their own way. When organizational and ideological tools were available, minorities resisted 'the efforts of management to exceed the historically acceptable pace of work'.[56]

The next chapter questions recent interpretations of the last fifty years of American labor relations and of the development of the UAW from the assumption that workers' beliefs were usually composed of contradictory strands.

2 Fifty years of labor politics, unions and the UAW

Current interpretations of the development of American labor relations since the 1930s tend to stress its discontinuities. The 'militant' 1930s are followed by the 'watershed' of World War II and the 'labor truce', which lasts throughout the late 1940s, the 1950s and early 1960s, and then by the 'labor revolt' of the late 1960s and early 1970s. The late 1970s and the 1980s are then viewed as a 'new era of non-adversarial bargaining'. For convenience of presentation, this chapter is divided into three sections which follow this rough periodization. Each section – on the 'golden age' of the 1930s, the 'labor truce' of the 1940s and 1950s, and the period from the 'labor revolt' to the 1980s – raises questions as to how far current interpretations are supported by the evidence of the Chrysler case. Indeed, the principal theme of this chapter is on both the *continuity* and the *contradictions* of the labor experience throughout these five decades. Neither labor market factors nor managerial strategies provide satisfactory explanations of the complex process uncovered.

In all five decades it is important to recognize a central continuity of the American labor experience: American labor never emerged from its minority status and this ensured that American management retained an anti-union combativity. Conflict never disappeared. If it was suppressed or controlled at one level of labor relations or at one moment it reappeared shortly at another level or time. Rather than viewing American workers as swinging between resistance and accommodation according to pressure from exogenous labor market forces and/or long-term economic cycles, both resistance and accommodation are seen as co-existing throughout the period.

As well as arguing the contradictory character of the labor experience against certain other recent interpretations, the chapter has another theme, centering on the involvement of political factors in shaping that experience. The 'golden age of militancy' has to be seen in the legitimating political context of the New Deal, the 'watershed' must be related to the context of wartime popular nationalism and the 'labor truce' to Cold War nationalism. The 'labor revolt' also took place in the political context of the civil rights movement and the Vietnam War. The political elements in workers' consciousness which came to the fore at specific moments were shaped by the political environments in which workers lived: primarily the national class, race and gender political environments but mediated by the specific workplace political environment. To understand the context in which the Chrysler Dodge Main experience unfolded, the political context in which these workers and managers lived out their lives cannot be ignored. Part of the purpose of this chapter, then, is to briefly remind the reader of that political context.

I. The golden age of militancy: the 1930s

Radical historians have referred loosely to 'the epidemic of factory occupations' in the late 1930s,[1] or to 'a couple of million in the 1936–37 sit-down wave',[2] or cited, uncritically, Bureau of Labor Statistics data that suggests 'nearly 400,000 workers participated in sit-down strikes at their peak in 1936–37'.[3] If nearly half a million American workers had been *actively* involved, the subsequent history of the American working class might have been very different. But at Dodge Main, probably the UAW's strongest large plant, only a third of the workers in the most committed department joined the sit-down. The sit-down tactic was used because the activists were too few to risk putting up pickets to keep the majority of workers out. As the Dodge Main strike bulletin stressed on March 11 1937: 'If they (the workers) went outside, some *scab* might come in and take their jobs. That is why we are staying in: *to protect our jobs.*' Why were the 1937 sit-downs so much a minority experience? The answer requires a review of wider political developments over the preceding decade.

The years from the election of President Hoover in 1928 to the entry of the United States into World War II in 1941 were ones in which 'prosperity' turned to depression,[4] the federal government launched a massive intervention in social and economic planning, and the structure of today's automobile industry was laid down. Possibly the most enduring change of the period was that which took place in the relationship between management and workers. In the 1930s the growth of union membership usually meant the growth of *organized* opposition to the arbitrary dictates of management, and successful unionism meant workers imposing their restraints on managerial autonomy. It is for this reason that many writers have seen the strikes of the 1930s as a 'golden age' of American labor. But it is necessary to situate the unionization process in a wider political process.

The story of unionization in the 1930s is well known. The number of union members rose from 2.8 million in 1933 to 3.9 million in 1936 – and then more than doubled to 8.4 million by 1941. As a percentage of the potential non-agricultural workforce, union density was 7.3% in 1933, 9.8% in 1936 and 19.5% by 1941.[5] Only once before, in 1920 and 1921, had it even approached the one in five mark; but this time union density remained above 20% for forty years. This expansion of unionism was accompanied by a fourfold increase in the most obvious indicator of industrial conflict: strike frequency. From an historical low annual average of 24.7 strikes for every million workers between 1927 and 1929, strike frequency rose to around 96 per million between 1934 and 1941.[6]

The rise in union density and worker combativity was the result of changing political allegiances as well as of stronger union organizations. Throughout the 1920s growing numbers of city workers (and coal miners) switched their votes from the traditional urban party, the Republicans, to the Democrats. For example, in auto city in 1920 the Democrats cornered just 19% of the Detroit presidential vote, but by 1928 their share had doubled to 37.1%.[7] The trend to city living and Democrat voting reflected many factors: the slowing down of immigration, the dawning of political maturity for the second generation of 'new' pre-1914 immigrants, the migration of nearly 20 million people from rural to urban areas in the 1920s, the severe income inequality that left most wage earners' families living below 'the American standard' in the mid 1920s, and the defeat of the old, rural, Protestant, southern and western, power base within the Democratic Party by its urban, 'new' immigrant, Catholic, Jewish and eastern elements.[8]

The 1928 trend became a landslide in 1932. The new president, Roosevelt, polled 22.8 million votes to Hoover's 15.8 million. Urban workers voted overwhelmingly for Roosevelt and against Hoover's passivity over unemployment, job insecurity and irregular or low pay. In Detroit Roosevelt took 59.4% of the vote and all Michigan's eight large cities went Democratic. Roosevelt won every major metropolitan center in the Midwest, the West and the South. American workers, without any direction from the American Federation of Labor, had reconstructed the pattern of American politics.[9]

Roosevelt's 1933 New Deal administration went on to play a major part in the process of change its own election had indicated was already underway. On June 16 1933 Roosevelt signed the National Industrial Recovery Act (NIRA), in which Section 7(a) legitimized union activity. The previously stagnating American Federation of Labor instantly launched an appeal to unorganized workers and called on its affiliated bodies to launch organizing drives. But the progress of unionism was far from straightforward. The size, growth and diversity of American industry in the 1920s had combined with the survival of predominantly craft-based unions to establish a wage structure with high differentials. Regional differentials of up to 90% were compounded by the common practice in much of manufacturing of paying skilled workers 100% more than unskilled workers, a division also marked along racial and ethnic lines and between unionized and non-unionized industrial sectors.[10]

Union membership for many, if not all, of the AFL's existing nearly all-white, all-male members in the late 1920s represented the protection of privilege as much as craft control on the job. The AFL's affiliated unions wanted union growth but without any reduction of differentials. They believed that differentials would be reduced if skilled workers in the unorganized industries were encouraged to join industrial unions with semiskilled and unskilled workers. This ambivalence completely sabotaged the AFL's 1933 drive to unionize autoworkers. The new Federal Local Unions were not empowered to form inclusive industrial unions. A year later the same indecisiveness seriously weakened the rubber workers when sharp clashes broke out between strikers and the police in Toledo, and general strikes occurred in Minneapolis and San Francisco, while in Detroit's Chrysler plants a union of semiskilled and unskilled workers, led by the populist 'Radio Priest' Father Charles Coughlin, rapidly dwarfed the tiny AFL locals.[11]

Managements continued to vigorously oppose all forms of unionism, and the New Deal legislation did not unionize workers on its own. Most major employers responded to Section 7(a) by setting up their own company unions. The National Association of Manufacturers took the lead in August 1933 by distributing a notice to employees telling them it was not the intention of the NIRA that 'employees should pay money into any organization'. The National Metal Trades Association, whose Detroit branch secretary was also general manager of the influential Detroit Employers' Association and whose members included GM and Chrysler, declared: 'The United States is an Open Shop Nation.'[12] This view was effectively endorsed by Roosevelt himself in March 1934 when he intervened to prevent a threatened auto strike and imposed a settlement that 'favors no particular union or particular form of employee organization or representation'.[13]

In May 1935 the Supreme Court declared the NIRA unconstitutional, but Roosevelt signed the National Labor Relations Act in July. The 'Wagner Act', named after its principal architect, established a National Labor Relations Board (NLRB) with powers to rule against employers' denial of workers' rights to organize and enter collective bargaining. Violently denounced at first as an interference with the rights of management, the Wagner Act laid down procedures which in the long term worked to encourage industrial rather than craft unionism. It provided that the union supported by a majority of workers in a unit would be the 'exclusive' legal body for 'all the employees in such unit for the purposes of collective bargaining'. And it gave the Board the power to determine the size of the unit. In another clause it obliquely served to give some legal basis for sectional shop stewards: to protect (non-union) minority rights it declared that 'any individual or group of employees shall have the right at any time to present grievances to their employer through representatives of their own choosing' – a clause that would be repeated later in the major union contracts between GM, Ford and Chrysler and the UAW.

At first the Board had little direct influence on labor relations. Not until April 1937 was it declared constitutional and its effective role in regulating labor relations in the automobile industry really began only in 1939.[14] But its passage gave a new impetus to the AFL's lagging unionizing drive in auto. In August 1935 the AFL called all Federal Local Unions in auto to send delegates to a meeting in Detroit. There, AFL president William Green issued them with a charter as the United Automobile Workers of America (UAW) but announced the new UAW would not be allowed jurisdiction over skilled workers. When he failed to get the convention to elect the pattern-maker, Francis Dillon, as president, Green simply appointed him to the job.[15] Within the AFL, John L. Lewis, the president of the biggest existing industrial union, the United Mine Workers, acted as the champion of the new industrial unions, and at the October 1935 AFL convention he supported the general case for industrial unionism and the United Auto Workers' appeal for approval of a broader industrial jurisdiction. Defeated on both issues, but with 38% of the voting delegates supporting him, Lewis decided there was a large enough core to press ahead anyway. He immediately organized a meeting of eight union presidents who had supported industrial unionism at the AFL convention, and they set up the Committee for Industrial Organization in November 1935.[16]

The formation of the CIO broke the craft mould of the AFL unions and created an organizational framework relevant to organization in the mass production industries. They required a different kind of unionism than that offered by the AFL. Skilled workers' craft control and job monopoly could be defended by a union structure external to the plant, with locals based on where workers lived rather than where they worked. But semiskilled restraints over managerial authority on the assembly line could only be maintained in each plant by on-the-spot collective force; and that required drawing all workers into a common organizational framework, not drawing lines between them. The CIO industrial union federation was created by the leaders of several existing AFL unions and so it brought with it a key role for the professional organizer and for centralized policy making and administration. Yet it also offered a form of union organization structure that corresponded to the labor process experienced by auto industry workers.

The formal suspension of the ten CIO unions by the AFL took place in September 1936. By then the CIO had already launched two key organizing drives: in the steel industry it aimed to take over the industry's works council–company unions from within;[17] and in auto it sought to unite four small unions, the AFL's UAW, Father Coughlin's Automotive Industrial Workers' Association (AIWA), Matt Smith's Mechanics Educational Society of America (MESA) and Arthur Greer's Hudson-based Associated Automobile Workers of America.[18] Unity negotiations broke down several times before the April 1936 UAW convention where the election of Homer Martin signified a victory for industrial unionism and for autonomy for local unions over the cautious, centralized craft leadership of the AFL. The merger into the UAW of the AIWA and of three large left wing Detroit MESA locals followed rapidly, and in July the UAW affiliated to the CIO just in time to secure its suspension from the AFL.[19]

In the November 1936 presidential election the CIO campaigned hard for Roosevelt, while the United Mine Workers' $500,000 campaign contribution made it the biggest single contributor to Democratic Party funds. The Roosevelt labor bandwagon achieved a massive 61% of the popular vote – a decisive rejection of the Republican candidate, Alfred M. Landon, who was also a leading member of the anti-labor Liberty League.[20] The result showed millions of American workers that they could successfully challenge the will of the world's biggest employers, and it helped legitimate that challenge.[21]

For a brief period the business community felt exposed: it could no longer rely upon the federal government nor in certain states upon the state administrations to back its managerial prerogatives with force. Many employers either recognized this new consciousness voluntarily or were soon forced to do so. In February and April 1937 first General Motors and then Chrysler signed provisional contracts recognizing the UAW, whose new status immediately encouraged an explosion of members.[22]

The 1937 contracts, however, were won by the active and short-term participation of only a *tiny* minority.[23] At Chrysler's biggest plant,

Dodge Main, where participation was greater than elsewhere, Gertrude Nalezty's experience was common. A second shift worker, she reported for work on March 8 when the sit-down began and was denied admittance by the plant guards. Her involvement was limited to passing her lunch box over the fence to the workers inside. After that she sat at home until the company called her back.[24] At Flint the sit-down was used by a still smaller minority to stop the movement of dies out of the plant. And its success depended on the strength and solidarity of the shopfloor minority, on the non-intervention of the state (police or national guardsmen), and on political support in the local community. The unionization that took place did so in the context of the 'radical' political climate of the New Deal. It was not an *independent* working class creation, and this is partly both explanation and cause of the failure of a political labor movement to develop in the US.[25]

The tactical and numerical weaknesses at the moment of auto unionism's greatest advance were reflected in the essentially *defensive* character of the movement's principal demands: for an end to piecework and for a 'fair' lay-off system. These demands did not challenge any crucial part of management economic power or its shopfloor authority. They altered the *style* of managerial control, but not its content. The sit-downers sought and achieved restraints on managerial authority; they altered the limits of workplace legitimacy but they did not seek changes in the law. As Brody has argued, 'The sit-down strikers perceived of themselves as fighting for legal rights already theirs; the company stood outside the law, not they.'[26] The workers' sense of legitimacy was underwritten *outside* the plant.

The sit-down movement was an important moment in the American labor experience and the business community unquestionably saw it as a major challenge to their managerial prerogatives. But it is important *not* to exaggerate the breadth or the radicalism of the movement: the 'golden age of militancy' is partly a myth[27] and an obstacle to understanding the legacy the 1930s left to following decades. This is clear in the case of the UAW. The speed of unionization and the resulting lack of mass involvement had contradictory consequences for UAW unionism: self-reliance implanted a strong tradition of local union autonomy;[28] while the isolation of the activists nurtured the roots of the 'popular bossdom' that set in from 1947.[29]

To the extent that it had the capacity to predetermine a policy and consistently implement it, the UAW's main aim from its foundation in 1935 to America's entry into World War II was limited to winning and then keeping recognition from the auto makers. This was a goal that fitted well with considerable local autonomy on other issues, and was reflected in a relatively democratic and open UAW organizational structure. Local union organization was only controlled very loosely by the international, factions were tolerated, and the first two union presidents, Francis Dillon (1935–36) and Homer Martin (1936–39) were both thrown out of office. The autonomy of the UAW's locals was written into the constitution in 1939 after Martin's unsuccessful bid to use his presidential position to split the four-year-old union.[30]

The sit-downs were soon followed by the recession of 1937–38. So the new union's impact on managerial authority over lay-offs and job classifications and rates remained slight. But the 1937 contracts did give union organization in auto the legitimacy it had lacked in 1933. The recognition of the UAW was largely responsible for transforming the minority of union members into an overwhelming majority. This was *management's* key contribution to mass unionism and the result was that different patterns of managerial authority developed in different plants. The 'powerlessness' of workers in the 1920s became a distant memory; but the 'power' that was gained was only partial and remained conditional on managerial approval. At Chrysler, top management's 'approval' of unionism took the form of an almost wilful disregard of what took place on the shopfloor accompanied by a highly combative attitude towards what it saw as external interference from a hostile union. The outcome was that Chrysler fought losing battles in 1937 and 1939 against the UAW that led to the shopfloor militants in its plants being legitimized and to a particularly enduring form of shopfloor unionism.

The pattern of minority worker involvement in CIO unionization drives in auto was repeated in the CIO's attempt to unionize the five steel companies known as Little Steel in the summer of 1937. The defeat of that attempt demonstrated the failure of the radical impetus of the sit-down strikes in auto to spread outwards, and to influence the four out of every five workers who remained non-union at the close of the 1930s. Moreover, the 1938 congressional election results showed a marked shift to the Republicans: the mobilization of an anti-radical backlash had begun and the progressive period of the New Deal was drawing to a close.

II. Watershed and labor truce: the 1940s and 1950s

Compared with the militant 1930s the decade of the 1950s has been seen as a labor truce, while views of the intervening watershed of World War II have stressed either workers' great spontaneity and political advance[31] or labor's wartime weakness[32] that allowed management to formalize labor relations on its terms. For most employers, however, the unions only became a 'power in the land' under the tight labor supply conditions of World War II.[33] Corporate labor relations departments were then constrained to reach agreements with union leaders who were simultaneously constrained to oppose strikes and accept binding arbitration. After the war company-wide and the industry-wide contracts went on being signed, but most American managements launched an intense and often prolonged struggle over work intensity and work discipline on the shopfloor in which they regained most of what they feared they had signed away. Their success muted managerial hostility to the international unions and helped create the appearance – although not the reality – of a labor truce.

In America, as in Britain, World War II encouraged the growth of unionization by providing full employment, a tight labor market and government action to legitimize union organization. During the first full year of war, 1942, the National Bureau of Economic Research recorded 9.8 million union members and by 1945 this figure had reached 12 million. The trend continued upward to reach 14 million by 1950 and then 15.5 million by 1960. Union density, as a percentage of the number of employed and unemployed civilians in the workforce over these same years, rose from 22.3% in 1942 to 28.9% in 1945, and stayed in the range 28.3% to 31.6% until 1958 when it began a long-term decline.[34]

Strike frequency after 1940, in contrast with the experience of the 1930s, failed to increase in line with union membership. Excluding the strike-prone coal industry, the annual average fell from 105 strikes per million non-agricultural workers in the formative years of the CIO between 1937 and 1941, to average 80 a year from 1945 to 1959.[35] The more union members, it appeared, the less frequent the number of strikes noted by the Bureau of Labor Statistics (BLS). None the less, many more strikes occurred than in the years before the CIO: between 1946 and 1959 annual average strike frequency outside coal was 27% higher than from 1931 to 1936. The impact of industrial unionism also changed the shape of these strikes. They were either bigger or lasted longer than in the 1930s or during the war, since there were more set-piece confrontations involving whole plants or companies.[36] Management–labor relations in the 1940s and 1950s also saw increased federal intervention, the establishment of specialized company labor relations departments and greater centralization within the CIO unions. Yet while shopfloor conflict tended to be increasingly channelled within an institutional framework, it could not be suppressed and often was not effectively 'managed'.

Government regulation of labor relations accelerated in the period of war preparations and during the first two years of America's direct involvement in World War II. In March 1941 Roosevelt established a National Defense Mediation Board to help mediate labor conflict in the arms-related industries. To the Board he appointed Philip Murray, president of the CIO, George Meany, secretary-treasurer of the AFL, and certain pro-New Deal industrialists like the chairman of Standard Oil and US Rubber's director of industrial and public relations. Within three months, the Board announced that strikers would be refused access to its service and, after Pearl Harbor and America's entry into the war in December 1941, the CIO formally gave Roosevelt a no strike pledge. In return, the recast National War Labor Board (NWLB) was given the power to include union security clauses in contracts. Workers covered by union security contracts who did not opt out of the union within their first fifteen days on the job would have to pay dues, usually under a check-off agreement, and to abide by union rules. A standard formula to this effect was launched in June 1942. Conceived not as a means of strengthening shopfloor unionism, but as a device to strengthen the finances and authority of the senior union officials, it was followed a month later by an NWLB ruling that the Little Steel wage award formula, limiting increases to 3.5% in 1942 while inflation was running at 15%, would be a maximum.[37]

The union leaders' readiness to accept wartime wage restraint and to police the no strike pledge persuaded the employers – mainly through government pressure – to legitimize the union presence in their plants. The no strike pledge tied the union leaders closely to the wartime industrial–military alliance, and encouraged constitutional changes that formally restricted local union autonomy. But the ties binding union leaders to the defense effort were not inflexible, as John L. Lewis' wartime record shows, and the shopfloor experience was still more complex. For while union locals benefited from the government's 'gift' of a stable and growing membership, very large numbers of workers experienced wildcat strike action and a degree of self-reliance in numbers far greater than those involved in the sit-downs of 1937.[38] In 1945 the biggest unauthorized auto industry strike of the war broke out at Dodge Main and spread rapidly to most of Chrysler's Detroit plants.

Union security clauses, however, meant that unlike the struggled-for unionization of the early and mid 1930s, workers often had little choice about joining unions during World War II. While their inexperience may have aided the centralization of the CIO unions, it should not be assumed that the new unionists were necessarily *less* conscious of their rights and interests against management. The presence of a core of pre-war militants ensured that union traditions were passed on in the older industrial centers, and, once introduced to a tradition that denied management the right to act arbitrarily, the new wartime labor force took over the pre-war frontier of control as if it were its own creation.[39] But in most plants the lack of conscious collective effort involved in establishing this new 'strength' often encouraged a passive reliance on the existing union structure. By the second half of the 1940s, the centralized, bureaucratic 'bossdom' this reliance encouraged, had become characteristic of virtually all the industrial unions.

The argument here is that all three elements in the bargaining relationship, workplace unionism, the international union apparatus and corporate management, were strengthened by World War II. The conjuncture of a tight labor market with a still largely unstructured shopfloor unionism did strengthen American workers' self-confidence. Many workers found they could fight and win on their own. Yet the war also increased the prestige of the central union staff machines as the recently established CIO international unions became more dependent on arbitration by the state and legitimation by the employers. Finally, the war also strengthened management: the power of US capitalism reached its zenith on a world scale, a process that owed much to the close working relations American employers established with a state apparatus they had formerly regarded with suspicion.

These consequences of war were experienced against the political background of a strengthened populist nationalism. On either side of the masthead of wartime editions of the *Dodge Main News* were the Stars and Stripes and the slogan 'Give it your Best'. The political context of American wartime nationalism, however, had few of the collectivist overtones of Britain's wartime rationing and promises of social reform after the war. America's war nationalism was about the flag, American superiority and the individualistic American dream. So when America's minority of unionists adopted the flags and slogans of the war effort this hindered the expression of workers' *collective* interests against management.

The no strike pledge, union security and restrictions on wage rises, provided the context for substantial wartime union growth as union leaders institutionalized closer relations with the government and the employers. The active backing of the CIO for the wartime mediation boards and the no strike pledge proved crucial in fashioning what became the three dominant features of *post-war* industrial relations: industry-wide wage agreements; grievance procedures and impartial arbitration; and strongly centralized unions pledged not to sanction strikes during the term of a contract.[40] But the institutionalization of these procedures was certainly not automatic in the immediate aftermath of the war.

After the war the balance of forces tilted in favor of the employers, but in the context of increased worker self-confidence. Managements were confronted with a legitimated union presence no longer constrained by wartime nationalism. Managements often bitterly resisted quite moderate catching-up demands, made by union leaders anxious to renew their base among the rank and file after four years of opposing strikes. A great strike wave swept America in the year following the surrender of Japan, as over five million workers walked out to defend wartime job conditions and restore earnings levels seriously eroded during 1945.[41] Managements were hostile both to the extension of industry-wide bargaining to planning and non-wage conditions, and to the continuation of labor's wartime gains and long, big strikes occurred throughout the rest of the 1940s.[42]

In these years more workers experienced strike action and for longer periods – in most instances without strike pay – than in any other period of American labor relations. Critically, however, these major confrontations between labor and management remained isolated from each other, and the unions failed to secure any new extension of bargaining rights or even to defend labor's wartime shopfloor gains. The unions secured some restoration of their members' real earnings, but could not move the employers on any of the wider issues of consultation and control. Most were forced to include 'company security' clauses in their contracts and so enshrined the wartime no strike pledge in peacetime.[43]

The mass production industry unions survived this contest, but the considerable shopfloor confidence of the war years was largely broken in a highly fragmented strike wave that failed to draw in the majority of non-unionized workers. The bitterness of defeat boosted the fortunes of more conservative officials who openly advocated compromise and survival. There were, of course, exceptions. Some companies, like Chrysler, didn't seek an immediate post-war confrontation because of their need to establish their post-war markets. In such companies the wartime frontier of control often survived despite changes in the broader industrial and political climate.

Politically, labor's industrial defeat helped create a basis for widespread political apathy and popular support for anti-communism.[44] The rightward electoral shift that had begun in 1938 became a landslide.[45] In November 1946 the Democratic vote plummeted from 25 to 15 million as more than 60% of the electorate stayed away from the polls. This was a major political defeat for labor since Republican candidates like Richard Nixon in California successfully red-baited the CIO's Political Action Committee on slogans such as: 'A vote for Nixon is a vote against the communist-dominated PAC with its gigantic slush fund.' Only 75 of the

318 candidates supported by the PAC–CIO won, and the Republicans gained majorities in both Houses of Congress and in many states' governments.[46] Two years later Harry Truman retained the presidency he had assumed on Roosevelt's death, but many former Democratic voters didn't cast their votes. Rough surveys indicated that as many as 30% of voters who considered themselves 'strong Democrats' and 45% of 'weak Democrats' didn't vote.[47]

The growing Republican and right wing Democratic strength in Congress reinforced the management lobby hostile to unionism, and it also fueled a strident anti-communism. In the 79th Congress (1945–46) there were just four investigations into communism, by the 80th Congress (1947–48) there were twenty-two, twenty-four in the 81st (1949–50), thirty-four in the 82nd (1951–52) and in the 83rd Congress (1953–54), when Senator McCarthy was chairman of the Senate's Government Operations Committee, there were fifty-one.[48] Anti-communism strengthened the already powerful pressures that were conservatizing the CIO union leaderships, and weakened the confidence of those who advocated continued resistance. During these years liberalism, as well as all forms of socialism, was systematically denounced as 'anti-American'.[49]

By February 1947 there were more than 250 anti-labor bills pending in both houses of Congress, and on June 23, 1947 Congress overrode President Truman's veto to enact the Taft–Hartley Act. This Act gave the National Labor Relations Board powers to outlaw secondary boycotts and 'jurisdictional' strikes and allowed state legislatures to ban union membership agreements – so legitimizing the spread of 'right to work' laws. It prohibited strikes by federal government employees and gave the President the power to order 'cooling-off' periods in disputes that he decided affected the national health and safety. It allowed employers to file damage suits against unions for breach of contract and, to secure NLRB recognition of union shops and condemnation of illegal actions by the employers, it obliged both local and international union officers to file affidavits swearing they were not members of the Communist Party. Most crucially, the Cold War nationalism that motivated the anti-communist argument of the Act played a major role in purging the unions of the radicals and of the radicalism that had played such a big part in the previous decade's union growth. Taft–Hartley represented a series of legal *and* political obstacles to the long-term growth of union density and to the effective shopfloor exercise of union bargaining power.

After token resistance, the CIO and AFL leaderships agreed to accept the Act. It was not really aimed against their bargaining relationship with management but against shopfloor union power and the ideological influence of leftism. By 1957 the NLRB reported that 250 international unions had made the necessary rule changes with some 2,750 officers having completed non-Communist affidavits, while 21,500 locals were in compliance with some 193,500 affidavits.[50] The implications for both organizing internal union opposition and shopfloor dissent, and even for the expression of political views independent of both the company and the union leaders, were considerable. If 200,000 successful candidates for stewards, committeemen and local officers had filed statements that they did not belong to the Communist Party, it is safe to assume that in the course of the 1950s at least four or five times that number of unsuccessful candidates had also done so. Across America, then, perhaps a million shopfloor union activists joined the millions of federal employees whose past and present political views were investigated under the loyalty program, Executive Order 9835, that Truman issued in March 1947.[51] Little wonder then that while anti-communist factions in the CIO used the opportunity to consolidate their power, much shopfloor struggle in the late 1940s and 1950s went underground.

It was in this political and industrial context that from 1941 to the late 1950s, under presidents R. J. Thomas (1939–46) and Walter Reuther (1946–70), the UAW focused on standardizing and improving wages and non-wage benefits in centralized bargaining. During these years the union's International Executive Board (IEB) only rarely authorized local strikes, and immediate struggle over shopfloor managerial authority was effectively abandoned at the national level. The role of the international union shifted perceptibly from supporting internally-resourced local union organizations to taking all the key decisions itself.[52] Two trends merged: the centralization of union power in the hands of a few well-placed international officers who saw wildcat action as a threat to their control,[53] and the growing recognition by the larger employers that in a period of rapid growth and technological change, it was to their advantage to encourage the construction of bargaining institutions outside the workplace.

In some companies restraints on managerial authority were largely eliminated in the late 1940s as union leaders bargained them away for more tangible economic returns – often after one or more major confrontations. Elsewhere, wartime restraints remained throughout the 1950s. Some employers failed to grasp the nettle of the legitimation of union membership and conducted a vigorous anti-unionism that in turn bred active resistance; still others lacked the financial base to decisively defeat labor. At Chrysler a strong tradition of sectional union activity survived that allowed the custom and practice of mutuality to operate over many aspects of job organization until the late 1950s. Their survival in a major American 'core' corporation raises doubts about the blanket characterization of the post-war period as a 'labor truce'.[54]

Indeed, even without the evidence of high levels of conflict in large companies like Chrysler and International Harvester, the terms 'truce' and 'compromise' would be inappropriate. They imply voluntarily entered agreements by two sides to cease hostilities in exchange for mutual benefits. Yet there was nothing voluntary about the location of the shopfloor frontier of control between management and managed in this period. The picture is one of consistent struggle in which, when the workers were defeated in one area, management stepped up its 'drive' to try and remove other restraints from workplace legitimacy. Managing shopfloor resistance remained a major problem for management during the 1940s and 1950s. Some companies did so with fewer strikes (less visible conflict) than others, but the problem was the same for them all. At the point of production, workers' experience was not of a 'labor truce' but of continuing managerial 'drive'. How visible open conflict was depended on the interaction of management with the local union traditions.[55]

The first effective curb on local union autonomy in the UAW appeared during World War II when the IEB implemented the no strike pledge and took disciplinary action against certain local officers who defied it. Although Walter Reuther was narrowly elected UAW president in 1946, partly on the basis of his leadership of the 1945–46 GM strike and on his radical reputation, his political support already came from an alliance of his own personal faction of anti-communist former socialists and conservative anti-communists mobilized by the Association of Catholic Trade Unionists. As anti-communism became a still bigger issue in 1947, around the foreign policy stance of the Truman Doctrine and the Marshall Plan, so Reuther secured control of the UAW IEB and set about red-baiting any opposition.[56] In 1949 Reuther won agreement from the UAW convention for the IEB to institute disciplinary action against members when their own locals wouldn't. In 1950 he tightened his absolute hold over the IEB by closing access to and centralizing his own caucus: afterwards the IEB only met in full during conventions. His proposal for biennial international conventions was accepted in 1951 and he finally succeeding in getting two-yearly local union elections made mandatory in 1957.[57]

While Reuther pressed for greater stability and continuity among plant-level officers he undertook a similar 'professionalization' of the union's direct employees. The 1950s saw a considerable expansion of the numbers of UAW international union staff. UAW membership rose by

21% between 1949 and 1960 but the number of UAW staff based in Detroit and in the regions rose by 40% (to 660). This increase consolidated Reuther's power. Dozens of these staffers were former militant opponents who were now brought into line; by 1961 their average age was forty-nine years and on average each had been an international union officer for ten and a half years.[58] Compared to the rapidly changing international staff of the 1930s and 1940s, in Reuther's period a permanent union bureaucracy was forged. It gave him total loyalty and was too old to ever return to the plants. In the 1960s this apparatus effectively took over from the old Reuther caucus. Reuther no longer needed his caucus once the old opposition strongholds of the River Rouge and Dodge Main were under his control, and as the union began to recruit significantly outside auto. As the union grew to over 1.5 million members, its size and the monolithic character of its international apparatus ensured that opposition could be restricted to isolated locals.

The centralization of collective bargaining, the bureaucratization of the union and the neglect of work intensity had different consequences for shopfloor and local union organization according to the size and tradition of the different locals. Where a local was small or politically subservient to the ruling UAW faction, and highly dependent upon the international in conflicts with its management, then the effect of the establishment of collective bargaining at international level was debilitating.[59] For the most part, the 1949 observation that because of 'the changed relationship between the union and the corporation ... the steward, while still important in the shop, seemed to be less powerful in the union than he had been in the thirties', appears close to the mark.[60] Only in the largest plants, and usually where strong shop steward or left political traditions survived as well, was there a countervailing influence which could turn the international's neglect of local working conditions to its own advantage, claiming them as a legitimate area for its own independent activity.

While Reuther consolidated control over the UAW on the basis of anti-communism, the auto industry employers gradually came to see the benefits of formalizing close company and industry-wide bargaining relationships with his machine. In 1948 GM offered an escalator cost-of-living clause in exchange for a two-year contract. In 1950 Reuther negotiated the 'Treaty of Detroit', a five-year contract including properly funded pension schemes, first with GM, and then with Ford and Chrysler. This represented a strategic shift for Reuther, from making reformist demands on the federal government, to extracting reforms from the auto companies – a political development that squared with the realpolitik of business unionism. Union leaders began to negotiate contracts that gave lifelong financial security to their existing members in return for shopfloor policies that provided the best environment possible for profitable production. *Fortune* magazine heralded the 1950 'Treaty of Detroit' with this assessment: 'GM has regained control over one of the crucial management functions in any line of manufacturing – long-range scheduling of production, model changes, and tool and plant investment.'[61] In December 1955 the AFL and CIO fused to form the AFL–CIO. The re-establishment of one national union federation was precipitated by the need for a joint response to the Republican Eisenhower administration elected in 1952, but it also marked the general acceptance of one form of business unionism or another by most CIO and AFL unions.

Despite the restoration of union unity, however, business unionism was not all pervasive. It was based upon assumptions of continuous economic growth and of a conservative ideological Cold War nationalism that would not survive unscathed through the next two decades. And the lifelong security it offered was conditional upon workers doing whatever their supervisors demanded and only taking any objections to the 'unfair' exercise of managerial authority through a lengthy grievance procedure afterwards. Business unionism's economic benefits were also denied to most black workers through racial discrimination in the job market. These qualifications gave rise to continuing shopfloor conflict even while union members' living standards rose by leaps and bounds.

A significant institutionalization of American labor relations in the 1940s and 1950s is not in doubt. But beneath the 'peaceful' surface a strong undercurrent of conflict continued, as shown in chapters 5 and 6, which demonstrate a high level of shopfloor combativity in Chrysler. When the political and economic climate changed again in the following two decades, the continuing presence of resistance along with accommodation became more apparent, leading to the analysis of a 'labor revolt'.

III. The labor revolt and the new era: the 1960s to the 1980s

The 'labor revolt' of the late 1960s and early 1970s has been viewed as 'an unravelling of the postwar truce' and as a confirmation of the historical correlation of long-wave economic cycles and managerial control strategies. Gordon *et al.* link it with an extension of bargaining to 'non-economic' issues, and, finally, arrive at the 'stronger conclusion' that 'the gradual erosion of the postwar labor truce ... constitutes a principal source of the well-known slowdown in productivity growth in the

Table 3 *Transport equipment industry*
BLS recorded strikes, 1961–78

Year	Strikes during term of contract as %	Strikes over plant issues as %	Year	Strikes during term of contract as %	Strikes over plant issues as %
1961	41.2	45.4	1970	40.9	35.2
1962	32.0	38.0	1971	27.1	28.9
1963	52.0	51.0	1972	26.3	26.7
1964	47.5	44.2	1973	26.3	26.9
1965	44.3	41.0	1974	15.7	20.8
1966	48.1	39.8	1975	19.0	31.4
1967	34.7	43.7	1976	17.7	24.6
1968	37.1	42.0	1977	10.6	13.8
1969	43.3	38.9	1978	9.4	11.4

Source: Peter Nolan and P. K. Edwards, 'Homogenise, divide and rule: an essay on "Segmented Work, Divided Workers"' (Warwick: SSRC Industrial Relations Research Unit, unpublished paper, December 1982), Table 3, 26.

US economy'.[62] Underlying their thesis is an assumption that there is a clear discontinuity between the labor experience of the late 1960s and the earlier post-war years.

The evidence, however, is more complex than Gordon *et al.* allow.[63] Official government strike data, for example, show a very different picture. Auto features strongly in their 'labor revolt' thesis but, in the transport equipment industry, strikes over 'non-economic' plant issues were actually higher in the early 1960s before the 'revolt' began. Another significant measure is that the level of mid-term strikes (generally accepted as largely unauthorized) remained constant from 1961 to 1970. Then, far from rising with the onset of the 'labor revolt', table 3 shows that both measures declined as a proportion of all strikes from the 1960s to the 1970s. The strike counts kept by the individual auto companies, however, do lend support to the thesis that something new was happening: strike frequency rates at Chrysler and GM doubled between 1960–64 and 1965–69.[64] Was there a national 'labor revolt' in these years or something less? The Chrysler evidence considered in chapter 9 suggests the reason for the contrast between nationally-kept and company-kept data is that what happened was piecemeal, local and isolated resistance. Fragmented shopfloor movements did appear for a few years and push back the frontier of control temporarily, but they failed to make permanent inroads.

It is difficult to estimate the influence of these different shopfloor movements. In an earlier period, they might have created permanent organizations or a consistent political expression of their radicalism.[65]

But the unevenness of the radicalization presented major obstacles. So did the retention among many workers of a powerful anti-communism – often, as with the miners, accompanying industrial militancy. Behind these political obstacles were economic and social ones. In the 1960s and early 1970s these shopfloor movements took place in the context of an economy whose rapid growth allowed certain limited reforms, against employers whose economic power was now truly global and within workplaces where union organization had developed a conservative 'powerlessness'.[66]

Moreover, in the 1960s and 1970s the unions still failed to make inroads into the 75% of America's workers who were unorganized. The absolute number of union members did expand, especially after 1962 when President Kennedy agreed to allow federal authorities to bargain with unions representing federal employees;[67] the National Bureau of Economic Research estimated that the number of union members rose from 15.5 million in 1960 to 21.1 million by 1975. But the total labor force grew faster: 26.3% union members out of a 59 million civilian labor force in 1960 slipped to 25.1% of 84 million by 1975. BLS statistics suggest an even greater decline in union density, from 28.9% in 1960 to 23.1% in 1975,[68] and a more recent estimate suggests that union density dropped still more dramatically in the second half of the 1970s, to just 20.9% of the total labor force by 1980, and since then to below 20% for the first time since the 1930s.[69]

Why did American unions fail to grow at the same rate as the growth of the labor force in the expanding economy of the 1960s and 1970s? The neo-classical economists' answer is simply that the benefits of unionism did not outweigh the disadvantages, and employers were able to persuade workers – through the stick or the carrot – to steer clear. But unionism is a collective experience that reflects the ideological competition between employers' and workers' interests as well as existing organizational potential. A major factor in the decline was that business unionism systematically lacked the independence and initiative necessary to mobilize new workers. This weakness was the result of three linked developments: the 1955 reunion of the AFL and CIO had strengthened the narrower, more conservative leadership and tradition of the older craft-based movement at the expense of any remaining combative industrial unionism; federal governments intervened more frequently in industrial conflicts and in wage settlements while labor's political clout waned; and instead of harnessing the groundswell of radicalism to strengthen unionism, international officers made common cause with management to suppress it.

The AFL–CIO decided to launch a massive new organizing drive at its founding convention in 1955: it never happened. Meany's view on devoting resources to union organizing was: 'We've done quite well without it.'[70] This policy was so negative it eventually led Reuther to believe he might be able to create a new, more dynamic labor federation, and he disaffiliated the UAW from the AFL–CIO in 1969. He had clashed with Meany over the absence of democracy within the federation and over Meany's refusal to countenance a serious struggle against the government or the employers to build union organization. A natural conservative, Meany tried to maintain a close relationship with successive federal governments. President Kennedy persuaded Meany to endorse pay controls in 1962, and Nixon did the same in 1972 after he appointed New York construction union leader Peter Brennan as Labor Secretary. This followed ten years of growing federal government intervention in wage bargaining and labor conflict. But the principal mechanism government used to influence the conduct of labor relations, besides negotiating with its own employees, was the invoking of Taft–Hartley. Kennedy, Johnson, Nixon and, in 1978, Carter all used Taft–Hartley against workers whose demands and threats of industrial action might trigger more general labor unrest. And what the federal government didn't finish, the courts did. In the early 1970s the Nixon appointees-dominated Supreme Court and various lower courts significantly reduced workers' rights.[71]

The failure of the conservatively led AFL–CIO to adjust to changes in the structure of American industry, particularly the growth of the service sector, stood in marked contrast during the 1960s with a major resurgence of radicalism – this time focused around black workers' grievances that had been growing since World War II. When wartime labor shortages and federal policy after the 1942 March on Washington Movement encouraged the auto companies to hire more blacks, the proportion of black workers in Chrysler's Detroit plants rose quickly from 2.5% to 15%. But this recruitment was accompanied by a major anti-black race riot by whites in central Detroit and few blacks were upgraded out of foundry and unskilled work.[72] Blacks began to be commonly accepted as semiskilled workers only in the late 1940s, first in the physically demanding body shops and then in assembly, but they were still excluded from skilled or white collar jobs. In the 1950s Chrysler employed only twenty-four blacks among 7,425 skilled workers and only one among 350 apprentices.[73]

Black workers in all blue collar jobs except laboring or foundry work held significantly lower seniority in the 1950s than most whites. So when the big lay-offs occurred at Chrysler almost every two years through the 1950s, they also tended to be laid off more frequently.[74] This was particularly true in the national recession of 1957–58 that was used by many labor relations departments to establish a new 'hard line' on work discipline.[75] In this recession managements used unemployment and lay-offs to police shopfloor practices and supplement the freedom of movement provided by their close relationships with union leaders, who were then often reduced to running after the employers reminding them of how useful they had been to them in the past.[76] Between 1957 and 1958 when total employment at Chrysler's four biggest Detroit plants fell from 45,584 to 22,776, the proportion of black workers collapsed from 20.3% to 14.7%.[77] By the end of the 1950s, many black workers appreciated that business unionism had not provided them with anything like equality or opportunity of earnings: its lifetime security was for someone else. A mass base was being created in the black community that would support the militant civil rights movement and black riots of the 1960s.

In 1957 the former Ford Rouge worker and first black UAW international representative, Horace Sheffield, called some other black Detroit union officers to a meeting in his basement and formed the Trade Union Leadership Council.[78] Three years later, after similar groups had formed in other cities, Philip Randolph, the veteran socialist and leader of the Brotherhood of Sleeping Car Porters, founded the Negro American Labor Council. Randolph opposed separatism but believed black workers should no longer wait for the existing white leaders to set them free:

> While the Negro American Labor Council rejects black nationalism as a doctrine and the practice of racial separation, it recognizes the fact that history has placed upon the Negro and the Negro alone the basic responsibility to complete the uncompleted civil war revolution through keeping the fires of freedom burning in the civil rights movement.[79]

But Randolph's demand that the AFL–CIO act to 'eliminate segregation and discrimination within international and local organizations' led to his being censured by the AFL–CIO's Executive Council for promoting 'antilabor' views.[80]

At the very same moment, however, the civil rights movement re-established collective militancy as a legitimate form of action. The Greensboro lunch-counter sit-ins of 1960 gently opened the door; the freedom riders of 1961 and 1962 pushed a little harder. By 1963 even the Kennedy administration, elected on a wafer-thin majority of 118,000 out of 68 million, was ready to acknowledge the need for legislation to guarantee the civil rights of Southern blacks. And Lyndon Johnson, taking over as President on Kennedy's assassination in 1963, felt he had to move still faster to exorcise his Southern Democrat origins.[81]

The 1964 Civil Rights Act and 1965 Voting Rights Act did not reduce tension straightaway: the federal government's recognition of certain black demands legitimated the continuing protests and helped to strengthen the movement for change, articulated most clearly by Malcolm X. In 1965 a black suburb of Los Angeles, Watts, erupted in a black rebellion that was echoed in dozens of other uprisings across the United States over the next few years; in 1966 the Black Panthers were formed in Oakland, California; in 1967 the biggest black uprising of all occurred in Detroit; and in 1968 Martin Luther King was assassinated in Memphis where he was supporting a strike of black sanitation workers, members of the rapidly growing municipal workers' union, AFSCME.[82] In Memphis and in parts of the auto industry, like Chrysler's Dodge Main plant, there were clear links between the struggle for black rights in society at large and black workers' rights in the workplace and in the union. Among black auto workers the disillusion with business unionism was still more complete since the ostensibly pro-civil rights UAW was still led by an all-white IEB right up to 1963.[83]

A similar, though less marked, connection existed between the Vietnam War and much rank and file discontent in the late 1960s and early 1970s. Not only did hundreds of thousands of young Americans come under the direct influence of the anti-war movement, but many of the hundreds of thousands of Vietnam War veterans, black and white, returned to work disillusioned with the standard managerial, nationalist and authoritarian ideology. Membership discontent with business unionism showed itself most dramatically in the miners' union. Despite Tony Boyle, John Lewis' successor, ordering the murder of his principal opponent in 1969, a rank and file movement, born out of a campaign for mine safety, still succeeded in ousting him. Big wildcats in the postal service and among teamsters also led to this discontent being described as a 'labor revolt'.[84]

In 1972 the 90% white workforce at the GM plant in Lordstown, Ohio, struck the country's most modern assembly plant. Gary Bryner, the young Lordstown UAW local president who ten years later was on the International Executive Board, explained:

> There's a substantial number of people that are Vietnam war vets. They don't come back home wanting to take bullshit from foremen who haven't seen as much of the world as he has, who hasn't seen the hardships.[85]

And in 1973 when news came over car radios being fitted on the lines that the Vietcong had entered Saigon, workers in several Detroit car plants began spontaneously hooting and cheering.[86] This was not, however, as much the sign of a new radical upsurge but of a collective sigh of relief at the end of a conflict which had divided Americans for nearly ten years. The end of the Vietnam War removed an important political issue legitimating the politics of confrontation from American politics and played a major part in limiting the influence of radical ideologies among students and among young and black workers.

The redistributive and demobilizing impact of the New Frontier and Great Society reforms of 1963 to 1965 should not be underestimated, however.[87] The black rebellions led to money being poured into inner-city aid programs, and occasionally into the pockets of former black militants who ran them, while police and FBI agents initiated a successful drive to destroy the remaining militant groups. By the mid 1970s the black middle class was larger, wealthier and more geographically dispersed than ever before. Above all, its job opportunities no longer lay exclusively within the black ghettos.[88] For the poor of those ghettos, federal and city poverty programs, food stamps and welfare payments provided a very thin safety net, but this itself was an advance on the 1930s: in 1982 a third of the adult population of Detroit survived on welfare.[89] Meanwhile, beginning with the election of Coleman Young as mayor of Detroit in 1973, the American political process appeared to provide a role for black politicians who stayed *within* the Democratic Party. The removal of Nixon from the presidency in 1974, and the election of Carter on a reforming platform in 1976, also added weight to the argument that the political system was working properly and that minority views should be organized through the Democratic Party rather than separately.

The emergence of these new 'minority' constituencies within the Democratic Party speeded the decline of the political influence of the atrophying AFL–CIO in the mid 1970s. Despite the election of the Carter administration and the largest Congressional Democratic majority since 1964, the well-organized opposition of business interests in Washington easily defeated the AFL–CIO's mild Labor Law Reform Bill in 1978. Lane Kirkland, soon to succeed Meany, was outraged. He accused the employers of mounting 'class warfare' and warned that industry's resistance to the proposals to assist union organizing 'may well mark a crossroad in the future of relations between labor and management in this country'.[90] Doug Fraser, the new president of the UAW, denounced GM's role in the successful filibuster and resigned from Carter's joint industry–union advisory committee in protest.

The defeat in Congress underlined business unionism's powerlessness on issues affecting the independent interests of working people. If it was a question that affected mutual interests of union and management, things might be different. The UAW appeared next at Congress in 1979 to campaign for federal funds to bail out Chrysler, and in the early 1980s it headed a drive to limit Japanese car imports that got quiet support from Ford and Chrysler. The AFL–CIO still had the strength to mobilize half a million union members to protest against 'Reaganomics' in the streets of Washington DC in November 1981, but it could not – or did not wish to – lift a finger for the dismissed PATCO air traffic controllers marching alongside them on 'Solidarity Day'.

By 1980 workers' fears of company bankruptcy and plant closures or lay-offs had created such insecurity that strike action (and other forms of open resistance to managerial authority as well) became 'illegitimate' in the eyes not only of management, the UAW and the courts, but also in the commonsense consciousness of virtually the entire workforce. Absenteeism rates, a measure of the confidence of the individual worker, collapsed:[91]

Absenteeism rate (%)

	Chrysler	Ford	General Motors
1979	7.3	3.9	9.2
1980	5.9	3.0	9.4
1981	5.6	2.4	9.6
1982*	5.1	2.1	8.0

* January to June

Union passivity was also strengthened by the fear of foreign competition. In the mid 1970s the US became a major importer of manufactured goods. The logic of world-wide competition finally began to dawn on American workers who found their labor relations executives, like Ford's Savoie in 1977 and Chrysler's Clancy in 1980, making pilgrimages to Japan. In many cases, the corporations paid for delegations of international officers to go, too. Post-war business unionism's remaining organizational independence from management was rapidly eroded when the unions agreed to help reduce labor costs in face of the 1979–82 recession. The UAW's return to the AFL–CIO in 1981 was not merely a retirement gesture from Fraser. It also signalled the UAW's abandonment of any pretense that it could harness whatever radical energy the late 1960s and early 1970s had possessed to a revival of unionism.

The re-emergence of homogeneity of perspective among union leaders and the defeat or stalemating of opposition movements among the postal workers, miners, steelworkers and teamsters by the late 1970s was a reversal for the radicalism of the previous fifteen years. The reversal dovetailed with growing job insecurity and a new resurgence of American nationalism with the Iranian hostage crisis of 1979–80. Reagan's 1980 election victory, the passive toleration of mass unemployment and the rash of concession contracts in the 1979–82 recession all followed. Chrysler, the auto maker with the highest level of worker–management conflict between 1938 and 1979, was the first to secure UAW agreement to concessions that froze workers' wages for two years and took away promised benefits while for the first time since the early 1930s strikes virtually disappeared.

Not all rank and file resistance disappeared. Solidarity with miners defying Taft–Hartley in 1978 was more widespread than for any other national strike since the 1940s.[92] At GM grievances rose to a new peak in 1979.[93] But this resistance had been made much more difficult and had retreated further underground. The declining power of institutional unionism *vis-à-vis* the employers was not compensated for by growing power in the hands of ordinary workers, while it was being recast by corporate labor relations departments.

In 1983 a Harvard professor of business administration confidently argued that the adversary era of labor–management relations, in which the '"law of the shop" has become more and more burdensome to our economic enterprises', was returning to an earlier, pre-1930s form of collaborative unionism:

> Before the 1930s, unions ordinarily envisioned themselves becoming involved in a broad range of problems associated not only with the difficulties of employees on the job, but also with the performance of the business enterprise ... It is time to draw on this older tradition of the US labor movement, and leave behind the concept of collective bargaining as primarily a rulemaking process.[94]

And Ernie Savoie, Director of Ford Labor Relations, believed Ford's employee involvement schemes were evidence of a qualitative transformation in relations between management and the UAW 'top people':

> More and more labor and management are coming to accept the fact that their relationship must also include a joint pursuit of their mutual converging interests. I see collective bargaining becoming more open – adding new structures under the collective bargaining umbrella – being more co-operative. These new layers institutionalize the zone of converging interest so that we may legitimize and foster appropriate mutualism in the years ahead.[95]

Savoie's assessment that 'things have changed permanently' should not be dismissed as wishful thinking. In the close 1982 vote that finally accepted concessions in still-profitable GM, plants with established quality of work life circles were more favorable to concessions than those without.[96]

The revival of what in 1940 Slichter called 'systematic co-operation'[97] is partly a simple reflection of the new balance of bargaining strength created by the 1979 recession: temporarily weakened companies faced by much weaker unions. But it is also true that this most recent development is a *new* aspect of an established trend, a trend which can be measured in the decline in union density since the late 1950s and the rising number of union certification defeats from the mid 1970s. The trend began as a steady growth of managerial power over labor and has been transformed, with concession-bargaining in face of Japanese competition in the 1980s and with labor-saving high technology, into enhanced managerial authority over work organization. Managerial requirements of improved labor productivity and product quality are being advanced within procedures for greater consultation and worker involvement which are not simple copies of a Japanese paternalistic labor relations system, although they have borrowed from that model. Rather, they reflect a much longer-term shift from point-of-production *bargaining* to institutionalized *consultation* and *cooperative* Taylorism.

In the mid 1950s the managements of the Big Three deliberately sought to extend the scope of bargaining from mere economic issues. Managements wished to introduce automation and tighter production standards and the resulting multiplication of plant-level grievances created pressures on them to extend formal bargaining. Partly to retain control over the local agreements that were becoming commonplace, and partly because the companies pushed them as supplements rather than alternatives to the national contracts, the Reuther administration agreed, experimentally in 1958, and throughout the industry in 1961, to allow locals to negotiate formal agreements with their managements. While the development was unavoidable, it was neither a devolution of *centralized* union control – the agreements had to be ratified by the international and lasted the full term of the national agreement[98] – nor did it represent the extension of workers' shopfloor frontier of control as it only took place once direct shopfloor bargaining was formally eliminated.

This extension of the area of formal bargaining was highly effective. It led to a situation where more local UAW-authorized strikes took place, and this gave new legitimacy to the idea of processing grievances through the procedure in order to win IEB support without having to take the risk of wildcat action. Both elements tended to increase the dependence of local union leaderships on the international union. Also, the international found itself obliged in the 1960s and 1970s, not merely to authorize local strikes at the termination of the national contracts, but also to authorize larger numbers of local strikes on strikeable issues that were effectively in defense of the local contracts. This spin-off effect of the greater participation by the international in local bargaining affected

General Motors and Ford as well as Chrysler. At GM only ten strikes were authorized by the international between 1942 and 1956, while in the five years after 1961 the international authorized fifty-four. At Chrysler, with less than a quarter as many separate locations, the total of authorized strikes rose from just three between 1942 and 1956 to eleven between 1962 and 1967 and thirteen between 1968 and 1972.[99]

The extension of plant-level bargaining also helped to stabilize the position of the international union leadership. The mechanism by which this happened was complex. While it added to certain management costs, local bargaining further fragmented the common interests of UAW locals. A layer of full-time elected local leaders emerged who had very little influence over either the outcome of national or local contracts but who could be – and from the mid 1960s frequently were – thrown out of office by a discontented membership after poor local or national contracts. The bargaining system thus made it more difficult to construct a united opposition to the international leadership while the union's structure made the local officers increasingly dependent upon favors from their managers and on the full backing of the international's election machine to get re-elected. Plant-level conflict was increasingly channelled through the international – a tendency which became still more apparent after 1970 when the UAW ran deeply into debt in a nationwide strike against GM.

The heavy costs incurred in the 1970 two-month GM strike led Reuther's successor as UAW president, Leonard Woodcock (1970–77), to attempt to avoid further national confrontation and to exert bargaining pressure through the encouragement of some local leaders to mount carefully controlled individual plant strikes.[100] In return the local officers were given greater job security under a rule change raising the duration of office from two to three years. The new international strategy of confronting the auto makers locally rather than nationally led to the numbers of authorized strikes in the second half of the 1970s rising significantly above the level of the late 1950s and early 1960s as the figures for Chrysler and GM show:[101]

Annual average number of authorized strikes

	Chrysler	General Motors
1957–67	1.8	7.7
1974–79	5.5	19.2

In this period, what remained of local union autonomy became subordinated to the new local bargaining strategy of the international union as locals carried out Woodcock's policy. Subsequently, under Doug Fraser (1977–83), both authorized and unauthorized strikes virtually dis-

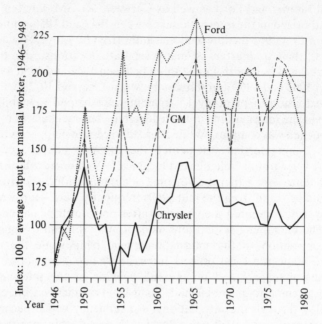

Fig. 3   Passenger car output per manual employee, Chrysler, Ford and General Motors, 1946–80

appeared as the recession forced the international to accept concessions and lay-offs in the interests of the industry's survival, in a context in which local union autonomy virtually disappeared.

The period from the 1960s to the early 1980s can be seen, then, as one in which there was both resistance to management, as illustrated by the 'labor revolt', and a countertrend of accommodation and passivity, which ultimately dominated. This analysis still leaves the question of whether the labor revolt was 'a principal source' of declining growth rates in the 1970s?[102] The question itself, although posed by Gordon *et al.*, echoes standard management thought[103] and is especially important in the case of Chrysler. The narrative chapters of this book suggest Chrysler workers restrained managerial authority for longer than workers at Ford and GM. Was this why Chrysler went bust? If it was then it appears logical that a national labor revolt would have such an effect on the national economy.

The evidence discussed in chapter 10, however, places little responsibility on labor for Chrysler's near bankruptcy in 1979. The reasons went much further back. In the mid 1950s worker-imposed restraints made Chrysler management rely more than GM or Ford on manipulating total employment to change output. Yet even then most of the responsibility for its low output per worker was management's. Chrysler built more complicated cars with less new investment than its rivals. After the labor relations watershed of 1957–59, as figure 3 shows, car output per head at Chrysler moved in line with Ford and GM for ten years. Chrysler workers did not advance their shopfloor restraints over managerial authority in the 1960s as they had during earlier growth periods. Poor job motivation continued to impact negatively on workers' job performance,[104] but it was not translated into additional restraints over management. In the 1970s, Chrysler's output per worker again moved out of synchronization as new investment was cut in the wake of the failure of management's product, design and marketing strategies. Productivity only rose when crisis-invigorated management cut the labor force by almost half. Chrysler workers' independent impact on business policy cannot be held responsible for the company's falling productivity and bankruptcy.

It has also been argued that the emergence of new technology, concession bargaining and the self-disciplining quality circle in the late 1970s and early 1980s represent strands in a new political collaboration between designers and producers that could mark 'the end of Fordism'.[105] But it does not follow that an extension of consultation to company survival plans, product quality and design or health and safety and the number of pay phone booths actually weakens or qualitatively changes managerial control. The test is whether such consultative bargaining leads a management to act differently or otherwise than in its own interpretation of its profit-making self-interest. The evidence of consultation about plant closures at Chrysler suggests the UAW's impact has been marginal while, in certain surviving plants, product and quality suggestion schemes never took off. It is true that Chrysler incurred 'efficiency' costs through improving the work environment but other companies that did not consult the unions have made similar improvements. Similarly, while federal safety checks and workers' compensation and insurance legislation and expectations of racial and sexual equality were often bargained over, the *source* of what could later become restraints on management decision making was not union strength.[106]

The shift in the scope of bargaining to so-called 'non-economic' factors is not a sign of a new, higher-level challenge to managerial power.[107] Rather, the development of bargaining over plant efficiency and social issues in the 1960s and 1970s should be seen as a process gradually leading to equally limited consultation rights over company viability in the 1980s. What began with management agreeing to negotiate on what it saw as issues that did not compromise its shopfloor authority, developed into quality circle and employee involvement programs as combativity collapsed in the recession.

Far from facing an 'erosion' of the existing organization of the labor process and an 'end to Fordism',[108] Chrysler used the 1979–82 recession to reinvigorate managerial 'drive'. Its pattern of labor relations closed dramatically to the industry norm and became a pattern setter. The 'norm' it approached and overtook was not marked by a weakening of the dominant managerial control system but, if anything, by a system of managerial authority more independent of collective worker restraint in the early 1980s than at any time since the 1930s. The widespread adoption of tightly disciplined team-work systems has secured a key objective of scientific management: the self-monitoring of work effort.

This chapter has argued that several different interpretations of American labor history, the golden age, the World War II watershed, the labor truce, the labor revolt, and the onset of non-adversary bargaining, do not fit the Chrysler experience. The narrative of chapters 3 to 10 considers the detailed evidence.

Part II
Autocracy and resistance, 1928–1941

3 From company picnics to Coughlin

The Great Depression of 1929–33 underlined the powerlessness of all semiskilled and unskilled workers. The South Carolina mill owner who declared, 'We govern like the Czar of Russia',[1] was not an exception. Managerial absolutism ensured that workers' lives were dominated by insecurity. But even in an industry as hard-hit as auto, the Great Depression did not have a homogeneous effect. In pockets of relative job security the anger workers felt against Hoover in the 1932 presidential election was expressed collectively. Accounts of the unionizing process in the 1930s as unproblematic are inaccurate. Managerial ignorance, prevarication and prejudice interacted with a complex workers' world view that had as much ethnic and religious solidarity to it as class consciousness.

This chapter shows in section I how Chrysler strengthened its market position from 1929 to 1933 while keeping unilateral control over its workers. In 1933 the New Deal's endorsement of labor unions appeared to threaten Chrysler's autocratic paternalism, and, like many other employers, he responded by setting up a 'union' based on a works council (section II). However, as shown in section III, Walter Chrysler not only promised joint decision making, he also had to contend with a highly concentrated workforce at Dodge Main whose works council representatives came under the influence of the populist 'Radio Priest', Father Coughlin. The combination of these factors led to the formation of a Chrysler-based union with mass support. 'Coughlin's union' was organized independently of the company and, as outlined in section IV, in 1936 it became a key component of the UAW.

I. Chrysler expansion in the Depression

On May 29 1928 53-year-old Walter Chrysler bought the ailing Dodge Brothers Company. The 'rescue' was the biggest he had attempted since quitting General Motors nine years earlier – of a going concern whose $132 million assets were actually greater than Chrysler's own $104 million. The major asset of Dodge Brothers was its 'Main' plant, an eight-storey plant on a 30-acre site in Hamtramck, a city suburb of Detroit. Dodge Main's 30,000 workers were soon turning out about a quarter of a million cars a year, including the new Plymouth and DeSoto models as well as the existing Dodge line. The acquisition transformed Chrysler from being one of many makers of medium-sized cars into a major producer. Once he had included the 3,160 dealers of the Dodge organization, Chrysler had around 8,000 dealers throughout the US and Canada and was represented in all price classes of the market between $720 and $2,945. Chrysler overnight became America's third largest automaker.[2]

Compared with Ford and the largely local managements of several of the more expensive car-making firms in Detroit, Chrysler Corporation, like General Motors, had an out-of-town, professional management image from the start.[3] Chrysler himself came from Kansas, and had risen from apprentice mechanic to GM Buick president. K. T. Keller, who headed the management team that dramatically reorganized Dodge Main in 1928, had been an apprentice machinist in Pennsylvania and, subsequently, general manager of GM's Canadian operation. But their GM backgrounds did not mean Chrysler Corporation adopted the multidivisional decentralized organizational structure that characterized GM after 1925. GM had grown through the acquisition of many small (and not so small) companies and plants, and the experience of many little empires all competing with each other provided the basis of its genuinely pluralistic management structure. This experience did not appear relevant to Walter Chrysler. After he broke from GM in 1919 he was hired by a group of Chicago bankers to rescue first Willys–Overland and then the Maxwell Motor Car companies. The Maxwell rescue led him to launch the Chrysler Six, a medium-priced high compression-engined car that was so successful he got the bankers' support in transferring all Maxwell Motor's business and property to the new Chrysler Corporation on June 6, 1925. Largely financed by Chicago and Wall Street banks, and based on a handful of plants, the new corporation did not change its centralized, unitary form of management structure for another twenty years.[4]

Market conditions in the late 1920s proved ideal for Chrysler. With demand for cars jumping by 56% from 1927 to 1929, the Dodge purchase enabled the company to more than double its output and to finance itself. Chrysler Corporation's annual average pre-tax return for 1925–29 was 11.2% – enough, as table 4 shows, to survive the recession and to

Table 4 *Chrysler production(a), market share and profitability(b),*
1925–45

Five-yearly average	Passenger car production (000s)	Car market share (%)	Return on sales (car and non-car) (%)
1925–29	316	10.03	11.16
1930–34	292	15.51	0.34
1935–39	724	23.14	8.36
1940–41	907	24.24	7.95
1942–45			6.13

Source: Chrysler Corporation, *Financial and General Fact Book*, June 1973; Wards
Automotive Year Book, 1969, 79.
(*a*) Based on new passenger car registration from 1925–34.
(*b*) Before tax operating margin as a percentage of net sales.

continue to increase its market share. The boom of 1927–29 was followed
by the deep recession of 1930–32 that cut the number of establishments in
the motor industry from 210 to 122 between 1929 and 1933.[5] Economies
of scale had become decisive. In the 1920s any company capable of
selling over 10,000 cars a year survived. But after 1931 companies that
sold fewer than 100,000 cars lost money.[6] The harsh climate effectively
eliminated much of the competition and the survivors, GM, Ford and
Chrysler, claimed the spoils: their combined market share rose from 59%
in 1927 to 87.5% five years later.[7]

In 1933, the first year of recovery, Chrysler built nearly the same
number of cars as it had in 1929. Its market share rose from 8.2% to
25.4%. Dodge Main did particularly well. Walter Chrysler designed his
cars with a high proportion of interchangeable parts to keep costs down,
and so Dodge Main manufactured parts for Chrysler's top-selling Plymouth car as well as assembling the DeSoto and Dodge cars.[8] Table 5
compares the annual change in new registrations between the top-selling
Chrysler cars to those of Ford and GM. Between 1931 and 1941
Chrysler's Dodge Main and Plymouth plants expanded output nearly
three times faster than GM's Chevrolet Division and five times faster
than Ford's River Rouge plant. This expansion provided Chrysler's
production workers with more regular work that at Ford or GM, with a
particularly sharp disparity in 1933.

During the early years of Chrysler's growth its workers faced virtually
unlimited managerial control. In the late 1920s and early 1930s Walter
Chrysler combined a not particularly generous paternalism with support
for strict plant discipline enforced by the foremen.[9] At his Kercheval

Table 5 *Car registrations of Chrysler, GM and Ford leading models, 1931–41*

Year	Chrysler		General Motors	Ford
	Plymouth % change	Dodge/DeSoto % change	Chevrolet % change	Model A/V-8 % change
1931	+ 47	− 18	− 6	−50
1932	+ 19	− 35	−45	−51
1933	+123	+101	+47	+20
1934	+ 21	− 5	+13	+71
1935	+ 27	+103	+23	+56
1936	+ 30	+ 48	+42	− 9
1937	− 7	− 13	−17	+ 2
1938	− 38	− 41	−40	−53
1939	+ 22	+ 68	+29	+32
1940	+ 26	+ 12	+43	+13
1941	+ 3	+9	+ 3	+11
Average annual change 1931–41	+25%	+21%	+8%	+4%

Source: Chrysler, *Facts*.

assembly plant a 'Good Cheer Fund' provided workers with company picnics and a legal advice bureau. When Chrysler took over Dodge, he inherited its marginally better provisions: a group life insurance package, free dances for employees, a welfare department that might give a worker a small loan, and legal advice for workers.[10] A contemporary account provides an indication of the favoritism and poor working conditions that prevailed before the Great Depression. Robert Dunn quotes a trim worker at Dodge Main in 1927: 'In Department 66 only the bosses and their friends are working. The other workers are sent home.'[11] Another man who worked nearby in Department 64 reported in 1928:

> We are allowed to stop work about 15 minutes to bolt our lunch, but we are not provided with a place to eat it. We either sit at our benches in the dusty room or, when there is nothing else for one to sit on, we have to sit on the floor. Besides, they work the sweepers on another shift and they are sweeping the floors right under our noses while we are trying to eat our lunches.[12]

While conditions in Chrysler's plants were not the worst – contemporaries viewed the Briggs body plant with most horror[13] – they were quite bad.

During the three successive years of collapse of the American car market after 1929, however, endemic job insecurity led to shopfloor discipline being tightened. Some restraint of output continued despite the absence of unions, as Mathewson's notable study demonstrated. He found foremen often played an organizing role in holding up work so that lay-offs would be postponed.[14] In a large automobile plant, where the workers agreed among themselves on a ceiling for bonus earnings on grinding valves, Mathewson quoted a worker who believed the foreman and the general foreman supported the ceiling: 'They don't want the rate cut any more than we do. It just makes the men sore and causes a lot of trouble.'[15] Such restraints were not, however, universal. Close relationships did develop between skilled men and foremen who had formerly been skilled workers, or between workers and foremen in areas of the plant where superintendents and plant managers allowed a certain flexibility of output. But where final processes were involved, with continuously moving conveyor lines, pockets of better working conditions were eliminated as auto profits and production crumbled in the Great Depression.

The general experience of semiskilled and unskilled auto workers was that while conditions were extremely tough in the car market boom of the 1920s, they became worse as the Great Depression took hold. The most loyal and hard-working employee was not safe. The proportion of auto workers laid off for anything from a shift to a few months rose from 49.7% in 1930 to 86.2% in 1932. Still more devastating, and against the trend in US manufacturing, the number laid off who were also 'separated' – that is, told there would be no guarantee of more work in the future – rose from 70.2% in 1930 to 98.9% in 1932. The effects were considerable. Previously those regularly laid off and separated had been the traditional 'disposable' semiskilled and unskilled sector. By 1932, the entire workforce, including the 10%–15% of skilled workers, was affected, creating a common grievance.

Job insecurity was compounded by insecurity over pay: average weekly earnings for those still at work in automobile, body and parts plants fell 43% from $35.14 in 1928 to $20 a week in 1932.[16] John Zaremba, a graduate of Brown's Business School, Chicago, had worked as a time study man for GM in 1920 and as a clerical worker at Dodge Main from 1921 to 1923. Unable to get clerical work in the Depression, he started back in Dodge Main as an operator in the heat treatment department in 1932. Zaremba often went to work to be told by the foreman or superintendent not to bother clocking in. But the bonus, or lack of it, was an even bigger grievance: 'The bonus was a farce at all times. We never knew what we were going to receive as pay, whether it was going to be 50c, 61c, 71c or 76c ... the amount of the bonus was a "secret". Everybody would work and work and work. It seemed the more we worked, the less bonus we got.'[17] John W. Anderson, a University of Wisconsin graduate, was hired as a metal finisher at Dodge Main on December 2, 1932:

> To hold my job I had to work continuously from 12 to 14 hours a day, seven days a week from the day I was hired until 7 pm on Christmas Eve ... On December 24 the foreman told me, 'You're being laid off until further notice. We'll call you when we need you.' During those 23 days I worked almost 300 hours and at 52 cents per hour I earned about $150. There was no premium pay for overtime or working Saturday or Sunday, yet we metal finishers were among the highest paid in the industry.[18]

Pay was high for short periods, but workers never knew how long the work would last. The pool of 75,000 young unmarried men in Detroit, called the 'suitcase brigade', was hired and fired without respect or sentiment.

In December 1933 after the auto recovery had begun, a report on the Dodge Main drop forge department highlighted three areas of uncertainty for its workers: peak employment in the department had been 250, it was then 230, and in the 'slow season' varied between 75 and 130; hourly rates varied widely from 54c to 96c while hourly earnings – including the bonus – varied still more, from 65c to $1.85; finally, the hours worked each week ranged between 30 and 35.[19] All three variables, whether an individual was laid off or recalled, the rate and bonus, and the number of working hours, were determined by the foreman, general foreman or superintendent.

Managerial authority was arbitrary. Often the supervisor had the personal authority to recruit family or friends or workers from a similar ethnic background.[20] The alternative was to queue from 3 a.m. outside a plant's employment office that opened at 8 a.m. Those lucky enough to get inside might have to wait until 9 p.m. to be told whether they were hired or not.[21] Foremen had the power of instant dismissal. Workers tied to moving lines had to request their foreman's permission to go to the bathroom.[22] In much of Dodge Main workers were not allowed to speak while working. Gertrude Nalezty started in Dodge Main's showcase first floor Wire Room in 1934: 'Before the union you had to work fast. The supervisors were on your back all the time. Once the whistle blew you could say "Good morning" or "Good afternoon", but that was that. You couldn't talk to one another while you worked.'[23] Here again was ground for grievance. Workers were systematically being denied the basic rights and dignities of citizenship.

II. 1933: Year of change

In 1933 economic trends coincided with a political watershed. US unemployment continued to rise until March 1933, but in Detroit the situation improved. Chrysler recovered its pre-depression production levels in an industry producing 41% more cars than in 1932. Sales of its principal model line, the Plymouth, made at the Dodge Main and new Plymouth Road plants, rose 123% in 1933 above 1932 sales.[24] Jobs in the auto makers and especially in Chrysler began to seem more certain. Critically, March 4, 1933 also saw the inauguration of Franklin D. Roosevelt, the 'New Deal' President. Elected in November 1932 he had stood 'for the building of plans that rest upon . . . the forgotten man at the bottom of the economic pyramid' and promised unemployment compensation and federal relief to prevent starvation.[25] By the time of his inauguration a new political atmosphere was already encouraging a minority of workers to assert basic democratic rights in the workplace and 1933 saw the biggest strike explosion of American labor relations.[26]

In Detroit the 1933 strike explosion began in the Briggs plants that supplied Ford with its 'white' car bodies. Briggs plants were known as 'slaughter houses' and their working conditions were considered some of the worst in the industry. In January 1933 new labor hired at its Highland Park plant to cope with increased demand for 1933 models quickly found management cutting the hiring rate for metal finishers from the 52 cents promised (and being paid at Dodge) to 35 cents an hour. After the third reduction in successive weeks, the men stopped work and demanded an explanation. Their foreman told them: 'If you don't like your job why don't you quit?' and, when they kept stopping or working slow, insisted: 'Either go to work or quit!' They walked out and the presence of a few Communist Party members in Briggs, with the assistance of the CP's Auto Workers' Union (AWU), turned the flare-up into the first big auto industry strike.[27]

The Briggs strike showed that, with organization, workers could direct their anger effectively against the auto companies. Those who struck and stayed out were not rehired when the strike was called off on May 1. But their action forced Briggs and several other companies to increase their rates and stopped the spate of piecework price cutting.[28] It also led to the dispersal of several now-experienced strikers to other Detroit plants and helped encourage a major strike wave after June 1933 when Roosevelt signed the National Industrial Recovery Act (NIRA). A strike of dingmen (metal repairers), a key group of autoworkers with substantial acquired skills, quickly broke out at Dodge Main. It was against 'Chiselling by the Chrysler Corporation at all plants – Trying to break in new dingmen while there are dingmen still out of jobs – Chrysler Corporation trying to flood dingmen labor market and cut wages'.[29] Within forty-eight hours it was 'squelched' – even this highly skilled group was scared of being marked out as troublemakers. But Chrysler's refusal to listen to the fears of such a key group determined many individual workers to consider union membership as a way of changing management's attitude.[30]

On August 26, 1933 Roosevelt issued a 'Code of Fair Competition for the Automobile Manufacturing Industry' under the terms of the National Industrial Recovery Act. The code was published as a 5c pamphlet and distributed widely in Detroit making a considerable impression on both workers and employers. This was not because its minimum conditions were generous to the workers. Its minimum employment conditions were entirely acceptable to the National Automobile Chamber of Commerce: a 43c an hour minimum wage in cities with populations over 500,000; those employed not to be worked more than an average 35 hours a week; and a special clause, exclusive to the automobile industry, that allowed the employers to discriminate 'on the basis of individual merit'.[31] But the Automobile Code did repeat the Act's Section 7(a):

> Employees shall have the right to organize and bargain collectively through representation of their own choosing, and shall be free from the interference, restraint or coercion of employers of labor, or their agents, in the designation of such representatives or in self-organization or in other concerted activities for the purpose of collective bargaining or other mutual aid or protection.[32]

Union membership gained a formal legality and became 'American' overnight. In Detroit the Auto Workers' Union, the Industrial Workers of the World, the newly formed Mechanics Educational Society of America and the American Federation of Labor all recruited thousands of workers.

Union membership, however, did not instantly appear 'legitimate' to most workers. Union 'legitimacy' depended crucially not on the law but upon three other elements: management recognition, a high level of worker involvement and evidence of its effectiveness. In 1933 each of these elements was missing when the first attempt was made to unionize Dodge Main. The passage of Section 7(a) prompted AFL president William Green, under pressure from the only major industrial union, the United Mine Workers, to assign four full-time organizers to the country's half a million auto workers.[33] They were not exactly the most dynamic team, and they were given a hopeless strategy: first to organize all the autoworkers into federal (AFL) locals covering each plant; and then to divide up those recruited into their respective AFL craft unions. William Collins of the International Association of Machinists established his headquarters in Detroit, and within a month of the launch of the Automobile Code, the first AFL meeting was held at Dodge Main.[34]

Nineteen workers attended the Dodge inaugural union meeting on Sunday afternoon, September 24, 1933, but only five knew each other. John Panzner, one of Collins' staff, chaired the meeting and explained the Federal Labor Union charter, Local No 18277, that had been issued to Dodge employees. He then organized the election of officers. Harold Padget was ready to run for president as he had been laid off from the trim department in 1929 and was still not back at work. Jack L. Andrews was elected vice-president and wrote the names of those present on a blackboard so they could get to know each other. He was a company spy.[35] Eight days later the five workers from the fifth floor trim department cushion line who attended the meeting were fired. Harry Ross recalled his foreman coming up to him and his partner on the cushions, a man who had worked 20 years at Dodge Main, asking, 'What have you two guys been doing? I have just got orders to fire both of you.' Zaremba survived: he had given the spy a fictitious name.[36]

In October Panzner spoke to the second Dodge meeting, 'about how we should git the employees together and about forming a council of all locals to work hand in hand and to git things a rolling in this City to git all Factorys organized and to have a strong union in the Automobil distric.[sic]'[37] Later, the local drew up a program of demands to submit to the management. It raised the issues affecting all autoworkers in the early and mid 1930s: the bonuses and the piece rate system; job security and employment; regulation of the speed of work; favoritism; and payment for lost time.[38] But at the same moment two developments occurred to undermine these early moves to unionization. From the AFL Executive Council came instructions forbidding AFL organizers to put toolmakers, die makers, maintenance men and machinists into federal locals.[39] The movement to build an industrial union was sabotaged by the policies of the craft International Association of Machinists.[40] While from the auto makers came a powerful response to the formal legality to union organization offered by Section 7(a).

The employers were not united in their response, although they were almost entirely hostile. Henry Ford responded by strengthening his repressive regime to prevent the unions getting into his River Rouge plant. The Edward G. Budd Company of Philadelphia, body builders and owners of the British Pressed Steel Company plant at Cowley, found that at least a quarter of its workers joined the AFL union. It then simply defied the new Labor Board's recommendation that it should bargain with the union.[41] Chrysler and GM, by contrast, dressed up their anti-unionism in legal clothes by launching company union schemes.[42] These were works councils, usually of elected long-service employees and staff representatives who would funnel grievances to management without the need for the involvement of non-factory personnel or collective bargaining. They became very popular among employers determined to prevent 'outside' interference with their managerial prerogatives, but who baulked at outright law-breaking.[43] There were still, however, significant differences between the Chrysler and GM works council schemes which subsequently played a large part in shaping their shopfloor union traditions.

Walter Chrysler put his personal imprint on the plan for 'Employee Representation in the Plants of Chrysler Motors' in October 1933. He wrote in a letter distributed with the plan: 'As a former shop-worker I have long looked forward to the time when the Employees and the Management of the Chrysler Corporation would sit down around a table to discuss and decide matters of mutual interest to all of us.'[44] And the proposals stated baldly: 'Purpose. This is a Plan which provides an opportunity for the Employees *to have an equal voice with the Management in deciding jointly* all matters affecting wages and working conditions' (my italic). Neither the handful of AFL members nor the even smaller numbers of members of the Communist Party's Auto Workers' Union tried to mobilize resistance to the company union plan. Its hint of coming improvements in wages and working conditions was too promising to be opposed, even though the Dodge Main Joint Council was to be made up of fifty-three supervisors and staff and fifty-three elected employee representatives, while issues could only be decided by a two-thirds majority. The plan was adopted with 95% in favor in a secret referendum and the first employee elections were held early in 1934.[45]

GM's company union plan, drawn up in July 1933, was much more modest.[46] For several years GM had run the Industrial Mutual Association of Flint which provided club houses, bowling alleys, billiard tables and all the trappings of a self-running benevolent society that in practice was at GM's beck and call.[47] Confident from this experience, GM did not feel obliged to seek the double-edge legitimacy of Chrysler's plan by calling a ballot or promising joint decision making.[48] It simply imposed its plan. And the following year it issued a policy statement on labor–management relations which made clear that its 'collective bargaining' did 'not imply the assumption by the employee of a voice in those affairs of management which management, by its very nature, must ultimately decide upon its own responsibility.'[49]

These early differences between the Chrysler and GM schemes would have profound consequences.[50] The Dodge Main works council unified the highly concentrated plant in a period of rapid expansion, and brought together potential organizers. But it did not provide the genuine representation Chrysler had promised; nor was managerial authority significantly less arbitrary. In this situation the organizational encouragement of Detroit's nationally known 'Radio Priest', Father Coughlin, was decisive and Dodge workers formed an 'independent' union modelled on Coughlin's National Union for Social Justice. In contrast to the fate of the GM company union scheme, and certainly against the intentions of its creator, Chrysler's scheme acted as midwife to an active shopfloor trade unionism.[51]

III. The sources of militancy

The size and concentration of Dodge Main contributed significantly to the unionizing process. In the mid 1930s some 35,000 workers were employed working on two or three shifts in a total floorspace of 5.1 million square feet.[52] As figure 4 shows the complex was highly compact, with nine major buildings linked together. Henry Ford, the Dodge brothers and Walter Chrysler believed in integrating the manufacturing process. The reinforced-concrete construction was supported internally by concrete columns that divided the working space – already confined to long segments no more than 100 feet wide – into narrow aisles just 25 or 30 feet across.

Casting, forging and heat treating were carried out in single-storey buildings for extra ventilation. Other buildings were multi-storey, parts being received and stored on the ground floor, which also housed the heaviest machinery. Higher floors carried the conveyors that snaked almost randomly through the complex. The eight-storey body building was connected to the pressed steel building on the second, third and fourth floors, and to the no. 2 assembly building on the fifth and sixth floors. Once the body-in-white, painting, and enamelling processes had been completed the bodies were taken by other conveyors and elevators up to the higher floors of one of the two assembly buildings for trimming. The cars then passed down to the second floor final assembly lines. There, the bodies were dropped on to the completed chassis before the cars were driven down a ramp and out to the test building.[53]

The high degree of integration and the physically constricting work situation facilitated contact between workers with a common interest in collective organization. It ensured that news of disputes and grievances was spread quickly throughout the complex. This heightened sense of plant-wide identity was strengthened by the works council that brought

Detroit (following Babson (1984), 242)

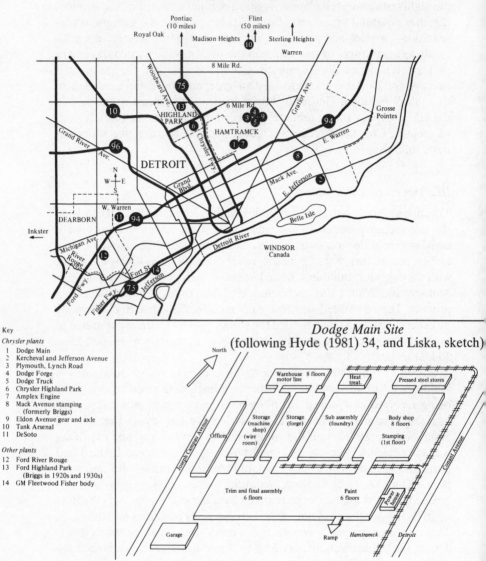

Key

Chrysler plants
1   Dodge Main
2   Kercheval and Jefferson Avenue
3   Plymouth, Lynch Road
4   Dodge Forge
5   Dodge Truck
6   Chrysler Highland Park
7   Amplex Engine
8   Mack Avenue stamping
      (formerly Briggs)
9   Eldon Avenue gear and axle
10 Tank Arsenal
11 DeSoto

Other plants
12 Ford River Rouge
13 Ford Highland Park
      (Briggs in 1920s and 1930s)
14 GM Fleetwood Fisher body

Fig. 4   Detroit and Dodge Main

together some fifty workers from all parts of the plant. Between the first works council meeting, early in 1934,[54] and the last, in February 1937, at least 150 different workers met together once or twice a month in company time. It was a far cry from most GM plants,[55] where the chairman of an eight- or ten-person works council would either conduct all discussions personally with the plant manager or invite him or a single management representative to attend meetings.[56] The Chrysler works councils fostered an 'us' against 'them' consciousness among a sizable layer of manual workers.

Chrysler workers' expectations of a new era of democratic rights aroused by FDR in 1933 were first endorsed by Walter Chrysler and then effectively dashed in 1934 and 1935. Though promised discussions on 'wages and working conditions', the workers were fobbed off, as District 23 employee representative Zaremba complained: 'It was nauseating for us to listen to the company recite about holes to be reparied in the floors and windows to be repaired in the departments.'[57] Richard Frankensteen had worked at Dodge from 1926 to 1928 while he attended night school at the University of Detroit, and had then graduated from the University of Dayton, Ohio, in 1932. He was back in the Dodge trim department in 1933 and was elected District 7 employee representative the following year. Along with most other works council representatives he found Chrysler's 'democratic' experience frustrating:

> As for the Works Council, we bargained for clean windows and floors without grease, and many things that were important, but meaningless in take-home pay. When it came to dollars and cents, when it came to economics, we were powerless.[58]

This resentment was felt sharply by those taking part, and began to surface when Chrysler's growth got into full swing and workers' job security returned, accompanied by a growing conviction that it was legitimate to challenge arbitrary exercises of managerial muscle.

An awareness of workers' rights developed particularly strongly in Dodge Main because it was located in Hamtramck, the 'Poletown' of the United States. In 1940 there were twenty-two foreign language publications being published in Detroit,[59] and a high proportion of Dodge Main's workers were first- or second-generation Poles. Many of them, from the late 1920s and mid 1930s, were followers of a very special Catholic priest, based in the Detroit suburb of Royal Oak, who was known throughout the United States as the 'Radio Priest'. Father Charles E. Coughlin began his demagogic Sunday night broadcasts on the WJR radio station in 1926 and continued with only a few interruptions until 1940. To an audience which, in the early 1930s, frequently reached up to forty million people,[60] he preached a virulent anti-communism in harness with vehement denunciations of prohibition and advocacy of the equality, class collaboration and 'social justice' for industrial workers.

Coughlin's radical philosophy of social justice was based on Pope Leo XIII's *Rerum Novarum, On the Condition of the Working Class* (1891) which argued that Catholic clergy should fight for just and moral reforms in industrial society. Pope Pius X's encyclical of 1912, *Singulari quodam*, took this further and acknowledged workers' rights to form trade unions, but added: 'Trade unions must not engage in any act or theory which does not concur with the teachings and instructions of the Church or of the relevant religious authority.'[61] Along with many other young priests in the 1920s Coughlin interpreted this as direct encouragement to intervene in the existing unions or to construct unions exclusively for Catholic workers.

Coughlin's appeal was directed at workers hit hard by the Depression and who wanted to get good-paying jobs in the land of opportunity. He attacked employers who denied workers jobs or employed them as 'modern industrial slaves'. In July 1930 he told a congressional enquiry into domestic subversion that 'The greatest force in the movement to internationalize (i.e. Communize) labor throughout the world is Henry Ford.' In the 1932 presidential campaign Coughlin strongly attacked Hoover's record, and he openly endorsed Roosevelt with slogans such as 'Roosevelt or Ruin' and 'The New Deal is Christ's Deal'.[62]

In 1934, when Roosevelt distanced the presidency from Coughlin who had begun making unacceptable political demands, Coughlin responded by trying to turn his Radio League of the Little Flower into a more organized political pressure group. His National Union for Social Justice, launched in a radio sermon in November 1934, was intended, Coughlin said, to allow his listeners 'to organize for social united action which will be founded on God-given social truths'.[63] The National Union's preamble began:

> Establishing my principles upon this preamble, namely, that we are all creatures of a beneficient God, made to love and serve Him in this world and to enjoy Him forever in the next; and that all this world's wealth of field and forest, of mine and river has been bestowed upon us by a kind Father, therefore, I believe that wealth as we know it originates from the natural resources and from the labor which the sons of God expend upon these resources.
>
> It is all ours except for the harsh, cruel and grasping ways of wicked men who first concentrated wealth into the hands of a few, then dominated states and finally commenced to pit state against state in the frightful catastrophes of commercial warfare . . .[64]

The Union for Social Justice never got off the ground – largely because Coughlin could never delegate responsibility – but its momentum carried over into his Detroit autoworker constituency.

Coughlin opposed his supporters joining the AFL in 1934 and 1935. The AFL's craft structure was hostile to Coughlin's constituency of unskilled or semiskilled recent immigrants and, in any case, the AFL's skilled workers were predominantly Protestants and the AFL was infiltrated by 'racketeers' and 'gangsters'. But Coughlin did encourage the transformation of Chrysler's employee representation scheme into an 'independent' union based on his Catholic principles of industrial unionism.[65] His contribution to the unionizing process was his prestige as the best-known Catholic priest in North America. The respectability his profession carried encouraged many Catholic immigrants as well as a key layer of Protestant native Americans to see union organization as morally justified.

IV. An 'independent' union

In the spring of 1935, frustration grew among the second wave of employee representatives elected in January and February. It became increasingly clear Chrysler was not prepared to allow the Works Council to become a bargaining forum. On Coughlin's advice the employee representatives met on their own on April 9, 1935 and decided to issue dues cards for an Automotive Industrial Workers' Association (AIWA). An eight point charter, probably drawn up at one of the regular Friday evening meetings of activists held at Coughlin's house,[66] was adopted. The objects of the AIWA were similar to those of Coughlin's Union for Social Justice:

> To promote the interests of those engaged in the automotive and allied industries by improving working conditions, by fostering better cooper- ation between employers and employees, and by promoting and fostering legislation tending to better the welfare and interests of the said employees.[67]

The AIWA's first year book, issued on December 14, 1935, was dedicated to 'our advisor and supporter Father Charles E. Coughlin, the friend and educator of the masses'.[68]

The improved effectiveness of Coughlin's Dodge Main supporters began to make itself felt quite quickly. In July 1935 an AIWA employee representative on the Dodge Main works council proposed Chrysler operate district-based seniority lists to govern lay-offs and recalls. This was defeated by fifty votes to forty, but at the same meeting twenty-five votes were recorded for a still stronger challenge to managerial authority, the right of employee representatives to take a witness in with them when they met management. A week later Frankensteen was amazed when he won the coveted two-thirds majority after several staff workers used the cover of the secret ballot to vote for a 10% rise in earnings. Most representatives felt entitled to challenge management on the *terms* of subordination while in 1935 only a minority challenged its *content*. The proposal was summarily rejected by Chrysler vice-president in charge of manufacturing, W. J. O'Neill, the Dodge Main general manager who chaired the Joint Council. Two months earlier he had instructed the representatives: 'I don't want you fellows to think because you don't get a 15% increase, and 65c rate, that this isn't Collective Bargaining.'[69] But this is what they did think, especially when management then sacked J. H. Campbell, the chairman of the employee representatives' side. A management representative explained: 'He made a slur on the President of the Chrysler Corporation when he made the statement that there were hidden profits.'[70] Instead of being a forum for management–employee togetherness, the works council fostered anti-management resentment by legitimizing the articulation of certain demands which management then turned down.

Other contradictions in Chrysler management's new industrial relations policy presented still greater opportunities to the AIWA. Chrysler provided the employee representatives with 'their regular average pay from the Company for the time actually spent in serving on such Council or Committee'.[71] And soon after the Joint Council began operating, the Chrysler workers' representatives were allowed paid time off to follow up grievances. The 'Policy for Works Council and Employee Representatives Meetings' allowed them a monthly meeting on their own in addition to the Joint Council one, and it stated, 'If for any reason the employee representative feels that in the normal discharge of his duties it is necessary for him to leave his work during working hours the permission of the foreman must be obtained before he takes such leave.'[72] In 1935 the AIWA organizers used these privileges as company union representatives to act as *de facto* shop stewards.

The AIWA constitution allowed locals to be set up by any group of twenty-five or more workers and established a shop steward system:

1. Every local shall have at least one shop steward and as many more as they find necessary.
2. Each shop steward shall have contact men who shall report and be responsible to him.
3. The duties of the shop steward shall be to aid the Financial Secretary in collecting dues and to see that each member's grievances are

properly taken care of. He shall report to the Local at least once a
month.[73]

By October 1936, when the first major clash occurred between the UAW
and Chrysler, management was hoisted on its own petard. It wanted to
stop the stewards going around their departments organizing meetings,
but had to agree when a shop steward–employee representative asked:
'Are the Representatives permitted to leave their work for business
reasons as they have been permitted in the past?'[74]

The privileges accorded to the employee representatives had not led to
greater identification with the company. Under the impetus of beliefs in
Catholic social justice and the New Deal, in a period of economic
growth, these privileges had been transformed into their opposite: a
tradition of elected departmental representatives being paid by the
company to progress grievances and industrial action *against* the
company. And there was more. Alongside, these company-recognized
stewards had developed a layer of union-recognized stewards who,
frequently operating in the same way, were often indistinguishable from
them. The AIWA was known in Detroit as 'Coughlin's Union', and often
decryed as a 'company union', but, as events would demonstrate, it too
was much more than that.[75]

The AFL local based on Dodge Main still existed, but its membership
was tiny. Its activities were largely restricted to endorsing correspondence conducted by Collins or Green with Chrysler management or the
Automotive Labor Board. In its first year, the only recruitment recorded
in the minutes was of twelve members in April and eight in May 1934.
Such was its impotence that Andrews, the company spy, remained
vice-president until October 1934 when he turned his attention to Dick
Frankensteen, the trim department worker who was soon to found the
AIWA.[76] On March 24, 1935, the local called a special meeting to take a
strike vote. Twenty-nine voted in favor and none against, yet no strike
ensued, for in mid 1935 the AFL had only 178 members in all of
Chrysler's Detroit plants.[77] In April 1935 the local agreed 'shop stewards
be appointed from each department', but could only find ten men present
(including the ubiquitous Andrews) ready to serve. With attendance
dropping in the fall, the local virtually disintegrated. It was renamed
Local 3 of the United Automobile Workers after a national meeting of
federal locals in August 1935. However, when it called a special meeting
to send a delegate to the UAW's first national convention in April 1936,
it only reached a quorum of nine out of its fifty members.[78]

So weak was Local 3 that some members, including John Zaremba and
Harry Ross, decided to work both in the company union scheme and in

building the AIWA. Once the AIWA was established, they found themselves paying it 25c and the AFL $1 a month. The joint work of Frankensteen, Harris, McIntyre, Ross, Cousins and Zaremba and, in particular, the regular meetings with Father Coughlin, paved the way for the AIWA and UAW to merge in 1936.

Two groups of workers played leading roles in the process of unionization: one was of those like Frankensteen and Zaremba[79] who had high school and college educations but who had been unable to find white collar work because of the Great Depression.[80] Also in this group who could be called 'organizers-through-career-frustration' were men like Leon Pody, a former businessman ruined by the Depression, Richard Harris, formerly an insurance salesman, and Harry Ross, whose father had wanted him to go to college. The Hamtramck Poles in this group were skilled workers such as Walter Rogowski, a former mechanic, and Joe Ptasynski, a former tool and die maker, who could not get skilled work.[81] The second group, of 'organizers-through-politics', was made up of immigrants from continental Europe or the British Isles, like the Probe brothers and Pat Quinn in the Dodge trim department, who brought with them expectations of some form of union organization. Of course, many others from different backgrounds played a part in the unionizing process; but these two groups provided disproportionately more organizers. They were young and had under five years' employment in the industry when they began to organize. Their personal or political responsiveness to the absence of social justice in the plant, together with needed organizational skills, pushed them to the fore. For them the differences between the UAW–AFL and the AIWA were minor factors compared to the imperative of building an organization that could bring dignity to their working lives.

Negotiations about a merger began soon after the newly formed CIO sent Adolph Germer to Detroit with this purpose in mind in December 1935, but it only took place after the South Bend UAW Convention declared its independence of the old craft-conscious AFL. Although the Convention did not bar Communists from holding office, it did unanimously express 'unalterable opposition to Fascism, Nazism and Communism and all other movements intended to distract the attention of the membership of the Labor movement from the primary objectives of unionism.'[82] Coughlin, who spoke at the Convention, welcomed its industrial union orientation and its anti-communist declaration and believed his AIWA, with an estimated 10,000 members in Chrysler plants, could become a leading force in the union. The AIWA negotiators, president Frankensteen, Frank Szymanski and Dave Brann from Dodge Main and AIWA vice-president R. J. Thomas from Chrysler's

Kercheval plant, all destined to be important figures in the UAW factional struggles of the late 1930s, were cabled by Coughlin: 'There can be but one for success. I urge you to amalgamate'.[83]

With Coughlin's backing, the merger was assured – although members' fears of 'outside' unions led to a sizable 35% voting against in a referendum.[84] The AIWA, the Hudson Motors' independent union and parts of the MESA joined, increasing the UAW's membership to some 25,000.[85] Frankensteen, who was also elected the first president of the enlarged Local 3, was given a seat on the UAW's International Executive Board and put on the UAW payroll as Detroit organizer. On August 2 1936 'a meeting of all Locals in the Dodge Plant' was held 'to form one big union of the entire plant'.[86] Overnight, six months *before* winning formal recognition from management, the UAW gained a mass membership in Chrysler plants and inherited a continuity of organization from 1933.[87]

4 Fair play with the management: 1936–1941

During the late 1930s the mass production industries were at the center of a major battle between American management and workers over the frontier of control. But the contribution of each side to the eventual location of that frontier was complicated by the varied experience different managements and groups of workers brought to the fight.

Section I of this chapter considers Chrysler's 1936 attempt to curb the UAW, its failure and how it rebounded to help establish an independent shopfloor union tradition. Section II considers the interfirm differences between managements and labor traditions that led to the 1937 sit-downs and contracts being experienced in a different way at Chrysler than at General Motors. The factional struggles within the UAW from 1937 to 1939 reflected different views on the source of union strength, and the outcome had a big impact on Dodge Main, the union's largest organized plant, as is shown in section III. Both GM and Chrysler tried to use the disarray of the UAW in 1939 to their advantage. But when its summer confrontation ended in defeat, GM implemented a new strategy of limited recognition and containment of the union challenge. Section IV argues that Chrysler took a different route, ploughing ahead with its own confrontation over the issue of control of production standards, and when it lost, failed to draw any significant conclusions. As the US economy geared up for World War II, Chrysler management found it had encouraged workers to view mutual agreements made on the shopfloor as a 'right'.

I. 1936: Year of advance

The strength of the newly amalgamated UAW was swiftly put to the test by Chrysler. On August 26, 1936, 3,000 Dodge workers received letters telling them: 'It does not appear at this time that our requirements will afford an opportunity to recall you to work.'[1] This was a deliberate attack. Harry Ross, dismissed first in 1933 and then reinstated by the Automotive Labor Board in 1934, was thrown out once more. So were hundreds of other shop stewards and union activists. Foremen were given special forms to record the names, badge numbers, class of worker and date of original employment of 'undesirable' workers and those 'we wish not to be returned'. In the first category, the Department 76 list contained eighteen names, all men with between two and five years' seniority in Dodge. Some of the 'remarks' filled in by the body-in-white foremen were:

> Talks too much – continually objecting to the amount of work.
> Strong union man – hot headed. Liable to cause trouble.
> Agitator.
> Employee Representative. Active in Union.
> Trouble maker – Walked off the job, hot weather, July 10 1936.
> Communist.
> Strong union man – Does a lot of talking. Contact for Symanski.
> Hard to handle – liable to cause trouble.[2]

The firings came during the model changeover, a bad time for any immediate response, so the stewards waited until rehiring for the 1937 model began. Then, following a leafleting campaign on the theme 'What security have you? *None* unless you act NOW', Local 3 organized a series of after-work departmental meetings to take strike votes. These began on October 1 and were to build up to open mass meetings on October 14, 16 and 18. By October 12 the trim, warehouse, hammer, metal polishing, heat treatment, foundry and pressed steel departments had almost unanimously backed the strike call (a total of just eleven workers voted against).[3]

The strength of resistance to Chrysler's obvious intimidation flowed partly from growing economic security and partly from rising political confidence. Economic security returned to most autoworkers as year-on-year growth between 1933 and 1936 nearly doubled their average earnings:[4]

Model year September–August	Average annual male earnings in the auto industry $
1933	749
1934	1,014
1935	1,294
1936	1,399

1936 was also Keller's first full year as Chrysler president, and he presided over the company's biggest operating margin on sales (11.4% before tax) since 1927. In the 1930s Chrysler was one of the most efficiently managed companies in the auto industry. It secured considerable economies of scale by using a high proportion of interchangeable parts on different models. As a result, by 1937 its factor costs for each Plymouth car were the same as for each Chevrolet, despite producing only two-thirds as many.[5]

In 1936 sales of Chrysler's principal products, the Dodge and the Plymouth lines, reached the high point of the 1930s. Keller would dearly have loved to have kept the UAW activists out of Dodge Main on the 1937 models. But he faced a dilemma: at a time when every car which Dodge Main turned out was certain to be sold, was it worth risking immediate profits to defeat a union that nationally still had under 50,000 members? Keller decided not. On October 16, 1936, rather than face a strike, he announced the recall of all 1934 seniority workers including those previously 'separated'. The following week the retreat became a rout when all 1935 men were recalled, and on November 11 Chrysler conceded – three years before GM – time and a half overtime pay.[6]

This union success showed Detroit's autoworkers that the 'Big Three' could be forced to make concessions and it came just before Roosevelt's re-election to the presidency in November 1936. If the Chrysler victory was the spark to the subsequent wave of sit-downs, the flame was Roosevelt's massive defeat of the Republican candidate Alfred M. Landon, a strongly anti-labor politician.[7] The Democratic electoral victory appeared to legitimize the *shopfloor* unionism that had just shown its power, and it put Chrysler management still further on the defensive. This breakthrough was experienced personally by large numbers of Dodge Main workers as *participants* in a struggle. *Self-organization* was seen to produce results, rather than reliance upon a tiny number of activists, the international union or upon 'enlightened' management. 'Do-it-yourself' unionism became part of what can usefully be called the 'plant consciousness'[8] of Dodge Main and most other Chrysler plants; so too did workers' direct participation in rule-making – a process that elsewhere was largely determined by international officers.

The establishment of rights to shopfloor industrial action and rule-making encouraged a tremendous expansion in union numbers, confidence and organization.[9] In December 1936 the Local 3 regular business meeting agreed to hold departmental meetings throughout the plant to 'elect their Chief Steward, stewards and captains. Each elected man to be given a 30 day trial, if not competent then he should be removed.'[10] In January 1937 regular meetings of chief stewards, who wore black lapel buttons, and sectional stewards, with blue or white buttons, started up.[11]

The constituency of the chief stewards tended to approximate to that of departmental general foremen and their superiors, the superintendents. Sectional stewards were elected by work groups or appointed by the chief steward to cover every twenty-five workers or one for every sectional foreman or forelady.[12] By March 1937 there were 180 chief stewards in Dodge Main – representing a ratio of 1 to every 111 workers – and between 400 and 800 sectional stewards.[13] The steward system had arrived. It was not an exclusive elite or activist-only organization, but was seen by all union members – and many non-unionists – as a legitimate way of representing *all* interests within the department or section. This gave the stewards the authority not merely to speak for their members, but also to lead.

Within three years three major struggles took place that helped root this shop steward organization more deeply in Chrysler plants than in those of GM: the 1937 sit-downs and resulting contracts; the bitter internal UAW factional struggle; and the 1939 Chrysler strike. The result was to differentiate the union tradition between Chrysler and GM and to allow Chrysler workplace unionism to survive the 1938–39 recession and enter the war period of bitter conflict with management stronger than before.

II. Sit-downs

The two major auto sit-downs of 1937 were very different, despite the similarities between the contracts that ended them. The GM sit-down strike, experienced at the time by most participants as a victory, appears to have prepared the ground for subsequent defeats. While the Chrysler strike, which was seen by many Dodge Main activists as a defeat,[14] appears to have contributed to a longer-term advance in workers' rights.

When it became clear GM was going to compromise in its 1937 sit-down battle with the UAW, Chrysler tried to buy its way out of conflict. It agreed at a works council meeting to pay a 5% premium to all second and third shift workers.[15] But UAW candidates had just won forty-six of the fifty-three districts on the Dodge works council, and its negotiators, led by Dick Frankensteen, were in no mood to settle for minor concessions.[16] After the agreement-to-bargain contract was signed with GM on February 11, 1937, the UAW believed it could win *full* bargaining rights covering all Chrysler workers. At this point Walter Chrysler intervened from semiretirement to insist that Keller resist these demands and to take charge of negotiations. The union's strength was still untried; there was a chance it might crack. But even more important, only by resisting the UAW momentum might management retain any initiative in determining the form of future collective bargaining. In particular Walter Chrysler had noted GM's refusal to recognize shop stewards in its contract, and was determined to turn the tide back in his plants.

It was, however, too late. When Frankensteen was told on March 8 that Chrysler would not recognize the UAW as the bargaining agency for all its workers, it took just one phone call to John Zaremba inside Dodge Main to set the sit-down in motion. Zaremba raised his right hand in the pre-arranged signal and his blue button stewards told their sections:

> 'Shut it down!' From my department it snickered around ... It crossed the docks again. People are waiting for a signal there too. 'Shut her down!' And this is just how it happened. Within five minutes after the signal was given from the outside, there was not one piece of machinery moving.[17]

The Dodge stewards organized the rapid closure of the plant and also ran the sit-down. The chief stewards became the Dodge Strike Committee on the first evening. Then they immediately decided to bar superintendents, foremen and office staff from the factory.[18] And after about two weeks they also threw out the security guards, to discover their cache of handguns, ammunition and tear gas.[19]

The sit-down tactic was employed because of its success at Flint, and because a walk-out by the minority of union members could not have halted production for long. The unionization process at Chrysler involved a substantial minority of workers taking action with the passive support of the majority. There were already between 11,000 and 13,000 UAW members in Chrysler plants when the GM sit-down began in December 1936, and somewhere between 15,000 and 20,000 out of Chrysler's total workforce of 67,000 when the Chrysler sit-down started.[20] This strength proved most important. At GM the proportion of UAW members before the sit-down was tiny, so the layer of union activists who experienced the struggle was much thinner than in Chrysler plants where as many as 6,000 workers[21] were actively involved. After four days the 450-strong Dodge body-in-white Department 76 boasted 'the best record of any group in Dodge Main: over one third of its total membership sat in voluntarily. When one third of these were forced to go home (by the Strike Committee to cut the costs of feeding them all), there was a fight for the privilege of remaining.'[22] The *Dodge Strike Bulletin* was distributed to workers inside the plant and to those who came to offer support on the outside. The same writer explained in its first issue why the sit-down movement commanded such support:

> The men in the factory seem to be real Americans, good citizens, some property owners. They want to have real collective bargaining which rightfully belongs to them and guaranteed by the US Government. They want to have fair play with the management; they have Democracy within their Union. They want Democracy within the automobile industry as well as Democracy within the whole country.[23]

The sit-downers' demands were legitimate; their aspirations were 'American'. Their movement could be supported by *all* working Americans, from Communists to Catholics.

What had happened between 1933 and 1937 was that workers' beliefs in the legitimacy of unrestrained managerial autonomy had been undermined. The New Deal's politics of 'responsible citizenship', the defensiveness of the business community and the emergence of union organization capable of articulating the new demands of 'worker citizens' accomplished the change – thanks to a healthier climate in parts of the American economy. And at Dodge Main, the longer history of continuous organization, its origins in a Catholic-backed movement and the status union representatives were accorded as a result of Chrysler's works council scheme, all contributed to a higher level of mass involvement in the sit-down than elsewhere.

The Dodge stewards' independence from UAW headquarters was shown when Chrysler began to process injunctions against the occupation. The UAW President Homer Martin got cold feet but the *Dodge Strike Bulletin* warned:

> There are some people who are going around spreading the propaganda that we can win this strike just as well by leaving the Plants and forming a picket line outside the Plants. Boys, this is Treason. Lets get these rumours stopped, also the stoolies that are spreading it. Our Chief of Police, Patrick Quinn, a former member of the IRA, knows just how to deal with traitors. Get on your toes and let Pat do his stuff.[24]

After Chrysler got an injunction the pressure to pull out increased. To avoid a confrontation Martin secured an agreement from Chrysler that it would not attempt to run the plants if the evacuation went ahead, and from Governor Murphy that if necessary he would place state police on the gates to stop strike-breakers. The activists in Local 3 still held out – against the advice of the UAW's Chrysler negotiators – saying they would evacuate only if Chrysler conceded sole bargaining rights and re-opened the plant within seven days.[25] When they finally left, after several votes at an all-night meeting with Martin,[26] they still maintained their active strike subcommittees, including a flying squadron which kept up a picket on the UAW–Chrysler negotiations in the Michigan State capital of Lansing.

On April 4, however, Martin wound up all these Dodge strike committees because 'third degree methods were being employed in questioning suspected different people', and he accused their pickets of delaying 'the satisfactory settlement of the present strike'.[27] He blamed 'the Communists' for the trouble and used it to justify launching an anti-communist, anti-socialist purge within the growing numbers of UAW staff.

The four-week Chrysler strike ended on April 6 after John L. Lewis reached a GM-style agreement with Walter Chrysler that failed to win the sought-after full recognition. Many Dodge Main workers strongly opposed the settlement, but management had not cracked their solidarity nor, despite certain of its copycat GM provisions, did the first contract withdraw legitimacy from the shop stewards. So although Chrysler merely conceded bargaining rights to the UAW for its own members in the seven struck Chrysler plants, union membership continued to spread throughout the entire workforce.

A comparison between the Chrysler contract and that of the industry leader, GM, reveals differences that reflect the greater involvement of the Chrysler workforce and the poor strategizing capacity of Chrysler management in the area of labor relations. The first complete GM contract was signed four days after the Chrysler strike began. It excluded any reference to 'shop stewards', and only recognized a new body, the 'Shop Committee' of between five and nine (depending on the size of the plant) elected committeemen as the proper channels for grievances. It has been rightly called 'a combative, hard-nosed, but fundamentally legal labor relations strategy'.[28] One of GM management's first tasks in the seventeen UAW plants was to work out the shape of the new large committeeman constituencies with the local UAW officers.

In the Chrysler agreement, management was as insistent as GM that the word 'steward' should be kept out and it too set up small plant committees. But, in addition, Chrysler was forced to recognize unspecified numbers of 'District Committeemen', with full rights to negotiate during working hours, and to agree that the numbers of districts would not be changed. When the UAW printed out its version of the final Chrysler contract of April 14, 1937, it overcame the problem of terminology with an insert:

> District Committeemen (*Chief Stewards*) may perform their duties of conferring with foremen or other designated representatives of the plant management, or with the Labor Relations Supervisor of the plant,

during working hours without loss of time or pay. A District Committeeman shall always notify his foreman before leaving his work. [my
italic][29]

This insert provided, from the very first Chrysler contract, for *two*
parallel systems of plant bargaining. There was the existing chief steward
system – they retained their rights to take paid time off work, as did their
'assistants' on the second and third shifts – and, in what was assumed to
be a superior position in the plant bargaining hierarchy but was not
necessarily accepted as such, there was the Plant (Bargaining) Committee.

In reality the situation was even more complex. To counter the rank
and file criticism that the 'steward system' was being sold out by their
negotiators, Frankensteen had to write an introduction to the Agreement which explained the continuing role of chief stewards and the
continuing function of 'regular' sectional (blue or white button)
stewards:

> Regular stewards have no authority to deal with the Management but
> they have official capacity for the Union as contact men during lunch
> hour, before work and after work, and during this time can pass out
> grievance slips to those who desire them, collect dues, and serve other
> interests of the Union ... Each District shall have a recognized Chief
> Shop Steward to present grievances or, in the case of second and third
> shifts, an Assistant Chief Steward with equal power (to all effects and
> purposes).[30]

In Chrysler, the UAW endorsed the 'official capacity' of sectional
stewards as grievance gatherers and general 'contact men', while at GM,
by contrast, the most that was promised was that the steward system
would be fought for in the next round of negotiations.[31]

Additions to the GM collective bargaining agreements in 1937 and
1938 illustrate the greater clarity of GM's approach to its new relationship with the UAW. GM appreciated, almost from the start, that the
union structure was not homogeneous and that the interests of the
international union and the locals were not always identical. In response
to the rash of wildcat strikes that followed the victory over GM in 1937,[32]
UAW president Martin was persuaded to send a company security clause
to GM confirming its right to discipline union activists:

> The Union agrees that it is the responsibility of the Management to
> maintain discipline and efficiency in its shops and the right of the
> employer to hire, discipline and discharge employees for cause is
> expressly recognized, subject to the right of appeal through the griev-
> ance procedure.[33]

Then, in the 1938 GM contract, management not only negotiated an explicit ratio of 'one committeeman for each 400 hourly-rated factory employees working in that plant', but it also secured a ruling against shop stewards: 'Shop Stewards shall have no function under the grievance procedure and can handle only their own individual grievances with the foreman, same as any other employee.'[34] At the same time GM added to the visibility and prestige of plant committeemen by giving them two hours a day paid by the corporation to pursue grievances.

While most American managements in the 1930s were totally opposed to 'outsiders' negotiating wages and conditions for 'their' workers, after 1937 GM quite consciously operated a dual policy aimed at limiting the impact of unionism on the shopfloor. Inside its plants it undermined the position of departmental and sectional shop stewards to the benefit of its large-constituency committeemen. And at the same time, whenever possible, it negotiated with, made demands on and insisted on the involvement of even more remote figures: the international officers.[35]

Alfred P. Sloan, GM's President from 1923 to 1937 and its Chief Executive Officer until 1946, wrote later: 'What made the prospect seem especially grim in those early years was the persistent union attempt to invade basic management prerogatives. Our rights to determine production schedules, to set work standards, and to discipline workers were all suddenly called into question.'[36] GM policy was no less hostile to union organization than was Chrysler's, but it was significantly more flexible. It recovered very rapidly from the clear defeat it experienced in the 1937 sit-down strike determined not to allow the initiative to remain with its workers. Industrial relations were prioritized in a way they had not been before; and while GM finally only abandoned its hope to live entirely without the UAW in 1940, it instantly developed a pragmatic response aimed at forcing the UAW to accept responsibility for wildcat strikes and at maintaining management's rights over the crucial areas of the labor process.

Chrysler, on the other hand, lacked both the foresight, the will and the means to develop a similar sophisticated strategy. As far as it was concerned most militant trade unionists were communists – beyond the pale. Walter Chrysler told the UAW's top negotiator in Lansing in April 1937: 'Mr Lewis, I do not worry about dealing with you, but it is the Communists in these unions that worry me a great deal.'[37] The anti-union prejudice and autocratic structure of Chrysler management was not a good combination for dealing with the much more complex job control problems created in its plants by the presence of mass trade unionism.

The wider layer of activists, the early tradition of self-reliance, and

Dodge Main's unique position as the UAW's largest unionized plant before 1941, added another feature to the form of trade unionism being rooted there. Elsewhere, in smaller plants or ones with only a handful of activists, the massive UAW membership expansion, from 88,000 in February to 400,000 by October 1937, often led to the appointment to a staff position of the only really experienced shopfloor organizer. For this reason, or because of the sheer volume of new members lacking in organizing experience, many other UAW locals quickly entered a *dependent* relationship towards the international UAW machine. But when Frankensteen, Ross and a few others became staffers, there was still a large experienced cadre in Dodge Main whose organizing experience dated back longer than most UAW staffers, to 1933 and 1934. Dodge Main showed a degree of independence from the UAW headquarters' staff and from the bureaucratizing process that overtook the UAW in 1937.

III. Factional struggles, 1937–1939

The thirty-month factional struggle in the UAW from 1937 to 1939[38] also played an important role in strengthening the sectional, problem-solving shop steward tradition in Chrysler plants.[39] Both at the local and at the international level, the left-wing 'Unity Caucus' was identified with the growth of shop steward influence and, less clearly, with the development of a tradition of 'independent' (from the UAW machine) action. The right-wing 'Progressive Caucus', on the other hand, was seen as advocating tight centralization with all decisions on action being taken by the UAW headquarters. The final decisive defeat of the right-wing Homer Martin faction in 1939 was therefore a major political and ideological boost for do-it-yourself unionism.

The battle between left and right was nowhere more fiercely fought and complex than at Dodge Main. In 1936 the plant was the principal Coughlinite stronghold in Detroit. But the demogogic Coughlin had become increasingly opposed to Roosevelt and the New Deal, and in June 1936 broadcast that the Union Party he had just set up would support congressman William Lemke for President of the United States. Roosevelt, Coughlin told a Cleveland meeting in July, was a 'betrayer', a 'liar' and a 'double-crosser'. Coughlin promised to deliver nine million votes to Lemke or retire from public life.[40] In August 1936 Coughlin turned against the UAW when it joined the fledgling Committee for Industrial Organization and was suspended from the AFL. Zaremba gave a more colorful account of Coughlin's change of heart:

> All of a sudden, like lightning out of the sky on a clear day (we were visiting Coughlin's home) he said to Dick Frankensteen, 'Say, Dick,

you know what?' 'What?' 'I guess I will have to talk against your unions.' 'Why?' 'Because Fisher (Lawrence Fisher of Fisher Body) told me that if I do not speak against you fellows, he is not going to pay the balance for the organ in the church.' And Dick took it jokingly, he thought it was a joke between gentlemen. He said, 'Well, I guess you'll have to talk against us.' Lo and behold, the next Sunday a tirade came from Father Coughlin over WJR radio station against the workers.[41]

While Fisher's organ could have played a part, it is more likely that Coughlin's view of the CIO as 'communistic'[42] and of Roosevelt as a 'betrayer' prompted the break with his mainly Democratic Party Dodge Main followers. In making it, however, so he began a process that ultimately led to the isolation of his conservative anti-communist ruling bloc in the plant.

During the 1937 sit-down the Catholic faction was still strong enough to stop the *Daily Worker* being allowed through the fence into the plant. Stamping plant chief steward Barney Hopkins went further. He read a 'protest against the Communistic literature passed out to Union men at the plant gates and to the pickets. We demand that something be done to prevent Communism from entering our rank and file. If Communism is to enter our ranks then labor's cause is lost.'[43] After a considerable debate the strike committee agreed the outside pickets – organized by a leading Dodge Main Communist – should stop 'all literature (being) indiscriminately peddled in the street in front of the plant'.[44]

By the end of the sit-down strike, however, discontent with the evacuation from the plant and with the final settlement had swung Dodge Main opinion in the direction of the militants. At the first Local 3 membership meeting after the return to work, a call by Local 3 president, Dick Frankensteen, to delay rushing into a new election was narrowly defeated by 300 to 290 votes by those he called 'a click [sic] who are trying to get control'.[45] But while the activists were becoming more militant, the majority of Dodge Main workers were still well satisfied with the old leaders. When the 9,517 votes for Local 3 president were counted on May 16, 1937, the conservative AIWA slate had a fair majority: Frankensteen polled 60% ahead of C. 'Pat' Quinn, a center slate candidate who had been chief of security in the sit-down, who took 29% of the vote, while the left slate candidate, Communist A. J. Walden, former chairman of the outside strike committee, polled just 11%. The position of Local 3 vice-president was won even more convincingly by another former Coughlinite, Ed McCann, with 65% of the vote.[46]

When UAW president Homer Martin launched his drive to reduce the Communist Party and Socialist Party influence in the UAW leadership, local faction organizations, mirroring the national caucuses, sprang up at Dodge Main. The 'Unity' Caucus was led by IEB members Wyndham

Mortimer, a Communist, and Walter Reuther, a Socialist Party member. Unity stood for breaking with the Democratic Party: 'We want independent political action . . . We want to see a Farm-Labor Party in the US based upon our labor movement.' And it argued for strong shop stewards' organization: 'We want enlarged powers for the shop stewards. We want them a regular part of the union structure. They should have powers to decide on shop problems, clearly stated in the union constitution.'[47] By contrast, the 'Progressive' caucus of Martin and the former AIWA leaders Frankensteen and Thomas, was silent on these issues. It focused instead upon 'responsible' unionism:

> The UAW must at all times protect its right to strike, its greatest weapon. However, we will fight mercilessly against any person responsible for using this weapon irresponsibly or without authorization, in such a way as to place it in jeopardy by giving our opponents the chance to take it away from us.[48]

The difference about whether shop stewards had the right to 'decide on shop problems' or were always obliged to get 'authorization' came up often and quite sharply in Dodge Main, where Martin's Progressive views clashed diametrically with the structure and tradition of Dodge unionism and workers' experience of Chrysler management.[49]

The March 1938 Local 3 elections were held in an atmosphere of extreme bitterness, illustrated in these verses about Dodge Main's leading right-wingers by a Unity caucus shopfloor poet:

> Hitler hides his face in shame
> His methods are so clean
> When compared to the tactics of
> The monster MARTIN–STEEN . . .

> And here's McCann, a sorry specimen
> Without an honest breath
> Besotted – Windy – redbaiting yes man
> As sneaky as a cat
> With all his brains in his pratt . . .

> Brothers meet Mr Frank Szymanski
> That big little pot-bellied boy
> To whom the death of every 'Polock'
> Would be everlasting joy . . .

> There they stand, that happy lot
> Of dictators big and small
> By the sword they all have risen
> And by the sword they'll fall . . .[50]

The 1938 Progressive election pamphlet was printed on green paper, starting the tradition of a green slate representing the more conservative faction in the plant. It was 'not endorsed by any Political Party, but . . . by R. T. Frankensteen, International Vice President, President of Dodge Local 3'. But despite its AIWA credentials, it failed to make headway. Progressives Frank Reid and Ed McCann retained the presidency vacated by Frankensteen and the vice-presidency on a turnout nearly a third smaller than the previous year. But the three other full-time local positions, recording secretary, financial secretary and treasurer (a Communist) were held by the Unity slate, which also defeated six Progressives for other positions on Local 3's executive board.

The set-back for Local 3's Progressive caucus coincided with Frankensteen's growing disillusion with Martin. These two factors led Frankensteen to begin discussing a change of caucus allegiance with leaders of the Communist Party's auto work.[51] In May 1938, when Frankensteen finally switched to the Unity caucus after a deal with the Communist Party, his former supporters were thrown into disarray. A month later Frankensteen was one of five international officers suspended by Martin. On the Dodge EB the right-wing majority slipped: they got only five votes to support Martin's action, and a mild protest was actually carried by twelve to eleven.[52]

In November and December 1938, when the national factional struggle was reaching its height, the paper-thin Progressive majority on Local 3's executive and plant committees, tried to reinforce its power by undermining the chief steward system. The EB ruled 'that when a Chief Shop Steward has completed his business with the Plant Committee members, he should immediately leave the plant committee room.'[53] It also decided to give the plant committee a monopoly on the use of industrial action: 'No Chief Shop Steward shall take any action without the knowledge or permission of the Plant Committee of Dodge Local 3. That all Chief Shop Stewards shall receive orders in writing, same orders must possess at least a majority of signatures of Plant Committee members.'[54] When this rule was ignored, the executive threatened to discipline disobedient stewards:

> Any Steward of Dodge Local No. 3 who causes or sanctions any interruption in production without first receiving permission from his officers of his Unit and the Plant Committee, that such a Steward be reprimanded, and shall be held fully responsible for the action taken, to the Executive Board of Dodge Local 3.[55]

This so clearly laid the stewards open to managerial discipline that a second vote agreed to keep the resolution out of the minutes.

These attempts to impose a GM-style bargaining system at Dodge Main lasted only a few weeks. The isolation of the Reid–McCann right-wing Catholic faction was finally completed early in 1939. R. J. Thomas, the former AIWA vice-president and president of the Kercheval Chrysler plant, finally deserted Martin, who then suspended fifteen members of the International Executive Board and set about building his own UAW. Two months of heavy in-fighting followed. Armed guards were put by Unity caucus supporters on the Local 3 hall, and financial secretary Ross refused to countersign the check for outstanding international dues McCann wanted to pay over to the Martin headquarters.[56] At one stage McCann was found guilty of trying to pack the big Local 3 debate on the Martin versus the IEB issue with black workers who were not even employed at Dodge.[57]

In March 1939 Martin organized his own UAW convention and affiliated to the AFL. The presence of two UAWs encouraged GM and Chrysler to try to recover the managerial control they had lost in 1937. 'Buck' Jones in the Pressed Steel unit, Department 74, wrote a UAW–CIO 'Reconstruction Song':

> Hold the fort for we will help you,
> UAW is strong,
> Frankensteen is one who will do it,
> Now that Martin's gone.[58]

The struggle culminated in elections for Local 3 officers and for delegates to the 1939 UAW–CIO Convention in Cleveland. In them the right mounted the first major red-baiting campaign seen at Dodge with leaflets attacking Zaremba:

> FACTS
> *Did you know* that the Department from which our militant Recording Secretary John A. Zaremba comes is the only department in the Dodge Plant that is still unorganized?
> *Did you know* that Zaremba claims that he does not belong to the Communist Party?
> *What do you think*?
> *Let's judge 'John' by the company he keeps.[59]

The few Progressives left inside the UAW–CIO's Dodge Local 3 were on the defensive as Martin's staunchest supporters had already joined the UAW–AFL. Their election platform began:

> 1. We are not opposed to the CIO.
> 2. We are strongly opposed to wild cat strikes and breaking of our contract. We believe those who are responsible for such acts should be disciplined. BUT we also believe in being very firm in insisting that the Corporation lives up to its side of the contract.[60]

But their 'More Unionism, less Communism' campaign suffered a crushing defeat. Reid was the only Progressive elected to the Cleveland UAW–CIO convention out of twenty delegates. And the 'CIO slate' of Pat Quinn for president and Zaremba for re-election as recording secretary then swept the election of local officers and plant committee members. 'The CIO is Americanism' slogan, complete with photograph of John L. Lewis, won the day.

The UAW–AFL was not seen as 'legitimate' in Dodge Main despite its leadership of old Coughlinites for two main reasons: it opposed the plant tradition of on-the-job problem solving and the shop steward system on which it depended; and it stood outside the political circle bounded by John L. Lewis, the CIO and the New Deal. As a result it failed to recruit any significant group of activists. Even Frank Reid kept a foot in both camps, staying in the UAW–CIO and reporting to the Local 3 executive board on AFL meetings.[61] The breakaway union finally collapsed in Dodge Main after the overwhelming 85% vote for the UAW–CIO in a Labor Board election on September 27, 1939.[62] By early 1940 all bar a handful of UAW–AFL supporters had made their peace and been readmitted to Local 3.

The effect of this center-left victory on shop steward organization in Chrysler plants, formerly a bastion of right-wing power in the union, was considerable. The anti-steward rulings of the Reid–McCann period were turned over in September by a new Local 3 constitution which reflected the more rank and filist tone of that year's UAW–CIO convention.[63] The primacy of the steward over the plant committee on departmental issues was restored: 'The Plant Bargaining Committee shall not invade the jurisdiction of a Chief Steward, except at his or her invitation, or at the discretion of the Executive Board.'[64] It built into the rules rank and file control over chief stewards' freedom of action, establishing that 'The Chief Shop Steward cannot settle a grievance unless it meets with the approval of a majority of the union men affected.' And it boosted sectional shop stewards:

> The Chief Shop Steward may appoint or elect, if the group wishes, as many deputy stewards as may be necessary to aid in his or her duties. There shall be at least one deputy steward for a group of 20 or less. In case of isolated groups there must be a deputy steward in the group ... It shall be the duty of the deputy stewards to attend all steward, unit and special meetings.[65]

This constitutional advance for sectional bargaining infuriated Chrysler management and helped create the conditions for a new struggle over the frontier of control in October and November 1939.

IV. Equal control of production

The ground chosen by Chrysler for a major confrontation in 1939 was its authority to determine production standards. Anticipating the market recovery of 1940–41 Chrysler management seized the opportunity provided by the union split. Yet it again underestimated the hold of union organization. Management refused to extend the contract after March 1939 for more than a month at a time on the grounds that it didn't know which UAW it was really dealing with. In May, at the end of the 1939 model run, it fired leading leftist 'Pat' Patrick, the plant committee chairman, for allegedly intimidating a foreman.[66] Then, in September 1939 after calling the 1932 to 1934 men back to work for the 1940 models, it announced that it would not renew the contract and introduced a major speed-up.

The speed-up at Dodge Main was particularly harsh for the day and night shifts in three departments: the body-in-white (3,000 workers), the paint shop (1,800 workers) and the crankshaft department (150 workers).[67] During the 1939 model year the body building's arc and gas welding lines had worked at twelve bodies per hour; the management now set a new rate of twenty and on October 6, 1939 fired twenty men for not fulfilling their new production target. That day the paint shop superintendent fired men in three different sections: on the body spray line, where the speed was raised from 46.5 to 48 an hour; on the wet sand line, where twenty-four men had been sanding twenty-seven cars an hour and were told to do thirty-six; and in the enamel spray section where workers refused to spray eight more cars an hour than the thirty they claimed was their maximum. In the crankshaft department the line speed was the same as for the previous year's model, but the crankshaft weighed 90 lbs, 3.5 lbs more than the 1939 model year crankshaft. Management fired some workers there for handling three or four less an hour. It sent the rest of the workers in all these areas home.

For the next two weeks the same thing happened every day in one area or another of the plant. Men would come to work, be instructed to work at the speed dictated by management, be told they had no right either to bargain about it or to put it into the grievance procedure because there was no contract in effect after September 30, and then the foremen would fire a handful of workers. In axle unit 113, the supervision fired four assistant chief stewards, two chief stewards and two deputy stewards between October 6 and October 10. By the end of the second week Chrysler had fired a total of 105 and disciplined another 23 Dodge workers, and the UAW–CIO's IEB, now led by former Chrysler workers R. J. Thomas and Dick Frankensteen, finally decided to take a *Chrysler-*

wide strike vote. International union politics meant Dodge Main was not allowed to be isolated.

The strike vote was held on October 15. In later years strike votes became used as bargaining ploys and were often poorly attended. But this vote was massive: 13,751 Dodge workers were for strike action with 1,324 against – a 90% majority. They were defending their new frontier of restraints over unilateral managerial autonomy. The top two strike demands were about workers' living standards and control of the labor process: '1. A general wage increase with a bonus for afternoon and night shift workers.' And '2. Joint fixing of production standards by the corporation and the union.'[68] Nor did management duck the issue. General manager Herman Weckler stated: 'Production schedules are the management's function. You may as well know now that we do not intend to give your union control of production.'[69] The strike began on October 18, 1939 and lasted 45 days.

Father Coughlin, whose self-imposed silence after Roosevelt's election victory in November 1936 lasted just six weeks and whose broadcasts were now strongly anti-semitic,[70] entered the ring with a blistering radio denunciation of the strike. His broadcast included a speech by David Brann, the leading UAW–AFL organizer at Dodge, who stated that 'shop stewards actually placed locks on the conveyor to limit production.'[71] Coughlin was outraged: 'Among the demands which the union are making through their leaders, they are asking for an *equal* control of production standards and a *total* control of discipline over all workmen in the Chrysler Corporation.'[72] Although Coughlin's influence was negligible by 1939 compared with five years earlier, his broadcasts were still listened to by enough Chrysler workers to reinforce rank and file awareness of the underlying issues behind the conflict.

Chrysler's determination to defeat the strike finally led it to a desperate attempt at creating a back-to-work movement among some of the 1,700 black workers employed in the Dodge foundry and in low paid janitorial jobs. It was assisted by Martin's UAW–AFL, which had proved its capacity at mobilizing small numbers of blacks earlier in the year. After some rioting on Friday November 24 between pickets and blacks trying to enter the plant to collect their paychecks, several prominent black politicians and organizations moved into action to prevent the movement growing. One pro-strike leaflet asked: 'How long will the Negro stand for Labor Dictation? What is happening is obviously on the part of the Corporation to get the Negroes to go into the plant to antagonize the white workers.'[73]

On Monday 27 November, Chrysler and the UAW–AFL organized a group of 181 blacks and 6 whites assisted by a 1,000-strong police escort to march through a mass picket of more than 5,000 workers waving American flags. The following day the number of black strike-breakers rose to 430. But this was still not enough. Chrysler had neither recruited sufficient black strike-breakers to come even remotely close to a mass back-to-work movement that could mobilize white workers as well, nor had it provoked the white workers into anti-black rioting. Under mounting criticism from fellow employers and from Detroit and national politicians, Chrysler surrendered the next day.[74]

The November 29, 1939 strike settlement formally recognized the union's steward system and institutionalized the sectional collective-bargaining tradition. It was crucial in cementing a job-bargaining tradition into the Chrysler workers' view of workplace legitimacy because it came as a *struggled-for* advance. Chief stewards and assistant chief stewards were named in the contract and given super-seniority, as were members of the plant committee and local executive board, and they won the right to move about their areas virtually at will:

> Chief Stewards and assistant Chief Stewards, during their working hours, without loss of time, or pay may ... peform their duties of conferring with foremen or other designated representatives of the plant management and of investigating grievances.[75]

They could also leave work to confer with other chief stewards or to telephone the plant committee. The form of unionism legitimated by Chrysler encouraged on-the-spot bargaining between a small-consti-tuency, elected workers' representative and the immediate supervisor. It was a form much more liable to encourage wheeling and dealing and a shopfloor tradition of custom and practice, accepted by both workers and supervisors, than was the much more remote individual-to-plant commit-tee structure at GM.

The settlement on production standards was more ambiguous than the legitimation of chief and assistant stewards. But it still provided a new and formal basis for the blossoming of restraints on management in on-the-job bargaining. Section 3 (1) of the contract referred to the rate of production being established 'on the basis of fairness and equity' for 'the reasonable working capacities of normal operators'. Section 3 (2) gave the foreman the power to 'adjust the matter' if the workers (or their blue button steward) complained the rate was too fast. And, if the foreman refused, it allowed for negotiations to take place between the chief steward and general foreman or superintendent at department level. Only then, 'should a satisfactory agreement not result, the matter in dispute shall be referred to the bargaining procedure' – that is, it would go to the plant committee. Finally, 'The management of each plant is authorized to settle such matters.'[76] These clauses put discretion to make concessions into the hands of foremen, general foremen and superintendents but gave workers the right to appeal to top plant management. The dual power situation created by the anomaly of competing chief steward and plant committee bargaining structures had been resolved in favor of the stewards. And in its unwitting legitimation of this situation, Chrysler also effectively withdrew from its own front-line supervisors the final authority to say 'no'.

The UAW, understandably, exaggerated its achievement. Workers had got their first all-round general wage rise since 1937 (although rates tended to be less than at GM plants), and all 128 workers fired and disciplined in October were reinstated. The *UAW–Dodge Main News* boasted:

> The workers are now allowed a say in the setting of production rates, one of the main issues in the dispute. Sole bargaining rights are granted, squeezing out the rump and other company unions. Seniority is retained no matter how long the worker is laid off. The 'no strike' clause is eliminated.[77]

More important than the form of words, however, was the confidence Chrysler's defeat inspired in shopfloor self-activity. In a typical incident in the body-in-white in 1940, the superintendent instructed the welders to raise their production. Art Shipley, their chief steward, suggested they continue working normally and so one welder was laid off. Shipley then called all the workers together to march down to the superintendent's office where, faced with a boom in orders, the superintendent called the man back to work.[78] A new hire into the body shop in October 1940 was highly impressed because 'the foremen were very nervous about giving orders to the workers'.[79]

The strike outcome was a nearly unqualified victory for the workers. In contrast with the UAW's victory over GM in the summer 'strategy strike' of 1939,[80] Chrysler management learned nothing from its defeat. Its labor relations function remained an adjunct of its New York-based attorney's office, far removed from workplace realities. The strike established the custom and practice of *mutuality* so firmly in the determination of standards at Chrysler that it would finally be up-rooted only in the industrial relations hiatus of the late 1950s. At GM, the 1939 defeat caused management to reorganize its structure so that labor relations became a top responsibility, with a strong central staff allocated to negotiate and administer contracts with the UAW. GM was able to adapt because it had 'an ingrained habit of "management by policy" – the development of a program of concerted action – to handle all important problems'[81] and could review mistakes in a way not possible in autocratically-managed companies. GM could access its massive power resources comparatively easily.

The apparent speed with which GM and Chrysler became reconciled to the presence of mass unionism after their 1939 defeats should not obscure two significant qualifications. First, GM's bitter resistance to the threat of workers exercising collective restraints over its managerial authority did not disappear: it merely took a new form. Second, Walter Chrysler and many other Detroit employers close to the strike-breaking National Metal Trades Association, whose Detroit branch secretary also doubled as the general manager of the Employer's Association of Detroit, remained openly hostile. The settlements at the close of the 1930s changed workers' attitudes more than they did these managers'.

By 1940–41 Chrysler management had seen restraints imposed over its autonomy to determine both labor costs (wage rates, hours of work) and important aspects of the labor process (speed and allocation of work, discipline). In its plants a qualitative movement of the frontier of control, the exercise of collective restraint by workers over managerial power and authority on the shop floor, had taken place in the workers' favor. By contrast, GM's Alfred P. Sloan reminisced some 20 years later in a way unthinkable for a Chrysler executive:

> So far as our operations are concerned, we have moved to codify certain practices, to discuss workers' grievances with union representatives, and to submit for arbitration the few grievances that remain unsettled. But on the whole, we have retained all the basic powers to manage.[82]

Despite the similar technology, product, marketing and casual labor market conditions faced by GM and Chrysler before World War II, the differences in union organization, management structure and workplace labor relations were already profound.

Part III
Overcoming resistance, 1942–1959

5 World War II: sound American unionism

World War II deepened the contradictions for managers hostile to unionism. It provided a political framework conducive to management reasserting its shopfloor authority but in an economic environment that after 1942 increasingly suffered from labor shortages. At Chrysler the resulting conflict was never resolved. Management kept making efforts to regain autonomy over the setting of workplace rules, but then backed down when the cost of pursuing a tough line got too high.

Section I of this chapter describes the changeover from peacetime to military production when management tried to reassert its unilateral authority. Section II examines an attempt by Chrysler in 1943 to reimpose unilateral management prerogatives over what was by then a largely new workforce. Finally, section III looks at Chrysler's adoption of a new intransigent strategy in 1944 aimed at rolling back wartime restraints by its semiskilled workers in preparation for the resumption of mass peacetime production.

I. Changeover to war production

The changeover from civilian to wartime production was particularly traumatic at Dodge Main. The first Office of Production Management order cutting schedules for the 1942 model year by 20% was issued in July 1941, and passenger automobile and light truck work ended in January 1942.[1] Yet Chrysler took well over a year to complete the changeover. With Federal funds providing the means to build a new tank plant and to tool up its Chicago plant for aircraft assembly, it felt no hurry or necessity to concentrate its war production at Dodge Main. In July 1941 Dodge management refused to transfer laid-off workers to the new Tank Arsenal at Warren, ten miles to the north. And in September, thirty-six Dodge Main paint shop workers were laid off for two weeks for refusing to give up the tradition of a twenty-minute relief period at the shift changeover. But on both occasions the new hard line was abandoned after the threat of strike action.[2] Departmental-level management was allowed to try to reassert its authority over job mobility and work breaks, but top management was not prepared at that point in its negotiations on future war orders to openly confront the UAW.

More effective in weakening the Dodge workforce's resistance to managerial authority was a 25% collapse in average Chrysler manual employment between 1941 and 1942. As car production ran down, the threat of industrial action lost conviction. Local 3 then turned to propagandistic means of fighting back, and proved it was still capable of mobilizing substantial numbers of workers. Just after Pearl Harbor, on the Friday before Christmas Day 1941, 15,000 Dodge workers left their work or came in from lay-off to attend a mass meeting called by Local 3 to protest against 'the war slacker' Chrysler. Local 3 acting-president Bill Hill, who took office when Pat Quinn took a UAW staff job, argued that 75% of Dodge's machining facilities were idle and only twenty-five Dodge workers were so far engaged on 'gun jobs'.[3] As late as June 1942, when 5,000 of the 19,500 employed at Dodge Main eight months earlier had still not been called back, the local staged another propaganda coup: 500 maintenance men worked a Saturday morning shift for nothing as a protest against Chrysler's half-speed plant conversion.[4]

In April 1942 the UAW's earlier endorsement of the no strike pledge was supported at a special union convention. The 'Victory through Equality of Sacrifice' program that was carried could have undermined existing collective shopfloor strength. It clearly limited the restraints union members could exercise on managerial rights to determine the hours and conditions of work:

> 1. No strikes during wartime.
> 2. Saturday, Sunday and holidays were to be treated as ordinary working days – overtime premiums would only be paid after eight hours had been worked a day or after 40 hours worked a week.
> 3. To increase the production of war materials.
> 4. To operate arms plants on a 24-hour, 7 day a week basis.[5]

But *who* would honor the no strike pledge in the plants? If no one raised it at the moment workers decided to strike, or if the only person who did was a discredited non-unionist or the foreman, then the no strike pledge would not work.

In a few Detroit plants, like the Chrysler Plymouth plant where there was a strong Communist Party presence, the stewards were ideologically and organizationally committed to the no strike pledge. That plant was virtually strike free – although even there the stewards were unable to convince the membership to agree to restore the incentive payment system being pushed by the CP.[6] Yet at Dodge Main, the sectional-union AIWA background of men like Earl Reynolds, who was elected Local 3 president in 1942, and of the key Dodge Main stewards meant that although they paid lip-service to the no strike pledge, they were reluctant to sacrifice their constituents' immediate interests to it. Between December 1941 and January 1943, sixty-six work stoppages took place in Chrysler plants.[7] Management protested: 'Pearl Harbor, labor's no-strike pledge and the national policy against striking did not change this Union's attitude and practices.'[8]

II. The 1943 offensive

By the time management fully reopened Dodge Main on war production in late 1942, union activists had been widely dispersed to other plants, into the services, and into new departments. In April 1943 former trim department workers who still had jobs were found to be scattered widely among Chrysler's Detroit plants:[9]

Bomber plant	400
Lynch Road	50
Highland Park	200
Tank Arsenal	(a number)
Scattered through	
Dodge Main	1,000
Trim Shop	125

Despite this dispersal, however, management still faced an entrenched union tradition at Dodge Main. Among those few still in the trim shop were the committeeman Jimmy Solomon and four chief stewards. Super-seniority ensured that a handful of those who carried the activist tradition stayed in the plant. It was not the majority. There was a high turnover, for example, among those holding Local 3 office: of the forty-one candidates who ran for election in February 1941 only six stood for office again in February 1943.[10] But a *core* survived. And in the tight labor market of 1943 they taught the new labor force where to draw the established line marking the 'frontier of control' on the new war jobs.[11]

The switch to all-out war production tipped the balance of forces on the shopfloor towards the workforce.[12] This was because on cost-plus arms contracts, managerial emphasis shifted from quantity and low labor costs to quality. Gertrude Nalezty, a Dodge wire room worker, recalled:

> It was very different during the war. Conditions working on tank wire were much better. They stressed quality. No-one cared about quantity.

There were always relief people ready to help out. We were working six days a week but we used to get off early as often as we liked. We'd just ask the foreman and nine times out of ten he'd agree. It was during the war we elected our first woman chief steward, Angie Neuman.[13]

In 1943 Chrysler attempted to prevent this relaxation of workplace discipline from taking place. It launched a general attack on production rates on war work, trying to reclassify and redefine them at rates below those on civilian work. If the issue was written up as a grievance, lower-level management would simply refuse to bargain on it with the stewards and refer it to the log-jam already before the War Labor Board (WLB).[14] In March 1943, Local 3 president Reynolds urged workers not to let management use the no strike pledge to tear up mutuality:

> It is the position of the Local Union that they are 100% behind the program of President Roosevelt and the War Effort, but we are not going to let the Dodge Management use this as an excuse to break down the morale of our members.
>
> Employees who worked on a job for a good number of years, and have seniority on the job, should not be moved, unless it is *mutually agreed*, and they are given a job that pays a higher rate. [my italic][15]

Two weeks later the *Dodge Main News* carried the headline: 'Rates still being chiseled – Chrysler Manager rejects all appeals for Fair Dealing.'[16] It seemed Chrysler was using the no strike pledge unilaterally to redraw workplace rules and habits of rule making.

In May 1943 Dodge divisional manager Otto Franke escalated the conflict from the issue of management's authority in setting production standards and moving workers between jobs, to its right to recruit directly into key jobs from outside the plant. He hired six new workers for Dodge Main's department 229, the signal mount, which was known as having well-paid jobs mounting radios and searchlights into their casings. This was seen as a deliberate challenge to an earlier seniority agreement under which management had to offer new war work to existing employees before it took on new labor. There was an immediate walkout. Retaliatory firings by Chrysler followed, and then sympathy stoppages in all Chrysler's Detroit plants. Reynolds saw Chrysler's action as a deliberate provocation and the *Dodge Main News* called it 'Treason'.

The incident highlighted tensions on the UAW's international executive board when Leo LaMotte, the ex-Plymouth plant worker who was the UAW's Chrysler Department Director, accused the strikers of 'Reutherism'. Coming from Frankensteen's home local, Reynolds deeply resented LaMotte's charge:

It is unfortunate that Mr Weckler (Chrysler General Manager) was able to bring to his assistance in his efforts at union disruption, certain union officials who chose to ignore the union issues involved ... I brand the charge that this dispute was caused by followers of Walter Reuther as an unmitigated lie. I have never been a follower of Reuther. This dispute was caused by Chrysler Management and by no-one else. LaMotte tried to make a political football out of our difficulties ... We want to sit down and negotiate matters, but if the Dodge Management want us to get things the 'hard way', 'getting things the hard way' will be the policy of Dodge Locals.[17]

The initial walkout reflected the strength of Dodge Main's 'do-it-yourself' problem-solving tradition and the contentiousness of the seniority issue in a complex where 90% of the workforce had just been moved to new departments or other plants and where there were wide divergences in the type of work and rates of pay. The issue was generalized when stewards at the other old AIWA stronghold, Local 7, the Kercheval plant and several smaller and newer plants where the CP had little influence called solidarity strike action.[18] This Detroit-wide industrial action by 27,100 workers coincided with War Labor Board hearings into the state of collective bargaining at Chrysler, set up following a break-down in negotiations on a new contract. LaMotte did not believe it was a coincidence and neither did Chrysler management which was certain there was an attempt to influence the War Labor Board to establish an impartial umpire system.[19]

In 1940 GM had introduced an umpire as the final stage of a centralized grievance procedure in a move advocated by Reuther,[20] and Ford had done the same in its first contract in 1941. Reuther saw two benefits accruing from the umpire system: it would be an external restraint on arbitrary management that would oblige it to adhere to a standard set of workplace rules; and it would create an appearance of judicial 'fairness' that would help channel rank and file anger away from the potentially dangerous conflicts he saw as a threat to the survival of the union. By 1942 his view of the need for a rigid grievance procedure, ultimately legitimated by an 'outside' umpire with the power of redress, was shared by all factions of the UAW's IEB. For similar reasons, believing it would encourage industrial peace, the War Labor Board of New Deal interventionists[21] also encouraged the erection of GM-type appeal structures. It saw them as a means of persuading workers against taking immediate action by holding out the promise of an impartial enquiry by an 'outsider'.

The labor-containment aspects of umpire procedures were not endorsed, however, by the whole business community.[22] In 1943 Chrysler bitterly resisted the proposal. Some umpire systems resulted from management, international union or WLB pressure, but on other occasions procedural changes were only conceded after struggles *against* management. The 'defusing' consequences of a 'struggled-for' umpire system were not necessarily identical to those where an umpire system was delivered as part of management's labor relations strategy. With two top managers and two UAW IEB members sitting on its existing final appeal board, Chrysler viewed 'independent' umpire systems as a get-out for the UAW to avoid disciplining workers who broke the no strike pledge and the UAW–Chrysler contract. It, and most other wartime managements, saw the 'outside' umpire system as a threat to managerial prerogatives.[23]

The solidarity action of May 1943 showed strong support by other workers, but it was also a bargaining mechanism through which local and certain international officers let the WLB know what was on their mind. Frankensteen's links with Dodge Main and R. J. Thomas' connections with the Kercheval plant may well have had more bearing on this action than has yet come to light. As it was, an umpire system did indeed turn out to be one of the outcomes of the strike. The National War Labor Board directive issued on August 27, 1943 extended the grievance procedure at Chrysler to include an impartial chairman at the final UAW–Chrysler appeal stage. But two other outcomes proved more significant in the shorter term: those fired for leading the walkout from the signal mount department were reinstated; and Chrysler renewed transferring workers into Department 229 in accordance with the transfer agreement.[24]

This was a fairly decisive management defeat. Workers had not been expressing a political anti-war militancy; nor did the action represent the 'balkanization' of Chrysler plants into competing sections.[25] The wartime *Dodge Main News* carried the Stars and Stripes and the slogan – 'Give it your best!'. Reynolds summed up Dodge Main's politics when he wrote, 'The only faction we propose to tolerate in our Local Union is a faction that stands for good, sound American unionism.'[26]

Chrysler was brought to a halt by 'sound American unionism' with the organizational base to defend restraints over the movement of labor and manning and production levels. And Dodge workers continued to do so: in September the 600 workers on day and afternoon shifts in the gun plant walked out when a steward was disciplined for refusing to move from one machine to another; in December, 150 day shift machine operators in the gyro compass department, some 60% of the total, quit work ninety minutes early to protest at the delay in getting a WLB hearing on a disputed job classification.[27] When the gyro workers finally got the WLB directive it was in Chrysler's favor. This too provoked a strike and the inevitable management denunciation: 'This is a strike against the government and the war effort.'[28] But for the workers the reality was quite different: for them it was a strike about work rules – how much a job would pay, who would work it and how the decisions were taken. Neither the no strike pledge nor disciplinary efforts by the international to impose external regulation of job behavior appear to have had much impact on the tradition of internal job regulation and local union autonomy at Chrysler.[29] These issues became even more important for the management as the end of the war approached.

III. End of the war

In 1944 Chrysler began planning for the post-war period. Highly conscious of the 'drift' in production rates and workplace discipline that had occurred since 1941, Keller instructed plant managers to restore work standards and manning levels to pre-war levels and not to negotiate with strikers. But this was a policy that bore little relationship to the shopfloor reality. Many supervisors simply could not operate either aspect, particularly in those plants increasingly hostile to the no strike pledge.[30]

At Dodge Main, where wartime production was characterized by individual bench assembly and machining work,[31] the new strategy had two aims. First, to speed up production and eliminate the wartime practice of workers producing at what they considered a 'fair' rate while a disputed standard went through the grievance procedure. And second, to overhaul the plant's facilities as quickly as possible to prepare for the reintroduction of automobile production.[32]

Early in 1945, then, as demand for war production began to slow down, Chrysler made its third wartime bid to reassert managerial autonomy. What happened is worth considering in some detail since the dense steward network at Dodge Main, the supportive role of Local 3's officials and their relative independence from the international, and the struggle's outcome – the confirmation of mutuality – would epitomize Chrysler's industrial relations over the next ten years.

On February 7, 1945 management issued a new work standard to the oil pump gear cutters working in the B-29 bomber engine parts department. It was based on a new time study method that included a 'Non-Production Time Schedule':[33]

	Of working day	
	(%)	(mins)
Personal use	3	14
Unavoidable delay	3	14
Fatigue	5	24
Tooling up	9	43
Per 8 hour shift:	20	99

The time study showed an automatic machine was capable of producing 225 parts a day. So, taking the 20% non-productive time off, the workers were set a daily rate of 184 over the full eight hour shift. This was a dramatic increase, since the workers had begun working the seven machines at 108 parts per day and when the new time study came out were completing an average of just 150. The stewards in the 1,100-strong B-29 department advised the men to ignore the new production standard and filed a grievance. Two days later the seven machinists were given a three-day suspension for not working to the new standard, and the whole Department workforce stayed away with them. The grievance was rejected at stage one on February 10 by their superintendent and at the second stage on February 21 by the labor relations supervisor.[34]

The following morning at 9.30 a.m., without waiting for the third stage involving an international UAW officer, the supervision sacked the seven machinists and a stock handler for 'loafing, insubordination and refusing to keep up production'. The machinists had refused to report their previous day's production, and the stock handler had refused to count it and report on them. One of the gear cutters was Earl C. York, the 47-year-old Unit 234 chairman and World War I veteran who had worked at Dodge Main for twelve years and had a son in the army in Belgium. All 743 workers on the day shift immediately walked out, many passing through other parts of the complex to let the stewards there know what had happened. By midday another 725 workers from other departments had also stopped. Pickets then appeared on the main gates and all but 500 of the 3,450 on the afternoon shift stayed out. By the next morning only 500 skilled maintenance and a few tool and die men out of the 9,400 workers on the shift crossed the pickets. Crucially, only eighteen of the one hundred Dodge-based interplant drivers who transferred parts and equipment between Chrysler's thirteen Detroit area plants, reported for work on Friday. And one of these was beaten up by two of the striking truckers after completing his shift. By the Saturday afternoon shift just seven out of the fifty-four interplant drivers reported and all Chrysler's Detroit plants began to grind to a halt. On Sunday a

Local 3 membership meeting voted to complete the stoppage by calling out all the maintenance workers still working.[35]

The UAW's intervention followed a classic pattern. Chrysler immediately contacted the international, complaining of war sabotage: 'Those who are leading this strike are apparently deliberately trying to sabotage the war effort because some of their members were disciplined for refusing to do their war work.'[36] R. J. Thomas was in London, so acting-president George Addes instructed the strikers to return within hours of the strike starting:

> You are hereby ordered by the International Executive Board of the UAW–CIO to return to work. The strike is unauthorized and is a violation of the union's constitution and no-strike pledge. Failure to comply with this order will necessitate immediate action by the International Executive Board.[37]

Local 3's executive members only got formally involved in the afternoon, when a special EB meeting was held to discuss the Department 234 strike. Their recommendation to the special business meeting of the strikers convened afterwards make it clear they were fully in support of the action. Their advice was:

> 1. Stay out long enough to force the Army to take over Department 234.
> 2. Demand a Congress investigation of Chrysler.
> 3. Call for the dismissal of the three Department 234 supervisors involved.[38]

This support, from executive members who were politically on the center-right of the UAW spectrum, reflected their opposition to Chrysler's new time study methods and their defense of the custom and practice that had developed on war jobs. Mike Novak, a strong anticommunist and supporter of Walter Reuther, had just been re-elected for a second term. A second generation Pole whose defeat of Reynolds in 1944 reflected the growing involvement of Hamtramck's Polish community in running Local 3, he was the first Dodge president without a background in the Coughlinite AIWA.[39]

The strike occurred a week after the UAW held a referendum on the continuation of the no strike pledge, and management's 'produce or be fired' ultimatum to the machinists reflected Chrysler's forecast of the national two to one vote majority to retain it. But the result was still undeclared and, as it turned out, it was very close in Detroit.[40] With his own re-election just accomplished and interpreting the situation as a kind of policy interregnum while the referendum votes were counted, Novak didn't hesitate. He threw himself entirely behind the strike:

We strike because we can't relax our principles. We've got to keep them as high as they were just before the war, so veterans can come back to good working conditions.

Servicemen are fighting against what we're fighting against. We are against speed-ups. We are against racial discrimination. We are against abuse of former servicemen. We are against lowering of our working conditions.[41]

After more than three years of war, patriotism and collective restraints over arbitrary management had become fused in the workplace consciousness of both the 'new' war workers and of many UAW secondary leaders.

In another plant the dispute could possibly have been contained among a small group of gear cutters. But at Dodge Main it generalized to a struggle over a key 'principle': the dismissal of workers and stewards for refusing to work to what the union called an 'unreasonable' production standard *while* it was being taken through the grievance procedure. A secondary strike issue was the workers' right to negotiate with the company and the War Labor Board while remaining on strike.

The strike lasted eleven days. It was Chrysler's longest wartime strike. Dodge Truck and Chrysler's Highland Park plants were closed through lack of materials, and another 1,050 workers were laid off at Chrysler's Windsor plant and the Tank Arsenal. On March 1 the stoppage spread to the Chrysler De Soto–Warren plant where the workers stopped in protest against the use of the railroads to transport critically-needed items usually carried by the striking Dodge interplant truck drivers. Nearly 19,000 Chrysler workers were on strike and another 5,250 were laid off.

The strike spread despite directives to return from the international IEB and the Regional War Labor Board. The strength of the 'do-it-yourself' union tradition meant the striking workers had the support of Local 3 officers to set up effective picket lines, regardless of the IEB. On the same day, in another wildcat strike, eleven Detroit Briggs plants voted to strike or were closed down by pickets from the Briggs Mack Avenue plant in protest against the firing of a committeeman and six shop stewards on February 27.[42] By the time the Dodge strikers finally went back the *Detroit Times* reported as accurate the opinion of most UAW IEB members that 'Every current strike in Detroit was inspired by the Dodge walkout.'[43]

The Dodge strike impressed other workers because of its size and strength. But it inspired them because of its success. The Dodge workers openly defied the management, the IEB, the Regional War Labor Board and the threat of being drafted.[44] They ignored patriotic bluster from the

Under Secretary of War and forced a special meeting of the National War Labor Board to be held in Washington while they were still out on strike. This agreed to a special inquiry into the dismissals and the gear cutters' production rate, and the walk-out ended. Three weeks later the inquiry found that the men should be reinstated but that they should produce 184 parts a day.[45] Thus while the management did eventually get its speed-up, it was only after 'due process' had been adhered to – including the entry into the plant of time study experts approved by the UAW. And the workers' resistance to management's reassertion of *unilateral* rate-fixing was effectively condoned.

The NWLB was not alone in feeling impotent before this strike. The workers and the Local 3 officers also got away with rank defiance of the IEB. After their original instruction to return to work was ignored, the dominant pro no strike pledge faction on the IEB worked full out to bully the Dodge workers back to work. The CP was beside itself with rage, accusing the Dodge workers variously of being 'enemy agents', 'followers of Reuther' and 'reactionaries' playing into the hands of anti-labor elements. A *Daily Worker* editorial stated:

> The strike of 14,000 at Detroit's Dodge plant which now threatens to shut down the entire Chrysler chain of plants is absolutely indefensible ... Only Nazi Germany and Tokyo can profit by its results ... The responsibility must be fixed whether it is from labor or management. If it should be proven that not enemy agents, but followers of Reuther incited the walkout, the effect is none the less serious in terms of lives of our fighting men.
>
> Responsible labor and government leaders should step in and act. If drastic measures are not taken, more of such strikes will be encouraged and reactionaries will exploit them to pass more anti-labor bills.[46]

An editorial in the *Detroit Labor News*, the publication of the Detroit and Wayne County AFL, was even more pointed:

> Hitler's helpers do it again; The Dodge strikers, who are dodging their obligation to the Armed Forces – not bullets – have again run out on the war ...
> Adolph shouldn't worry. His little helpers in America will take care of him.[47]

UAW acting-president Addes chaired one Dodge strike meeting and ran straight into the hostility engendered by the CP's attack on the strike. After he, Reuther, and Frankensteen had spoken, all urging a return to work, he opened the meeting to contributions from the floor and called a known 'leftist'. As a result, 'There were cries of "It's a frame-up!" "They've made a deal with the Communists." "Don't let them sell us out!" Several fist fights broke out on the floor, and the word went down the line to prevent "this deal with the Commies" by voting to stay out.'[48] Local 3's Novak had previously come to an agreement with Addes that he would support the call to return. But the fury expressed at the meeting swayed him to speak against, and Addes then left the meeting in disgust, saying he had 'washed his hands of the local'. Communists in Dodge Main, never particularly influential, were forced into a corner by their national policy from which they never emerged.[49] It was Reuther who finally fixed up the deal to which the WLB and Chrysler agreed, and he and Frankensteen who met the National War Labor Board in Washington and negotiated the return.

In May 1944 when Local 490 officers had supported a wildcat strike at the Chrysler Highland plant, the international union put the local under trusteeship for three months. But the offending president, an old Socialist Party member, Bill Jenkins, and his entire slate were re-elected in July.[50] That experience taught the IEB to be wary at Dodge eight months later. It was still Frankensteen's home local, but Reuther's alliance of anti-communist socialists and anti-communist Catholics was helping him build a base there, too. So despite Novak's open defiance, no action was taken against him or any of Local 3's officers: they were merely reprimanded.[51] Chrysler management had effectively lost this one, too. If it could not count on the UAW disciplining its members in wartime, what could it expect in peacetime? A Chrysler consultant speculated wildly in public:

> As industrial turmoil increases, more and more people will see the evils of collective bargaining and we should look to the time all federal labor laws are repealed.
> I condemn collective bargaining as an evil thing which is against public interest and which will increase poverty.[52]

Bruised by their wartime experiences, Chrysler's top management was desperate to eliminate shopfloor union organization. The consultant's speech was no accident: it coincided with the formation of a coalition of anti-union managements led by Chrysler's chairman, B. E. Hutchinson, aimed at stopping the accommodationist (to unionism) tendency being promoted by the US Chamber of Commerce.[53]

In Chrysler's plants where supervisors faced union stewards every day, however, it was a different story. There, a tradition of compromise and accommodation by mutual agreement had taken hold. Far from 'additional authority' being removed from 'the local union and the rank and file' during the war,[54] the opposite appears to have been the case: sectional industrial action appeared more legitimate than before. It was to be another ten years before Chrysler management developed both an effective labor relations strategy and the organizational capacity and front-line supervision to execute it. And it took another five years after that before management finally removed many of the restraints on its authority that were firmly embedded during the war.

6 Unionism, solidarity and militancy: 1946–1955

Chrysler slipped permanently from second to third place in the US auto league in the ten years following World War II. But these were boom years and growth allowed the corporation's autocratic management to survive – despite the survival of its 1920s structure of departmental 'empires'. Chrysler proved capable of doing what it had done in the past: make large numbers of well-engineered, conservatively-styled cars. This was sufficient, despite a declining share of an expanding market, to provide high profits and dividends to keep the dominant institutional shareholders happy, and to encourage a similar conservatism in labor relations policy. As a result Keller failed to undertake a reorganization similar to Ford's where, within six days of Henry Ford II becoming president in 1945, the labor relations staff function was upgraded to a Labor Relations Department. Chrysler continued to manage resistance with a combination of top-level autocratic intransigency and considerable front-line 'managerial discretion'.

Chrysler's management-by-habit continued despite major changes in the post-war labor relations environment. The Taft–Hartley Act, the unleashing of the House Un-American Activities Committee on the unions, and the victory of the Reuther faction in the UAW all weakened different aspects of workplace union strength. By 1949 Reuther had effectively broken the unofficial network of locals that provided the basis of the UAW democratic tradition.[1] But this shift in the wider balance of forces between employers and workers had little immediate impact at Dodge Main. Within the UAW, the fact that Local 3 was in the Reutherite camp for most of the decade after 1944 combined with the weakness of the CP at Dodge Main to make its independent tradition less of a target than was Ford Local 600.

Section I of this chapter examines the ways in which Chrysler's inappropriate management structure provided opportunities for continued worker resistance. Section II shows how Chrysler workers seized those opportunities because their sectional bargaining tradition was largely independent of international union pressure to centralize collective bargaining. Finally, section III sketches developments after the important 1950 confrontation with the UAW that precipitated Chrysler's gradual abandonment of total hostility to the union. By the mid 1950s a new labor relations strategy that aimed to get key local UAW officers to accept the external regulation of workplace behavior through the increasingly detailed national contracts was in place and was being consistently carried out.

I. Managerial crisis

Chrysler Corporation continued to be run as a centralized management autocracy after Walter Chrysler stood down as chief executive in 1935. His presence in the wings ensured there was no attempt to limit the responsibilities of his chosen successor or to shift to a multidivisional form. Thus by the time of Chrysler's death in 1940, K. T. Keller had inherited all the personal power and prestige that had belonged to Chrysler as well as his 'family' management structure. This meant that the key departments of engineering, production and finance, were virtually self-managing empires, run almost independently by various 'sons', and into which only 'K.T.' himself was allowed to intervene.

Keller dabbled in virtually everything, from insisting that only initials were used in the company directory to preventing the styling department from following the post-war trend to cars with lower rooflines. *Fortune* commented: 'K. T. Keller lived up to his promise not to knock anybody's hat off'; and one of his actual styling instructions was: 'We build cars to sit in, not piss over.'[2] But he made no serious attempt at developing or implementing a new business plan and he left Chrysler's large, overlapping dealer network unchanged. The fact that all Chrysler, DeSoto and Dodge dealers were allowed to sell the low-priced Plymouth line in 1929 had helped them through the Depression. But the continuation of this strategy after World War II allowed 10,400 dealers to sell the Plymouth as against 6,400 dealers selling the basic Ford lines.[3] This duplication had two important consequences: it gave the dealers greater leverage against Chrysler in bargaining over percentages, and it encouraged the lack of clear lines of managerial responsibility for the Plymouth, Chrysler's biggest-selling car. Without a clear managerial control structure, the presence of considerable managerial discretion and its resulting loss of control were virtually unavoidable.[4]

This weakness in management organization was compounded, para-

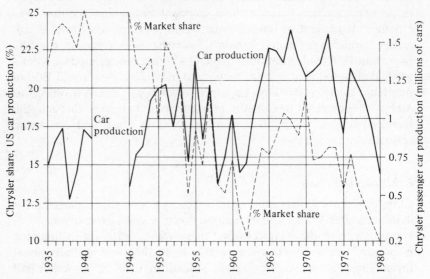

Fig. 5   Chrysler car production and market share, 1935–80

doxically, by Chrysler's immediate post-war success. The explosion of demand for cars that followed World War II allowed Chrysler to sell virtually all the cars it could turn out. By making only a few facility changes, such as moving most of the work in the Dodge wire room from benches onto a moving conveyor, Keller found he could outproduce Ford each year from 1946 to 1949.[5] The increase in production – from 540,000 passenger cars in 1946 to 1,120,000 in 1949 (see figure 5) – took Chrysler output some 20% higher than the 940,000 cars shipped in the pre-war peaks of 1937 and 1940. Yet it was this same management structure that had organized 68,000 employees in 1940, which was managing 95,000 employees in 1949, but spread out more thinly over more plants and including tank production and engineers working on the atomic bomb and missile weapon systems. Keller tried to maintain daily operational control by concentrating this rapid growth in the Detroit area, but none the less Chrysler began to exhibit clear symptoms of control loss in its financial and employment policies.

One significant area of corporate control loss occurred in the finance department. Walter Chrysler had hired B. E. Hutchinson, his financial right-hand man, as treasurer of the Maxwell Motor Car Company in 1921. Chrysler had been asked to rescue Maxwell by a bank consortium owed around $30 million. Pressure from these Chicago and New York bankers for internal financing became a permanent factor shaping

Hutchinson's approach to company finance, even after Maxwell Motor's business was transferred to the new Chrysler Corporation in June 1925. The combination of Chrysler and Hutchinson was highly successful. In 1928 a study of the financial history of the US auto industry described Chrysler as 'the only important producing enterprise that is the product of a receivership'.[6] A tradition of non-interference in 'B.E's' department developed in the 1920s and 1930s that was then carried on after Chrysler's death until Hutchinson's retirement in 1954.

Hutchinson's view was that profits were primarily the disposable income of executives and shareholders and borrowing should be kept to the absolute minimum. In 1948 he told *Fortune* magazine: 'The fundamental policy for Chrysler is to engineer good products, provide good facilities with which to make them, pay off your debts, and divide what is left with your stockholders, giving them as much of it as you can.'[7] Hutchinson operated a consistently high dividend policy financed by investing little and borrowing less. Between 1930 and 1945, Chrysler's best years, the depreciation of Chrysler property, plant and equipment actually exceeded new investments and Chrysler's ratio of fixed assets to sales was the lowest of any automobile company in the country. In 1941 Chrysler's 12c to the $ ratio of fixed assets to sales was only one-third that of GM.[8]

From 1935, when the debt incurred in buying up Dodge Brothers in 1928 was finally cleared, until 1954, Hutchinson's 'receivership financing' policy kept Chrysler from seeking any major new loan. In that eighteen-year period the corporation only paid a cumulative total of $2.5 million in interest on long-term debt. This compares with the final $2.4 million interest payment on the Dodge loan made in 1935 and with average long-term interest payments of $4.9 million each year from 1954 to 1961. The post-Hutchinson borrowing was initiated by the third Chrysler president, L. L. 'Tex' Colbert, who negotiated a $250 million hundred-year loan from the Prudential Insurance Company of America.

In the early 1950s Hutchinson heralded the onset of a declining market share by doubling the distribution of dividend payments (see table 6). Hutchinson's resistance to the reinvestment of 'his' average yearly operating margin of $161 million between 1946 and 1953 profits meant that dividends soared and Chrysler stock became increasingly popular. Just under 70% of the investment in new plant and equipment that did take place in these years was financed by the new stock issues of 1947 and 1949. But while the number of individual shareholders rose from 54,378 to 89,307 between 1946 and 1954, the major institutional investors maintained their controlling position.[9]

Table 6 *Chrysler production, market share and profitability, 1930–59*

Five yearly average	Passenger car production (millions)	Car market share (%)	Return on sales (car and non-car) (a) (%)	Dividends per share ($)
1935–39	0.724	23.14	8.36	0.75
1946–49	0.816	22.45	7.96	0.82
1950–54	1.072	19.30	6.78	1.62
1955–59	0.955	15.81	2.48	0.65

Source: Ward's Automotive Yearbooks; Chrysler Corporation (1973), *op. cit.*
(a) Before tax operating margin as a percentage of net sales.

On the shopfloor, however, top management's failure to use its considerable profits or to borrow to invest in new plant created a situation where front-line supervisors found themselves forced to use ageing machinery at ever higher capacities. The difficulties this entailed were compounded by the restraints on managerial authority maintained by workers exercising what they saw as their 'right to strike'. Together these pressures obliged departmental managers to rely heavily on alternating lay-offs and new hirings to control production levels.

The crude labor productivity index shown in figure 3 points to substantial differences between Chrysler, GM and Ford in the mid 1950s.[10] Output per manual worker increased by over 30% between the troughs of 1952 and 1958 at both GM and Ford, while at Chrysler it fell by 30%. Chrysler's loss of control over its employment requirements is demonstrated by a comparison with Ford's employment levels. While Ford and Chrysler annually produced within 100,000 cars of each other from 1946 to 1954, Chrysler managers hired 30% more hourly-paid workers in the first half of the 1950s than in the late 1940s while Ford expanded its hourly-paid labor force by only 20%. The companies' recruitment patterns were also different. In each of three boom years, 1949, 1951 and 1953, Chrysler took on an extra 20% or more hourly-paid workers, only to cut back by between 7% and 14% in the following years. While at Ford only 1953 saw a major new net intake of manual workers, a 31% rise, and this was only cut by 7% in 1954.[11]

The contrast in the recruitment of salaried staff was even more dramatic: Ford took on one-third more salaried workers between 1946 and 1949, against a mere 6% recruitment by Chrysler; and while Chrysler recruited salaried staff more rapidly in the early 1950s, its overall expansion of these technical, supervisory, clerical and managerial workers remained only half Ford's. The result was that while Ford recruited more supervisors, engineers, planners and sales staff to alter the structure of its labor force from one salaried worker for every 4.3 hourly workers in 1946 to one for every 2.7 by 1954, Chrysler's salaried-to-hourly ratio remained virtually unchanged. It employed one salaried worker to 3.8 hourly-paid workers in 1946 and one to every 3.2 hourly-paid by 1954. In 1955, Chrysler's historic employment high, when it employed an average 132,668 hourly-paid and 32,059 salaried workers, the ratio returned to 1 to 4.1.[12] Not only did Chrysler's top management have both policy-forming and day-to-day decision-making functions, but by comparison with its chief rival it survived with significantly fewer salaried staff.

II. Union tradition

The smaller Chrysler salaried labor force and the greater discretion plant and departmental managers had over recruitment than at GM and Ford fostered sectional bargaining. Departmental (chief) stewards and sectional (blue button) stewards coexisted at Dodge Main throughout the 1940s and 1950s. In large departments where the steward to worker ratio was very high, like the trim department with perhaps only six chief stewards on each shift representing some 4,000 workers, the blue button steward system was much more important[13] than in areas where there was a chief steward for every 30 workers. In the big departments these line stewards survived at Dodge Main for several years after the 1950 contract when their role as dues collectors was dispensed with by the check-off system – some nine years after Ford and four years after GM.[14] The blue buttons played a key role as passers-on of instructions and information when line or department strikes took place.

Blue button stewards were also the first tier of negotiators with management about production standards. Informal bargaining usually took place at model changes when management hoped to use engineering changes to reduce manning levels. The supervisors were often caught in a dilemma: if they insisted on formal procedures they would have to bring in the time study man to time a new job within hours of production starting up. Their 'scientific' study would then take place *before* the worker had progressed along the job learning curve. On the other hand, if they wanted to fix manning levels without the assistance of the time study department, they were forced to bargain with the line stewards. It was a problem that the uncertain economic situation of the early 1950s increasingly brought to the attention of the more far-sighted members of management.

Edie Fox was one of the first women to work on the final assembly line in 1949, and she remembered: 'The blue buttons were bargaining all the time. If there was a grievance they would either get the chief steward or, since you could never find the chief steward, in the interim they'd act as steward.'[15] Without an effective organization around him or her, a steward who took a militant line would be quickly isolated and dismissed. Chief stewards, who were aware of this, encouraged their blue button stewards to take on as much bargaining as the foremen would swallow. As late as the 1955 model year boom, the trim unit chairman wrote an article for the *Dodge Main News* called 'Tips to Blue Button Stewards on Bargaining':

> *Don't be sidetracked . . .
> *Keep the penal element out of the picture as much as possible . . .
> *Do not quarrel amongst yourselves . . .
> *Make sure that ALL workers know what the UNION is all about . . .[16]

Its basic rules could have applied equally to chief stewards in negotiations with foremen or superintendents.

While they survived the 1950s at Chrysler, however, the blue button stewards' role was already changing. In the early days of the UAW many sections regularly elected their blue buttons: they were direct representatives of the rank and file. The institutionalization of the chief steward system had changed this: blue button elections became a rarity in the 1940s. They were then always appointed by the area's chief steward, and tended to be those who had campaigned hardest for the chief steward's election.[17] This gradually weakened the representative basis of the system – especially in the 1950s when the blue button stewards came to be appointed mainly for factional reasons. Workers increasingly accepted management's view that blue buttons were less 'legitimate' than the chief stewards, and the flow of grievances upwards via the blue buttons slowly dried up.

The blue button system was also under more direct pressure from the chief stewards. The super-seniority and full-time negotiator status of the chief steward was often the reason many of them took on the job. The Chrysler chief stewards believed in the union tradition but preferred a quiet life. The 180 Dodge Main chief stewards in the 1950s rarely worked. Edie Fox recalled the situation in the trim and final assembly: 'Our chief stewards never worked. If they put our chief steward to work we would all stop. It was part of an established tradition: it came right out of the early years.'[18] From the late 1940s chief stewards started coming to work wearing a white shirt and a tie like the foremen; they were only nominally attached to a job and in certain cases management would only insist they weren't caught sleeping too often.[19] The continuing involvement of some blue button stewards in negotiations with their foremen became another factor in their eclipse. As major lay-offs began to occur cyclically every two years from 1952 to 1958, several chief stewards found they were opposed for election by workers who they themselves had appointed blue button stewards and who had gained their union and negotiating experience in that job. Increasingly, they preferred not to risk creating potential rivals, and so simply failed to give out new blue buttons when existing ones dropped out, were transferred or were laid off.[20]

The strength of Dodge Main workers' independence from company dictates and international UAW pressure lay in their belief that it was legitimate for them to respond to management's disregard of workplace-established rules by striking. At GM and Ford, by contrast, although wildcat strikes did occur from time to time they represented a departure from the norm. This difference between Chrysler and the other auto companies was not apparent in successive Chrysler–UAW contracts. In the 1937 Chrysler contract, as in that year's GM contract, strikes had been prohibited: 'The Union shall not cause or permit its members to cause, nor will any member of the Union take part in, any sit-down or stay-in strike or other stoppage in any of the plants of the Corporation during the term of this Agreement.'[21] Following the workers' 1939 victory the second contract acknowledged 'authorized' strikes, but only after 'all the bargaining procedure as outlined in this agreement has been exhausted, and in no case until after the negotiations have continued for at least five days, and not even then unless sanctioned by the International Union UAW of America'.[22] In the sixth contract, signed in May 1950 after a 104-day strike, the 'right to strike' was once more virtually ruled out. It became an offence to strike 'upon a matter on which the Appeal Board . . . has power to rule'.[23] And that constituted virtually everything since at Chrysler between 1943 and 1955, unlike the situation at GM and Ford, the Appeal Board chairman could even rule on production standards where the complaint was that the rate was 'too fast'.[24]

The constitutional 'illegality' of wildcats was clear. Yet between 1946 and 1956 Chrysler corporate headquarters recorded 1,434 unauthorized strikes. This large total did not mean that the contract prohibitions were irrelevant. They were available as a sanction. Especially from 1950, when Chrysler management slowly shifted from total opposition to union organization to trying to shape its union environment to its own liking, a growing proportion of wildcats ended in the dismissal of those the management decided were troublemakers – although management often still conceded the point at issue.[25] This made the leadership aspect of a steward's job much more difficult. Stewards had to find ways of calling strikes they couldn't be disciplined for. Claiming to be doing what everyone else was doing was ruled 'no defense' by the umpire as early as March 1945.[26] So one body-in-white steward, Steve Wisnieski, used to walk beside the body line with his hand in a particular position scratching the back of his head to give the signal. Another, Mike Kroll, always used to make sure he was in the department office talking about some trivial matter when a strike started.[27] Workers would often carry out the steward's wishes by going slow, refusing to work overtime, leaving to wash-up early or sitting-down on the job, without the formality of a meeting that could lay the steward open to discipline. And, as an extra-legal protection, the foreman would have to know that if a steward was fired his section and possibly the whole department would walk out in the steward's defense, making dismissal an embarrassment to the foreman and costly for the company.

The strike weapon was also regularly used over two other issues: 'fair' seniority rotas, and to defend workers disciplined for maintaining 'fair' production standards. On Wednesday November 30, 1949, the Dodge Main paint shop foreman, Simmons, called back some lower seniority workers while higher seniority workers were still laid off, saying, 'he would not call back in 100 men when all he wanted was a dozen or so sanders'. The result was a 10 a.m. walk-out to a union meeting where the whole paint shop decided to strike. The decision was particularly difficult because the unemployment benefit of those still laid off was automatically stopped if a strike broke out. But it was taken – and soon afterwards Simmons' superiors backed down. A *Dodge Main News* report ended: 'Unionism, Solidarity and Militancy does pay off'.[28]

A 'fair' production standard was another part of Dodge Main's plant consciousness during the 1940s and early 1950s. What this actually meant is very difficult to reconstruct. Jobs changed, sometimes every year; the technology changed, usually more slowly; and plant output targets changed, often from week to week. But many, if not most workers worked on jobs where it was possible either to get ahead of the production target or to 'double up' with another worker so as to provide extra relief time. A worker wrote of conditions in the body-in-white in 1949: 'We ran the job just as we saw fit and worked 40 or 45 minutes each hour. We'd get production ahead and then sit down to talk or rest or kid around. We never worked more than 45 minutes out of an hour, and sometimes, only 35.'[29] A final assembly worker recalled:

> The conditions on the assembly line, to me learning it, were really
> tough. But the standards were pretty much decided by the workers on
> the job. We would decide how much we could do. There was only one
> company time study man in the plant, so we didn't see much of him.
> We didn't have any relief – and we wanted it that way. We made our
> own relief. Without jeopardizing my job I could make 15 minutes for
> myself every hour. The foremen knew what was going on. But there was
> time to do good quality work.[30]

Ed Liska, who returned to the body-in-white in 1946 after five years in
the Army, recalled standards as very slack at least until the 1950s. 'We
had people just reading books, sitting down,' he said. 'We had enough
manpower to do anything.'[31]

How did they secure these conditions? Gertrude Nalezty remembered
workers' readiness to sit down and refuse to work as a common
bargaining practice: 'Most of the time people just sat down and wouldn't
work until they got what they wanted. For a while this was a real militant
bunch at Dodge Main and they really stuck together. Management tried
to get us to speed up. Some cases they got more work. Other cases the
workers banded together and upped production to where they thought it
was fair.'[32] In the final assembly it wasn't sit-down strikes that were most
common, but slow-downs, 'falling back down the line':

> If any work was added the workers would just go back down the line.
> We would just keep it up. To maintain control, we just didn't do the
> extra work. Generally the workers won. When I started on the final
> assembly in 1949 it was really unheard of to have a worker fired for a
> production standard dispute. Sometimes they would draw a line by the
> side of the line and if we fell back to that point then they would
> discipline or fire us. But if anyone was fired everyone would walk out. It
> only began to happen a lot in the late 1950s.[33]

Sectional action, or the threat to use it, was always present, as this one
of dozens of examples shows. In December 1949 time study men set a
rate of 640 pieces on the heavy gear case job in Department 107, the
Dodge Main transmission unit. The three workers, one on each shift,
were turning out only an average 513 at the time, but under pressure
raised this to 540. In the steadily deteriorating labor relations atmosphere that existed just prior to the 104-day national Chrysler strike, they
were given one-day disciplinary lay-offs just before Christmas. Eighty
fellow workers stayed off with them. Then, in January 1950, when they
persisted in their 'go-slow', management suspended them again – for two
days. The whole transmission unit then walked out at 9 a.m. to a meeting

in the Local 3 hall and decided to strike until the management backed down. The local executive board informally supported the strike, and management quickly backed down, discovering 'they may be wrong in the fatigue time they allow'.[34]

General foremen and superintendents had considerable autonomy from higher management as to how they ran their departments as long as they kept production flowing. So considerable bargaining strength remained with the work group on the shopfloor. The 'fair' production standard[35] was maintained by the right to strike. Only when sectional strike action was no longer a legitimate activity in the eyes of most Dodge workers was management able to regain its authority over standards.

The tradition of local autonomy at Dodge Main came under increasing pressure from the international union after the consolidation in power of the Reuther faction in 1947. But although the presidents of Local 3 were Reuther supporters from 1944 to 1949, and from 1950 to 1953, the international's attempts to assert control over wildcat strikes at Dodge Main failed. The local union tradition was still too resilient to be curtailed in a period when management was overtly hostile to *all* union activity.

Mike Novak, the first Hamtramck Pole to win the Local 3 presidency, was re-elected every year on a pro-Reuther ticket until 1949 when he was given a UAW staff job. During his period of office, Dodge Main, like all the other Detroit Chrysler plants, had shut down completely in the April 24, 1947 strike against the Taft–Hartley Bill.[36] And when Reuther subsequently decided to comply with the anti-communist provisions of the Act, including the swearing of non-communist affidavits by all candidates for local union positions, Local 3 fell in line.[37] Local 3 also backed Reuther's early idea of labor supporting an independent presidential candidate in 1948, and then, after he changed his mind, it too plumped for Truman.[38]

The year 1948 was the high point for the Reuther faction at Dodge Main. It cleaned up in the February 1948 elections, finally removing John Zaremba from the executive board on which he had sat since 1936.[39] But within a year of the rout of the left, the Local 3 leadership was in disarray. Anti-communism could cement an alliance on the UAW's IEB, but not necessarily sustain one in a plant where the left did not mount a serious threat but where management did. Once Novak, a strong personality with substantial ethnic support, stood down, the right wing split. Novak's closest supporters campaigned on the 'Green' slate around Art Grudzen with the support of Reuther and the Association of Catholic Trade Unionists:

Think Right – Be Right – Vote right
Vote the Grudzen–Reuther slate for
Pensions, Health Insurance, Job Security
Living Wage
Your Job Depends on
Good Leadership[40]

But they were opposed by a center 'Trade Union' slate around 'Big Ed' Bartelbort from the machine shop and Ed Domanski from the body-in-white. Their successful campaign – 'Pensions, CIO policy, Revision of contract'[41] – focused on the reopening of the unpopular two-year contract signed by Reuther after a sixteen-day strike in May 1948:[42] There was also a Zaremba–Van Horn left-wing slate of 'Fighting leaders for a More Progressive Union'. It stood for:

30c hourly wage raise
Pensions and health insurance program at company expense
All out fight against speed-up
Halt to discrimination in hiring and on the job against Negroes, women and workers over 35
Complete, honest repeal of Taft–Hartley[43]

The 'fighting' slate got nowhere, but the widespread feeling among Chrysler workers that they had been sold short with the 13c rise negotiated in 1948 led to the election of the Bartelbort ticket.[44]

'Big Ed' Bartelbort had started at Dodge Main in 1934 and was first elected chief steward for Department 108 in 1943. He was elected plant committeeman for the machine shop division in 1946, and represented the 'good sound American unionism' that dominated the activists' consciousness. But in 1949 he was not *for* Walter Reuther, so by definition he was seen as being *against*.[45] Local 3's oppositional stance was confirmed when, during the 104-day strike between January and May 1950, Dodge stewards led the Chrysler stewards' council to protest against Reuther's decision to allow maintenance and other workers into the plants during the strike.[46] In retaliation Reuther then reduced the voting strength of the Dodge Main delegation to the Chrysler Conference from 201 to 12, despite the fact that Local 3 represented one-third of the 89,000 striking Chrysler workers.[47]

The strike was over the UAW's demand that Chrysler guarantee to pay a $100 a month pension to workers aged 65. Reuther had made pension improvements his principal objective in 1950, and the demand implied that if federal social security benefits went up, so would the worker's total entitlement. Previously, Chrysler's liability had fallen when federal benefits were increased. To underwrite the new scheme the

UAW had called on Chrysler to follow the September 1949 agreement at Ford and pay 10c an hour per worker into a properly administered pension fund. But Keller refused to agree or to provide actuarial data to the unions. He maintained that costs were none of the UAW's business and was determined to demonstrate that Chrysler would not be pushed around by the UAW. Hutchinson was equally opposed but for his own particular reasons: he was against tying up $45m of 'his' money in the low-interest securities that a properly funded plan and fixed cents per hour commitment would demand.[48]

Keller delayed the negotiations until winter, when he believed the strike could be defeated, and then made his first and final offer on January 17, 1950. His intransigence made the first Chrysler-wide strike inevitable. After four months on strike, without any further negotiations, two factors forced Reuther to retreat on his fixed cents per hour demand. For the first time in a 'Big Three' strike the UAW had paid strike benefit, and the costs had drained the international's reserves; and on May 29, 1950 the still more important negotiations were due to begin on a new GM contract.

Chrysler, too, had been hit hard: it estimated a sales loss of $1 billion.[49] While GM and Ford car sales in 1950 jumped 38% and 47% respectively over 1949, Chrysler's only moved up 8%. For Chrysler this was disastrous: in 1949 Ford had produced the same number of cars as Chrysler, but in 1950 Ford made and sold four cars for every three Chrysler's.[50] Only one of the four months' lost production could be made up. Keller's obduracy did not even result in a major defeat for the UAW. The outcome was a contract stalemate: Chrysler did not agree to adjust benefits above the $100, but it did agree to establish a special pension fund. The exhaustion of both sides also expressed itself in their agreement to extend the contract for an unprecedented three-year term.[51]

The first sign of a more considered management approach to labor followed the end of the strike. Within weeks it was clear the Chrysler strike had been a major managerial misjudgement. The principle of non-interference by the UAW in actuarial matters, that Keller had sacrificed 500,000 cars to defend, was conceded by GM after just one week of talks. GM agreed to pay its pension obligations on top of the federal benefits – giving workers $117 a month; to establish a properly funded pension scheme; to pay a 50% disability pension to workers injured in its plants; and to pay half of workers' admission fees to the Blue Cross and Blue Shield medical care schemes. The best publicized feature of this 'Treaty of Detroit', as it was called, was its five-year term coupled with a cost-of-living bonus that had a downward movement limited to 3c an hour, and a guaranteed annual rise of 4c an hour.[52]

For Keller the GM settlement was a bitter pill to swallow. When Ford negotiated a mirror agreement with Reuther, Keller's discomfort got worse. It was clear that Chrysler had to fall in line soon or risk several more years of confrontation with the UAW, something its declining market share made appear unthinkable. So at the beginning of November Keller moved sideways from the post of company president to the position of board chairman. The new president was L. L. Colbert and it was he who immediately contacted the UAW to reopen negotiations. There was little to talk about, and only seven months after the May 1950 strike settlement, Colbert signed a new contract with UAW bringing Chrysler into line with GM and Ford. The December 1950 contract marked the start of a pattern-bargaining process in which the 'Big Three' gave almost identical benefits to all their UAW workers in successive long-term contracts covering the next twenty-nine years.

The long-term contracts helped regulate Chrysler's labor relations in several important ways. It provided an unprecedented degree of certainty about future wage costs, and so encouraged management to look at how to exercise control over labor productivity. The pattern-bargaining process gave Chrysler a direct incentive to catch up with the level of managerial control operated in its competitors' plants. And the 1950 contract also provided more assurance of opposition to unauthorized strikes from the international union than Chrysler had ever had before. This, too, acted to focus attention upon the shopfloor organization in its plants.

Chrysler's new president knew that the existing tradition would be extremely difficult to overcome as long as the whole union organization, from the local president and plant committee chairman down, supported sectional industrial action. He needed greater external regulation of their behavior by the international union, so he used the five-year breathing space to try and moderate the company's traditional hostility to the UAW while gradually building a closer bargaining relationship with Reuther and the UAW's Chrysler department.

To effect this change Colbert had to revamp Chrysler's own labor relations operations. From 1937 until 1950, relations with the UAW had been the joint responsibility of Nicholas Kelly from Chrysler's New York lawyers and of James Lee from its public relations firm. Chrysler's top executives had concentrated almost entirely on production decisions.[53] Increasingly, after 1950, executives, from Colbert down, took over decision making on labor relations and the function was then moved to Chrysler's Detroit headquarters.

While Colbert had partially conceded the need to live with the UAW presence, however, board chairman Keller never really accepted this.

There remained an ambiguity about Chrysler's attitude that made it difficult for Reuther's supporters to rebuild their caucus in the early 1950s. Then, when Colbert launched an all-out offensive against the local union tradition in the mid 1950s, Reuther's shopfloor advocates of compromise found conditions still more difficult. Yet the impact of ten years of defensiveness from attacks by both the management and the international union did begin to make an impression on the resilience of the Dodge Main tradition. The early 1950s was a period of flux.

III. The early 1950s: changes

After the 1950 strike Reuther kept up his pressure on the dissident Local 3 administration. At a Dodge Main stewards' council meeting, Art Hughes, the former war-time opponent of the no strike pledge, presented the UAW case for curbing unauthorized strikes. The defeated Reutherite of 1949, Art Grudzen, who was campaigning for Local 3 president again, was put directly on the spot. Balancing very carefully, he managed both to support international policy and to make an exception for Dodge Main workers who were responding to 'deliberate provocation':

> I want you to know that I am in accord with the International policy on unauthorized strikes. When a group of workers take the law into their own hands and walk off the job without following the democratic procedure of the by-laws of Local No 3 and the Constitution of the International Union, they are often, actually, doing a disservice to our Local Union . . .
> I wish to emphasize that I am not speaking of the many unauthorized strikes that are brought about by the arbitrary, dictatorial attitude and sometimes deliberate provocation of many by supervision and plant management. These situations we must fight when and where we find them.[54]

Thanks to the battle fatigue that had set in during the five-months' strike, the probably accurate rumours that Bartelbort had mishandled the strike finances, and the emergence of a rival center-left 'Blue Slate' from among Bartelbort's own supporters, Grudzen was elected president in July 1950.[55]

Grudzen's first speech as president reflected the contradictory character of right-wing Dodge unionism. He was a Reuther supporter whose election address promised 'responsible leadership in the settlement of the workers' grievances without resorting to "wild-cat" strikes'.[56] Yet a significant section of Chrysler management, backed by the still-dominant

Keller, made this an extremely difficult if not impossible task. It continued to deny the international union organization, the public recognition and private wheeler-dealer relationship which, by the early 1950s, the UAW was already receiving from GM and Ford. The continuing hostility to the international UAW meant it was not much of an advantage to be a Reuther supporter as Dodge president. Justifying continued sectional strikes taking place against the backcloth of the Korean War, Grudzen made a plea for greater managerial recognition backed by the threat of union mobilization:

> I stand four square behind President Phillip Murray of the CIO in supporting President Truman and our Armed Forces in the struggle which appears close at hand . . .
> Most of the unauthorized work stoppages have been and are caused by the Chrysler Corporation's refusal to directly negotiate with the union on a problem, preferring to hide behind the delayed action of the umpire procedure.
> So our big job in the coming year must be in the day to day negotiations. We must continue the fight to make the Chrysler Corporation bargain with our stewards, plant committee and officers on our plant problems and use the impartial umpire only as a court of last resort in fewer and fewer cases, as it was always intended.[57]

Grudzen found he could not openly break with the sectional bargaining and problem solving that Local 3 members believed were 'legitimate'. He was even forced to defend many of the unauthorized strikes in the last half of 1950:

> I caution those members who may unthinkingly blame their fellow-members for plant shut-downs; get the facts first, before jumping to the same conclusions that most newspapers do, that union workers are always at fault.
> Only a small number of unauthorized strikes have been caused by the workers, and your union has taken active steps to eliminate them.
> After all, I consider my most important responsibility is to keep you working every minute, until you, by your democratic ballot, decide to stop work as a group.[58]

Chrysler management entered the 1950s with a major problem: even 'responsible' unionists in its plants spoke the language of confrontation. But this problem was clearly, in part, of its own making. In 1952 Chrysler attorney Theodore Iserman testified before a Senate Labor committee against the 'monopolistic powers of labor unions':

The obvious answer (is to limit) the monopolistic powers of labor
unions as much as we do the monopolistic powers of business.
We should forbid great international unions to control the bargaining
throughout an entire industry, require them to restore bargaining
powers to Local unions, or other constituent units, each of which would
represent employees of a single company and its subsidiaries and would
be autonomous in its bargaining and striking. And we should forbid
these units to combine and conspire among themselves, directly or
indirectly, or to strike in concert.[59]

But while an older group of Chrysler managers remained bitter towards
the international for what they saw as the sabotage of Chrysler's market
share in 1950, there was a slow thaw. The focus of Chrysler's anti-
unionism changed in the 1950s from hostility to all unionism to a specific
opposition to sectional strikes.

At the end of the 1951 model year Dodge Main management used a
strike by workers demanding smocks to fire three stewards. The executive board ruled that 'no strike existed',[60] and Grudzen argued: 'We
could have won that grievance without losing time from work if cooler
heads had prevailed. And when I say that, I mean among both Union and
Management Personnel.'[61] Five days later management seized upon this
division and the Dodge labor relations director issued a threat to Local 3
officers and plant committee members that he would take 'drastic' action
to end further unauthorized walk-outs.[62]

Management's threat was immediately denounced by Alfred McNeil,
a militant paint unit steward and a Catholic: 'May I remind our
International Officers and the Officers of the Corporation that it was, in a
large part, due to these so-called "wild-cat strikes" that our UAW–CIO
was built ... We are not in Russia, and as free Americans we will not
tolerate Dictatorship by either the Chrysler Corporation or our International.'[63] But Grudzen remained silent and with sales of the 1951
models falling, management launched the threatened offensive. At the
end of June two more blue button stewards were fired when a shortage of
fenders made a stoppage not unwelcome – and when the section
returned after a protest strike their chief steward was fired for not
preventing it.[64]

These dismissals were, however, just a warming-up exercise. On July
24, 1951, a turning point in Dodge labor relations took place when
Chrysler fired Jimmy Solomon. As plant committee chairman and a
committeeman since 1942 for the largest of Dodge Main's six divisions,
the trim unit and wire room, he was a key figure in the Dodge union
organization. A well-known opponent of Reuther, Solomon was fired in
circumstances which led many activists to believe the UAW's 'top
leaders, it seems, are "involved" with the auto corporations'.[65]

Solomon's dismissal took place in the context of a standards dispute. The supervision in the trim department had imposed new production standards, and then given two-day penalty suspensions to a team of two workers on the seat cushion line for not reaching a new output target.[66] The first and the second shifts on their line walked out and pickets appeared at the plant gates before the 6 a.m. shift the following morning. No one crossed the picket line and the whole plant shut down. Grudzen immediately came under pressure from the international to end the wildcat, and the executive immediately called a mass meeting to hear the international reps., Art Hughes and Harold Julian, argue that the issue should be taken through the grievance procedure. It was attended by about 3,000 workers mainly from other areas of the plant, since most trim department workers stayed at home, and those present voted to follow the international's advice. Grudzen then ordered the removal of the pickets and the stoppage ended.[67] A vote of the whole plant had been used to force the trim unit to accept UAW discipline.

Five days later, Chrysler followed up its advantage. It refused to allow the two men to work at the old production standard while their grievance went through procedure and sacked them for not working to the new work schedule. Both shifts on their line stopped again, and Solomon then followed the normal practice of calling a mass meeting to consider the next move. Management, aware that Grudzen had advised him against this, promptly fired Solomon. Once again pickets shut down the plant. This time, however, Grudzen failed at first to convince a mass meeting to return to work, but three days later a noisy meeting of 11,000 workers agreed to go back on condition that the EB would immediately organize a strike vote so the plant could stop officially. This turned out to be the finish of Solomon. One steward believed open internal union feuding caused the vote to go back: 'The stench of the Right and Left Wing Factions have finally reached the nostrils of the membership.'[68]

It was early November 1951 and lay-offs and short-time working were in force before Grudzen finally called the strike vote. A total of 11,691 workers voted, but the majority for a strike was less than the two-thirds required by the UAW constitution. Solomon was out for good.[69] By proving it could dismiss the plant committee chairman (previously only done to the AIWA in 1935 and in the recession of 1939), Chrysler forced every steward to act with greater caution. Plant committeemen and chief stewards had also been taught a significant lesson by the international's cooperation with the management. The consolidation of the Reuther faction in office and the signing of the five-year contracts removed any remaining ambiguity about the international's attitude towards locally generated stoppages: the UAW was now publicly and privately committed to bringing Chrysler workers' strike weapon under its exclusive control.

One immediate consequence of Solomon's successful victimization was the dismissal in March 1952 of one of his chief supporters, wire room chief steward, Edith Van Horn. She was fired for distributing leaflets and holding meetings in the women's rest room attacking the Detroit hearings of the House Un-American Activities Committee (HUAC) where she was named as a 'Red'. Her dismissal was followed by a walk-out of virtually all the wire room workers.[70] Workers' reactions to the Detroit HUAC hearings were very different elsewhere in the plant. The previous Friday, Paul Henley had been subpoenaed to appear before the HUAC and had pleaded the Fifth Amendment. When he returned to the Dodge foundry, he was physically threatened by other workers and was escorted from the plant by security guards. The next day leaflets were given out at the plant gate attacking the witch-hunt against Henley. When he returned again to his job other workers refused to work with him and Chrysler fired him for 'violating the long-established rule against inflammatory and objectionable literature in the plant'.[71]

Management's conduct of these two cases bears witness to its continuing labor relations ineptitude. In both, the umpire eventually ruled that the company had not respected its own 'legality'. It had no evidence that Henley had distributed his leaflets, and supervision had never previously warned Van Horn against distributing hers. Both leftists were reinstated, Henley with back pay, Van Horn without.[72] These rulings were virtually unique during the McCarthyite Korean War peak when employers who dismissed workers because of the unrest caused by their political views were upheld in 80% of the cases arbitrated.[73]

The reasons for the umpire's ruling at Dodge Main were complex: there remained considerable support for Van Horn in the wire room and it was possible there could be another walkout; Chrysler's labor relations department had not prepared its case well, charging both with specific offences of which they were both innocent. Neither Chrysler nor the UAW believed there was a serious 'Red' problem in Dodge Main, and the credibility of the whole umpire system was still weak in Detroit and would not be helped by blatant disregard of the legalities. In the 1940s umpire decisions had overwhelmingly gone against Local 3: a breakdown shows thirty-nine clear rulings against Local 3 and only fourteen in favor from 1943 to 1949. But as Chrysler's labor relations strategy moved away from simple union bashing in the 1950s, so umpire decisions began to reflect more balance: from 1950 to 1959 there were only sixteen against to thirteen in favor.[74] The umpire system had to be legitimated as a source of 'fairness' and 'justice' in workers' experience as well as on paper before it could offer a genuine alternative to industrial action.

The growing acceptance of contract legality by Local 3 officers was threatened in 1953 when frustration with the 1950 contract erupted. Unauthorized strikes broke out across the whole auto industry,[75] fuelled principally by the discontent of skilled workers with the long-term contract. They had seen the Korean War boom send wages and overtime rocketing in the open shops not bound by the auto industry pattern, and many skilled men joined the breakaway Independent Skilled Trades Confederation.[76] In Dodge Main, the anti-Reuther 'Blue Slate' won every position in the local elections. The skilled plant committeeman, Joe Cheal, defeated Grudzen to become president, and the veteran Pat Quinn was elected vice-president.[77]

Aware that the successful blue slate would get no assistance from Reuther, management renewed its pressure on shopfloor custom and practice when Dodge Main employment fell below the June 1953 all-time peak of 32,000. In August, the new executive board called a strike vote, arguing that management was 'dictatorial':

> Collective bargaining, as it is known in America, has completely broken down in Dodge Main Plant. It has been replaced by a dictatorial management who insist that they and they alone shall dictate terms of employment, in hours of work, wages and working conditions . . .
> Continual hounding of workers for more work seems to be the general policy throughout the plant . . .
> Certain rights, such as wash up time, enjoyed by workers since the beginning of our Union are slowly taken away from them . . .
> We must remind Dodge Management that we did not organize to be apple polishers, nor did we organize for the greater glory of Chrysler Corporation; but we organized for the mutual protection against the dictatorial managements in Dodge Main Plant and elsewhere.[78]

But although there was an 80% majority for a strike,[79] the rapidly worsening economic situation that set in with the 1954 model year caused first 12,000 and then 20,000 lay-offs.[80] The strike call was deferred while the local called unemployment demonstrations demanding 'A Public Works Program Now'.[81] Management's tightening-up strategy survived – at least until the model year boom of 1955.

In June 1954, despite an attempt by Norman Matthews, the UAW Chrysler Director, to rebuild a viable anti-Cheal caucus,[82] the center-left blue slate was re-elected. For the first time, following constitutional changes brought in by the Reutherite majority at the 1951 UAW Convention, they were elected for a two-year term.[83] What was seen by management as a set-back for Chrysler–UAW relations caused it to issue a new challenge. Two trim department workers were fired for refusing to use a new method of installing window trim when the company refused to time study it.[84] Supervision was again trying to break with the custom and practice of sectional collective bargaining on the introduction of new work methods. The executive board responded to this challenge. It called a plant-wide strike, using the dormant strike vote of September 1953 as justification. But five days later the IEB ruled that the previous strike vote did not apply.[85] Chrysler immediately pointed out the lessons to Joe Cheal. Dodge Main's operating manager, Otto Franke, warned him and the international that unless they acted to 'prevent a recurrence' of the unauthorized strike, Cheal would be 'terminated' (full-time Local 3 officers were paid by the UAW but were on a leave of absence from Chrysler) and Chrysler would 'collect information necessary to file a law suit requesting damages against you and the Dodge Local Union'.[86]

The IEB expected the issue to die there, but the blue slate administration at Dodge Main stood in the classic tradition. Joe Cheal had been chairman of the AIWA's maintenance workers' local in 1935[87] and, like his vice-president Pat Quinn, had nearly twenty years of sectional union activity behind him. They were not going to let management have the victory so easily. When sales of the new 'Forward Look' 1955 models began to rise, the EB threatened a renewal of action unless management negotiated on production standards, the trim shop firings and on seniority.

Chrysler, squeezed by its lowest share of passenger car registrations since 1931, backed down. First, management signed a 'memorandum' agreeing that for every eight seniority workers recalled in any one department, it would recall two workers from the plant-wide 'Master Seniority List'. Particular problems that arose would be sorted out 'by mutual agreement between the Union and the Management'.[88] These seniority rules were felt, by a seven to three majority of the workers, to be 'fair'.[89] The agreement was partly forced by union pressure and partly conceded by a less antagonistic labor relations strategy that recognized the proposal did not raise labor costs significantly, since by 1954 at least 20% of jobs in most departments could be learned within minutes.

Then, in October, the two Department 99 workers fired in July were reinstated with back pay, and the Dodge Main labor relations executives, Clarence W. Johnson and Lewis B. Larkin, signed two documents that imposed certain restraints on managerial rights through to the end of the 1955 model year. The *Dodge Main News* was exuberant: 'The chief point in the agreement is that once the rates of production are set ... they cannot be changed unless a technological change takes place. Under this set-up foremen cannot, every few weeks, demand more production resulting in confusion and wildcat strikes.'[90]

Almost as important for the assembly line worker was management's agreement that 'on assembly line operations employees will not be required to make up skips'.[91] So if there were breakdowns or shortages, the supervision couldn't try to make up the lost production by running the line faster than the maximum scheduled speed. The company also put in writing a promise not to obstruct workers and stewards from complaining 'about a job being too fast' by insisting the protest was in writing before the company would negotiate on it: 'Facts will be made available for examination when a verbal complaint is made', the 'memorandum of understanding' added.[92] This, of course, was a key concession, since it confirmed *de facto* recognition of the blue button stewards, who were the ones most likely to bargain verbally with the supervision.

A second memorandum addressed the permanent aggravation of skilled workers: the use of outside contractors while some skilled workers were laid off. This agreement acknowledged the union request 'that since there are maintenance employees laid off that no work be contracted out on which they have customarily worked', and said it would 'review the situation in cases of this kind and give due consideration to calling back laid-off employees'.[93] This was Cheal paying his debt to Dodge Main's skilled workers. Their growing discontent had been a major feature of the Korean War period, when skilled workers in the 'Big Three' found their rates falling behind those in Detroit's open shops, and so demanded more overtime.

The two written agreements were Chrysler's version of 'peace in our time' – a holding operation that reinforced the legitimacy of struggled-for restraints. They show the extent of Dodge Main workers' frontier of control ten years after the end of World War II. Workers went on defending custom and practice while management continued to try to undermine the tradition of struggle on which they were based. Management had some successes. The threat to 'terminate' the Local 3 president, for example, had an effect. In May 1955, when a group of fourteen trim shop workers picketed the plant in protest against a three-day disciplinary lay-off of three women for failing to do their job, the executive board made certain it was *seen* to be trying to stop the strike spreading:

> Union sound trucks from Dodge Local 3, UAW–CIO, appeared at the scene early today to urge day shift workers to go to their jobs after it appeared the trouble might spread to the day shift.
> Despite the Local's statement that walkouts were never authorized, a group in the trim shop left their jobs at 10 a.m., resulting in the lay-offs of 7,500 others in the plant.[94]

When sectional stoppages continued at a high rate in 1955 and 1956, pressure from the international to keep to the contract and the threat to activists' jobs led to strikers becoming increasingly isolated. By 1955 strike action was still part of rank and file consciousness but the Local 3 leaders no longer openly defended its legitimacy in preserving custom and practice. Neither the Local 3 president nor the Dodge Main plant committee chairman would openly challenge contract legality again. The ground had been laid for the major managerial clawback of 1956–59, but for that to happen Chrysler's management structure first needed to be changed.

7   A cold one: 1956–1959

The late 1950s were indeed 'cold ones' for Chrysler workers as the informal labor relations system that had operated for nearly twenty years was redrawn in the image of the formal bargaining systems at GM and Ford. This chapter argues that the change did not result from a philosophical conversion of Chrysler management but because its declining market share forced a series of changes on the company. Management's restructuring and the sense of urgency created by the staccato effect of the four 1950s production slumps, led to an unprecedented consistency in labor relations policy. In certain ways, Chrysler approached, for the first time, the 'management by policy' that had characterized GM's labor relations since 1939.[1] This development was assisted by the agreement of the 'Big Three' auto manufacturers to conduct what amounted to joint bargaining with the UAW in 1958,[2] and by the onset of what industrial relations academics called a 'hard line' in management thinking.[3] For four years from 1956 the frontier of control moved in management's favor. There were moments when that movement was slowed, but it was never halted or reversed.

Section I traces the management changes that preceded the onset of open conflict. Section II considers the issues involved as the numbers of wildcat strikes in defense of the old informal bargaining system increased sharply in 1956 and 1957. Section III focuses on the traumatic year 1958 when the Dodge Local 3 was taken on and defeated in a stand-up fight.

I. Preparing for conflict

Chrysler's deteriorating market position from a 23% share of auto production in 1951 to 13% in 1954 was due to the cumulative effects of a weak product policy and of low investment compounded by conservative management. Management proved incapable of responding quickly to the new market conditions triggered by the Korean War when, over-night, a seller's market became a buyer's one, with the buyers demanding the modern styles that Keller refused to provide. Although Colbert was appointed chief executive in 1950, he had been with Chrysler since 1924 when he started as the first in-house lawyer and was unlikely to initiate any radical changes while 'K.T.' was still around.

The low market share of 1954, however, forced Colbert to initiate some changes. He appointed a new vice-president to plan towards developing a professional managerial structure. He attempted to decentralize Chrysler management by introducing independent divisional profit centers.

More significantly, Colbert also persuaded Keller to agree to hire the management consultants, McKinsey and Company, to undertake a major study of what was going wrong at Chrysler. McKinsey took nearly two years to report. When it did, after Keller's retirement, it proposed major changes in virtually every area of Chrysler's management. Colbert's decentralization experiment was put into reverse and the existing structure of seven totally independent vice-presidents coord-inated merely through a twice-weekly meeting with Keller, was recast into a committee structure of nineteen vice-presidents, all of whom were based at corporate headquarters in Highland Park. The plan was intended to free Colbert and his first vice-president, Edgar Row, to make corporate-wide strategic plans. Day-to-day decisions were to be the responsibility of Colbert's deputy, William Newberg, to whom the nineteen vice-presidents reported. The dominant influence of the engi-neering department was to be curbed, allowing car design to be fully modernized, and still further interchangeability of parts between the five model lines was to be introduced to secure greater economies of scale. Domestic production was to be decentralized away from Detroit, which in 1955 employed 81% of the company's total labor force, and with the construction of new, low-cost plants hundreds and thousands of miles distant from Dodge Main, it was hoped Detroit's labor relations prob-lems would be eased. Middle-level management was to ensure that Chrysler's new plants started to operate in the manner of Ford and GM plants. In its existing plants the plan was to redraw the frontier of control to achieve the same goal. The Plymouth car was to be given its own divisional profit center and its own dealer network, and Chrysler was also recommended to follow its competitors overseas.[4]

Knowing what should be done was not, however, the same as doing it. Highland Park was soon described by *Fortune* as being 'knee-deep in vice-presidents' without having added any new faces. At the same time only 15% of Plymouth sales were allocated to the new network as the other dealers resisted losing the staple custom the Plymouth provided.[5] Yet after Hutchinson's retirement in 1953 and Keller's in 1956, Colbert was finally left on his own with sufficient authority to implement the new McKinsey strategy in full.

The aspect of the McKinsey report Colbert chose to concentrate on was recovering managerial shopfloor control. This was not because he had any farsighted strategy, but because the workplace control issue could unite management in a way the highly contentious questions of product design, investment and management structure could not.[6] The figures demanded action: in 1955, when Ford and GM produced 115% and 70% more cars per manual worker than they had averaged between 1946 and 1949, Chrysler's labor productivity was 15% lower than in the late 1940s. On sales of $3.5 billion Chrysler's profit rate was just 2.9% in 1955, compared to 9.5% at GM.[7]

Colbert was acutely conscious of Chrysler's higher costs, and rather than depart from the market strategy of competing in all segments of the market, with the inevitable consequence of gaining fewer economies of scale, he made closing the 'work standards gap' his major aim. This ensured that Dodge Main played a central part in the events of the next three years. For although its share of the total Chrysler workforce decreased from about a third to a quarter and then a fifth in the 1950s, it remained a crucial symbol, in the eyes of management and of union activists, of what was viewed respectively as the worst and best in labor relations.

The Dodge Main time study department was built up and a major influx of 'crewcuts' undertook a complete study of the lines in all departments early in 1955. At first many workers treated them as a joke.[8] But this systematic operation was very different from the previous single job studies. As a plant-wide exercise, it threw into question *departmental* custom and practice. One department to experience this early on was Department 73. During the war the heavy press shop workers won a relief agreement, 'where the workers worked 50 minutes every hour and then shut down to rest for 10 minutes'.[9] In 1955, the pressure to standardize conditions throughout the plant meant management began to insist the press lines stopped for only three minutes in every hour and that production increased accordingly. Custom and practice that allowed heavy press workers eighty minutes' personal relief a day was not compatible with 'scientific' time study that only allowed for twenty-four.

The exercise also provided management for the first time with a total view of the labor input and costs of the press, body, trim and assembly lines. If production could be speeded up and/or manning levels reduced in these areas, then, management reasoned, pressure would be automatically increased on the sub-assembly, machining, off-track assembly and repair sections that fed the main lines. But 1955 saw Chrysler hit a new production peak of 1,361,835 of its 'Forward look' cars, and this postponed any managerial interest in precipitate action. The 1955 contract was signed after a mere six hours' strike by salaried UAW members to secure their inclusion in the new Supplementary Unemployment Benefit (SUB) pattern established by the Ford contract. Management also dropped its demand to limit chief stewards to three hours a day bargaining.[10]

The drive to improve productivity only took off again when demand for cars began to fall in January and February 1956, and as Keller's impending April departure left Colbert in complete control. In early February, the Local 3 EB called a strike vote against the speed-up:

> Our patience is at an end. We will not go back to the good old days, for the bosses, before we organized a union. We will not knuckle down to crackpot demands for more and more production. We will fight back with the one weapon we have at our command. We will strike if necessary to preserve decent working conditions in the Dodge plant.[11]

Nearly 10,000 workers voted, but despite a 96% 'yes' vote, a strike did not seem good sense to Cheal in a period of falling demand and lay-offs.[12] Management maintained its pressure and introduced the practice of issuing printed written warning 'tickets' to workers for not working faster.[13]

In June 1956, amid these deteriorating conditions, Pat Quinn became the blue slate candidate for president to succeed Joe Cheal, who was not identified with production workers' problems. Running against the former Reutherite president, Grudzen, the anti-speed-up slate had no problems, and Quinn was elected to the position he had first held in 1939.[14] It was as if he had been selected to personify the old tradition in the coming battle with the new.

II. Management initiates radical changes

Colbert formally launched his drive to intensify the pace of work in a letter to all employees in September 1956:

> We have developed new work standards. These standards are comparable to those of the same jobs at Ford and GM, and they are fair in themselves. Meeting these new work standards means only that each one of us will do, on his own job, as such work as the employees doing the same work at Ford or GM. It takes that much effort to give us the job security and progress we are all shooting for.

By measuring up to our new work standards each one of us will be able
to do his and her part to make sure that no one at Ford or GM is taking
over work that could be done in Chrysler plants.[15]

The letter was a declaration of war on a tradition of mutuality in
establishing standards to which both workers and their supervisors had
been a party for nearly twenty years. What made it significantly different
from lower key declarations of intent made previously was that this
statement of position accompanied a major managerial reorganization
and took place at the *beginning* of the 1957 model year.

Skirmishes over work standards took place from September 1956
through until March 1957, much longer than was customary on new
models. These months were characterized by supervision's readiness to
ignore the contract when it gave the workers a degree of restraint over
their actions. The provisions in the 1955 contract stipulating advance
notice of time study and suggesting the elimination of supervisory
'estimated standards' were disregarded when inconvenient.[16] The
UAW's response was to carry on as usual: a Chrysler conference
condemned Colbert's letter, there was an 84% majority for strike action
in a Local 3 ballot, and the *Dodge Main News* complained:

> Certain rights, such as relief time, negotiated work standards and
> wash-up time enjoyed by our members since the beginning of our Union
> are slowly being taken away from them ... Since the start of the 1957
> model Dodge workers have been subjected to a barrage of threats,
> intimidation and abuse. Time study men have been hired by the dozens
> and placed in the various departments to breath down the workers'
> necks.[17]

Reuther himself acknowledged there were more strikes pending on
production standards in Chrysler plants than in the rest of the UAW
combined.[18]

Reuther, however, had no interest in supporting strikes in defense of
pre-time study production standards in Chrysler plants once he had
successfully dealt with the main pocket of mid 1950s opposition at the
River Rouge. He told a Chrysler conference in October 1956 that 'the
leadership in the Chrysler plants must face this question (of production
standards) practically and realistically ... in line with a fair day's work.'[19]
Nor was there any likelihood of solidarity action between Chrysler plants
that had occurred in 1943, 1945 and 1947. Pat Quinn's Local 3 administration was both isolated as one of the few remaining anti-Reuther
administrations and from its own membership. The blue button steward
system had fallen away in most areas and, following the introduction of
two-yearly terms of office in 1954, the position of chief steward had

become still more remote. Like Joe Cheal before him, Quinn finally opted for a compromise on Chrysler's demands rather than a confrontation in the last year that gave Chrysler 20% of the market and its workers significant economic leverage.

Dodge workers recognized this was not an old-time quarrel over a few production standards; it was an argument about the frontier of control. Colbert's letter made this clear and this message was repeated six months later. Chrysler vice-president Frank W. Misch, in a speech to potential shareholders, told the New York Society of Security Analysts that Chrysler had completed a major cost-cutting exercise and, more explosively, that the UAW's leadership had cooperated:

> In September 1956 we took another major step in the direction of making our company more competitive on costs and improving its overall operating efficiency. For two years our industrial engineers had been measuring our manufacturing operations with a view to raising our plant productivity, which was not in line with that of our major competitors. With the start of production of our completely new 1957 cars, most of the assembly line operations would be basically changed. This change-over period was the only appropriate time to realign the assembly-line tasks. For many months preceding the start of Production of the 1957 cars, the analysis of work methods and standards was carried down to individual operations. The leadership of the UAW–CIO had been informed of our plans, with a full background of what was at stake.[20]

The international union was stung by this revelation into producing a special four page bulletin denying the charge of 'cooperation'. Its denial was not of the substance of Misch's argument – that the UAW had known what was going on – but was instead directed at Misch's argument that 'the tightening-up of production standards was a main factor' in Chrysler's 'recovery'. The UAW preferred to argue 'to the extent that it has made any recovery ... it was brought about by too long delayed technological improvements and a start towards production rationalization.'[21] The element of truth in this applied more to the machining areas, where automatic transfer equipment had been introduced, than to the production lines that were under the greatest pressure.

The high level of discontent with management and the international led in 1957 to 512 unauthorized stoppages taking place in Chrysler plants. At Dodge Main, four or five workers from areas experiencing the worst speed-up, the body shop and trim departments, had begun meeting together after being elected to Local 3's publicity committee in 1956. (Dodge Main was exceptional within the UAW in the late 1950s because

Table 7 *Dodge Main: Trim department selected hourly production standards, before and after the 1957 agreement*

Operation	Amount performed *before* 1957 agreement	Company demand winter 1956/57	Amount laid down by 1957 agreement	Actual increase worked (%)
Windlace	7	9	8	14.3
Door moulding	15	22	18	20
Cloth headlining	2.5 (team)	No demand	2.5 (team)	0
Installation of instrument panel to body	6 (team)	9 (team)	7.5 (team)	25
Chrome windshield moulding on hardtops	12	23	15	25
Lower belt chrome	6.5	9	6.5	0
Glass vent	6	10	7	16.7
Door pads on south line	30	36	0	0
Door pads on north line	26	36	28	7.7
Lower chrome windshield moulding	16	23	19	18.8

Source: UAW Research Department Collection, WRL, Box 79; data related to Chrysler speed-up dispute, 1958

it continued to elect all the members of its standing committees such as veterans, education and publicity, rather than follow most UAW locals and appoint them.) The militants elected included Edie Fox, a Trotskyist Socialist Workers' Party member who had worked at Dodge since 1948. On her initiative they formed a 'Rank and File' caucus to fight on the production standards issue and, to their surprise, tapped a great well of anger and frustration.[22]

Meanwhile, Quinn finally got Dodge management to agree to a compromise. The local agreement gave management considerable increases in production but promised not to change standards again in the 1957 model year. This did not amount to much since the 1957 models had only another five months to run. Dodge vice-president and former trim department chief steward, Pete Teliskey, described the benefits for Department 99. Out of the 900 operations in the department, he suggested production standards had only been increased on twenty-eight, while they had been decreased on fourteen. And he argued that since it was a written agreement: 'You know when you go to work how many pieces you are to do each hour for the balance of the '57 model . . . Work standards are to remain "as is" for the balance of the 1957 model year . . . No more tickets, no more threats, no more disciplines on rates of production.'[23]

Those who had to work the new standards, however, didn't see things the same way. At the first mass meeting on the new agreement Jimmy Solomon, the former plant committee chairman turned international rep, and the local officials were virtually shouted down and the meeting was taken over by opponents of the agreement. Thousands of the workers wore the 'Rank and File' buttons.[24] Table 7, listing the hourly production rates on ten trim department jobs before and after the 1957 agreement, illustrates why such anger remained. In sections where standards were not raised, the company's demands had made workers realize *they* could be next. It took Quinn and Solomon ten days and several mass meetings to persuade the membership to accept the agreement.[25] A few weeks later the rank and file caucus put up a full 'White slate' in the election of delegates to the 1957 UAW Atlantic City convention which, to the fury of the international and the Local 3 officer corps who were denied their customary vacation,[26] picked up twenty-two of the thirty-five places.

The Dodge Main 1957 rank and file delegation to Atlantic City created one of the last big stirs at any UAW Convention.[27] Heads began to be turned when they opposed the dues increase. The outspoken Scot from the paint shop, Alfred McNeil, lashed into the UAW officials: 'I am opposed to a dues increase because of all the trouble that we have had in the Dodge company. We have had representation that does not amount to 50 cents. I don't think any of our International reps will go hungry.'[28] When it came to a resolution commending the IEB for 'unwavering adherence to the policy of authorizing strikes where collective bargaining has proved futile', Reuther deliberately called Edie Fox to the microphone. She attacked the resolution, arguing that 'we, the rank-and-file members of our Union, have demonstrated a willingness to fight back but we are being discouraged in our efforts by our International leadership.' Her five minutes was immediately followed by a lengthy piece of red-baiting by Norman Matthews, the director of the UAW Chrysler Department. 'Where was this Fox girl?' in the hundred days' strike of 1950, he asked. He accused the 'so-called rank and file group' of only getting elected because they passed out leaflets while the blue and green slates had agreed not to conduct an election campaign this year. And he argued, 'I think it is about time this Convention should give us the authority to deal with these people in quick order . . .'[29]

The UAW's own figures did not support the argument that the international union had backed its locals. In February 1957, twelve Chrysler plants requested strike authorization, but only one authorized strike resulted, and only two other authorized strikes took place in the whole of 1957.[30] To cover up this poor record, Matthews conceded the opposition's demand that overtime in all Chrysler plants be stopped while the month-long strike by 4,000 workers in the Chrysler Los Angeles plant, Local 230, was taking place. 'Now,' he asked rhetorically, 'who is militant? Are these fakers that sit in this audience militant, or is the leadership of the Chrysler plants militant, plus the International Union, my friends?' Reuther himself wound up the debate, accusing the Dodge Main delegation of wasting time and justifying the intolerance of dissent shown by Matthews and himself: 'If the people who provoke these kinds of discussion will just think before they do, we would save a lot of time of this Convention. But they are not going to get away with untruths, because we are going to answer them.'[31] Reuther's convention bullying had nothing in common with the 'democratic' reputation he cultivated in liberal America.[32]

III. 1958: The decisive struggle

The year 1958 was a watershed for Chrysler. The company only produced 581,244 cars, its lowest output between 1947 and 1980. In line with this dramatic market collapse, mass lay-offs and severances reduced its hourly-paid labor force to 59,440 – a post-war employment low, undercut only in the 1961–62 and 1980–82 recessions.[33] The slump was made worse by the legacy of Chrysler's managerial crisis. Colbert had rushed his new 'Look it's 1960' models into production the previous year before they had been properly tested, and they had numerous structural flaws and rampant rust problems. A *Fortune* article appeared with the headline, 'Chrysler's private depression'. As the complaints multiplied, Chrysler lost its reputation for engineering quality at the precise moment the bottom fell out of the market. The vice-president for corporate market planning resigned and the McKinsey consultants were brought back to suggest a further management reorganization.[34]

The severity of the recession presented Chrysler, and many other managements, with the market power to exercise nearly total intransigence in labor relations.[35] The resulting conflict created another all-time record number of strikes in 1958, despite the labor force being 40% smaller than in 1957. The strike frequency rate shot up: more than eight strikes took place for every 1,000 Chrysler workers in 1958, compared with five in 1957 and with an average of 1.5 during the previous ten years. This greater strike frequency was the outcome of a conscious determination by management to reassert its authority. When these strikes happened, supervision was told to sit them out, and this led to a major increase in the average number of hours lost while on unauthorized strike. Chrysler workers lost an average of 17.4 hours a year on unauthorized strikes between 1947 and 1956; in 1957 this figure rose to 25.1 hours, and in 1958 to 91 hours. If the 4.6 million manhours lost in the two authorized strikes that year (including the key Dodge Main stoppage) are added to the 5.4 million manhours lost in unauthorized strikes, then each Chrysler worker lost on average a month's work in 1958: twenty-one full eight-hour shifts.[36]

The confrontations of 1958 flowed from management's three stage strategy. Once Colbert realized there was little to be done to improve Chrysler's sales position in the 1958 model year, he accompanied mass lay-offs with a renewed offensive on the production standards of those still at work. Fortuitously for the 'Big Three', the 1955 auto industry contracts expired that summer, so Chrysler seized upon the UAW tactic of 'working without a contract' to tear up remaining custom and practice agreements. Finally, aware that a major battle had to be fought if a decisive defeat was to be inflicted on workers and their organization and its traditions, Chrysler engaged the Dodge Main workers in a stand-up authorized strike, and beat them.

Local 3 president Quinn and plant committee chairman Steve Pasica became aware of the new management strategy on January 7, 1958. They were summoned to a meeting by the Dodge labor relations director and given two days' notice of a lay-off of a further 3,500 workers. This was not unexpected since a similar number had already been laid off since the start of the 1958 model year. What was unexpected was the news that the whole plant would be shut down for two weeks and that those called back on January 22 would have to work to a new method of determining production rates called 'Man Assignment Programs'.[37]

Before the new assignments, rank and file caucus member, Ed Liska, was already complaining about a speed-up in the body-in-white: 'The working conditions at the Dodge Plant have been at its lowest ebb since our Union was organized. Work schedules have been changed, not only in 1957 but 1956 as well. Nearly every worker has been putting out approximately 40% more production than in the past years.'[38] But by comparison with what was to follow, the initial pressure was quite slight. Management used the January 1958 two-week shut-down to unveil plant-wide man assignment schedules that increased production in the trim shop from ninety-two to ninety-seven cars an hour with 26% fewer workers.[39] Yet those working were the lucky ones: the 9,000 workers who were laid off did not start getting recalled until September 1959, 20 months later.[40]

The new man assignments finally finished off the old custom and practice of establishing a 'fair' standard between the worker, the blue button steward and the foreman. They allocated work on a different

Table 8 *1958: Increased shift production demands made by management at Dodge Main*

Department	1957		1958		Increase
	Production	Manpower	Requested Prod.	Manpower	%
Body in white	1504	2384	776	933	31.9
Trim (day shift)	744	1650	776	1201	30
Final assembly:					
Department 122	720	380	776	342	19.6
Department 123	720	490	776	450	17.3
Motor assembly	880	355	720	200	43.3

Source: UAW Research Department Collection, WRL, Box 79; document dated February 24, 1958.

basis to the old system. Before, the jobs came first and the labor force was divided up to cover them. The system created considerable anomalies since certain jobs took a great deal of time, while others could be finished much more quickly. Under the new system, the total available labor time came first, and the work was then divided up so each worker was allocated as close as possible to sixty seconds' work for every minute of the working day. The man assignments were prepared in the Industrial Engineers' (IE) Department, away from the shop floor. And the work load was the same in all areas of the plant, tying all direct production workers to a common effort and output. The increases in individual productivity demanded from the assembly side of the plant were considerable. A UAW document used in the negotiations that took place at the end of February 1958 gave figures of a speed-up demanded of between 17% and 43% (table 8).

Workers throughout Dodge Main tried to defend the old system by refusing to work to the new standards and in the second week of the new system hundreds were sent home for failing to keep up to the assignments.[41] In the trim shop at the center of the struggle, five workers were fired during the first two weeks of February while four others were dismissed in other areas of the plant.[42] When so many workers had been sent home that it was impossible to continue to run the plant, management simply sent all the other workers home. In the twenty-two days following the introduction of the new man assignments, the trim shop only worked an average of three hours and thirty-five minutes a day. But during those hours, the actual production rate, which had been sixty-eight an hour on the 1957 models, rose from seventy-five an hour on January 22 to hit eighty an hour regularly in February 1958.[43]

Aware that management was trying to provoke strikes, Quinn tried to

Table 9 *Dodge Main: Trim department selected hourly production standards, before and after the 1958 man assignments*

Operation	Amount performed after 1957 agreement	Company demand January 1958	Amount worked March 1958	Actual increase worked (%)
Windlace	8	13.96	9	12.5
Door moulding	18	31.4	19	5.5
Cloth headlining	2.5 (team)	5.8 (team)	3 (team)	20
Installation of instrument panel to body	7.5 (team)	15 (team)	10 (team)	33.3
Chrome windshield moulding on hardtops (a)	15	38	15	0
Lower belt chrome (b)	6.5	12.5	6.5	
Glass vent	7	17.6	12	71.4
Door pads on south line	30	48	30	0
Door pads on north line (c)	28	48	30	7.1
Lower chrome windshield moulding	19	40	34	78.9

Source: UAW Research Department Collection, WRL, Box 79; data related to Chrysler speed-up dispute, 1958.
(a) This job's production standard had been increased 25% in 1957.
(b) One of the few jobs to show no increase in either 1957 or 1958.
(c) Over 1957 and 1958 the standards for door pads on the north line were raised to equal those on the south line which didn't change.

keep everybody working – and so he made it known that anyone who was fired on a production standard issue would be put on the Local 3 payroll. Chrysler responded in kind, by announcing that it would oppose the payment of state unemployment benefit to those laid off, on the grounds that the local's support of those disciplined for refusing to work to standard was tantamount to an admission of an industrial dispute.

Reuther and Colbert then personally took over the negotiations. Their agreement, on March 3, was an even sharper declaration of management's rights than had been contained in the 1957 production standards agreement. This time Chrysler's concessions were merely notional. Colbert agreed to withdraw his threat to the unemployment benefit of those laid off, to reinstate the nine sacked workers and to restore the earlier production standards – except where improvements in method had been introduced. Where 'improvements' had occurred (and they were fairly widespread since the 25% cut in the labor force in January had necessitated a major redistribution of work) industrial engineers would look at the assignments again if there were any problems. In return, Reuther agreed to allow management to continue to revise production standards during the model year.[44] Management had won a significant victory. Table 9 illustrates the effect of the 1958 agreement on the same ten trim department jobs considered in table 7 earlier. The speed-up that had begun the previous year was thus continued in the much worse labor market circumstances of 1958, and it produced an average rise in productivity on these ten jobs of 28% over the two model years. While it is not possible to reconstruct any completely reliable comparisons between the pace of work in GM and Ford plants as against Chrysler, the marked difference that was frequently commented upon in the 1950s had undoubtedly been substantially eroded by 1959 and 1960.[45]

In June 1958 Chrysler workers, like those at GM and Ford, stayed at work after the expiry of the 1955 contracts. Leonard Woodcock, head of the UAW GM Department, said, 'We are going to rock and roll all summer.'[46] Reuther told the *Wall St Journal*: 'I think it's good for the union's soul to work for a while without a contract. It'll make the members aware of a lot of things that used to be automatic.'[47] Car sales were so low, the argument went, that there was no possibility of extracting any concessions from the employers until the start of the 1959 models. But like much of Reuther's 'strategy' bargaining in the post-war years, it was an analysis which looked at the industry from the vantage point of access to the boardrooms rather than from the stance of shopfloor workers. Reuther's idea may well have been that what the workers lost in the 'no contract' period they could regain subsequently. But, in Chrysler plants, what was lost was lost permanently and, since this included the tradition of sectional bargaining, it was never recovered.[48]

Chrysler seized the opportunity provided by the union strategy. Colbert wrote again to all Chrysler workers, this time letting them know there would be 'some change in arrangements for handling grievances' and reminding them that 'shop rules forbid collection of initiation fees, dues and assessments during working hours.'[49] Then, two days after the contract expired, Chrysler tore up the departmental relief agreement that still operated in Dodge Main's body-in-white, and laid off the thirty-five workers who acted as the additional tag relief men. The relief agreement in Department 76 had been introduced in 1938 on the grounds that the heat and dust in the body-in-white was much worse than in other departments. It provided each worker with a total of seventy minutes' relief a day: the seventh and eighth floor production lines stopped for five minutes every hour and workers were also relieved by tagmen for two fifteen-minute breaks, one in the morning and one in the afternoon.

Rather than strike immediately in defense of their relief agreement and jeopardize the supplementary unemployment benefit payments being made to those laid off, the body shop agreed to work the new system of twelve minutes' relief in the morning and sixteen in the afternoon. The *Dodge Main News* approved: 'The workers, sensing this trap refused to take the bait and decided at a meeting to meet the problem head on – knowing that while the company is having their turn at bat now, the workers' turn would come sooner or later and that they would get their just relief time back.'[50] But the 'workers' turn' didn't come in September when they were called back for the start-up of the 1959 models. Then, Chrysler threatened to fire workers who did not 'stay on the job 60 minutes out of every hour',[51] and by the end of September twenty-four men had been disciplined for taking the extended breaks and six had been discharged.[52] These men 'were picked by management to show fear to other workers in the department. All production workers did exactly the same things that the [first] 26 men did but they were not penalized.'[53] By October the 'just' relief system had gone for good.

In June, on the third day of 'working without a contract', management instructed all chief stewards to work on their assigned jobs for six hours a day including the first hour of the shift, the first hour after lunch and the last hour of the shift.[54] At first, this provoked a show of resistance from the Dodge stewards and local executive. Within a week a majority of stewards and committeemen had received first a one-day penalty lay-off and then three-day penalties for refusing to abide by the restrictions.

The situation was moving fast towards mass dismissals of the Dodge stewards. The international reps, Solomon and Addis, advised the local executive to accept Chrysler's terms. But the EB wanted to show more fight and so launched a new plan. The stewards and plant committeemen were to work for *all* eight hours a day and so effectively withdraw from all grievance machinery with the management. The unreal approach of 'fighting' management restrictions by self-restriction didn't go down well. Two days later, swamped with complaints from stewards not ready to work full-time or who saw the move as dangerous for the future of shopfloor union organization, the EB rescinded its decision and accepted Chrysler's terms.[55] These amounted to a redrawing of the bargaining map. Blue button stewards were no longer to be recognized, and foremen and superintendents were told to ignore 'the chief stewards when they try to settle a grievance without reducing it to writing'.[56] *Informal* bargaining was banished – and with it the scope for lower-level managerial discretion on which the tradition of sectional negotiations had developed. In future, *all* sectional and departmental grievances would have to be registered in the labor relations department so that settlements would no longer be determined by the individual supervisor but by corporate policy. The labor relations department had finally become an authority within the corporation.[57]

President Quinn summed up the results of the 'working without a contract' strategy in August: 'Since June 1, the date our contract with Chrysler expired, the number of management-provoked walkouts has steadily increased as Chrysler management continues to put on the pressure and to take away many recognized practices – such as relief time, wash up time, seniority rights etc. Up to this point there has been no walkouts in our plant, but many of our negotiated practices have either been drastically changed or eliminated altogether.'[58] He was, however, still in favor of seeing things through. Although Chrysler's Twinsburg, Ohio plant had finally struck rather than work under the new conditions on the start-up of the 1959 models,[59] Quinn was opposed to such a move at Dodge Main. But there were workers arguing that even a long strike would be preferable to the permanent erosion of working conditions. Liska reported from the hard-hit Department 76: 'We do not know how other departments' workers feel about the working conditions, but the consensus of workers in our department reveals that they are willing to go on a long strike to bring back the humane working conditions in our department, and I might add, that if a contract is signed and the working conditions are not improved, the members of our department will be very much disappointed at our union leaders.'[60]

Although Quinn was only re-elected in June on the blue slate for Local 3 president, he became increasingly dependent on Reuther. In September he argued against precipitate strike action 'because of the present (national) contract negotiations and a request by the International Union that the workers be kept on the job'.[61] It was not that Quinn believed they should accept the new conditions. He told the workforce: 'No honest union member could stand by and watch the gains they have made over the past 20 years go down the drain in a few short months.'[62] But his strategy was to rely upon Reuther to restore these 'gains' in the national contract negotiations.

The argument that the 'workers' turn would come sooner or later' ignored the reality that the legitimacy of the old workplace rules depended on their acceptance or toleration by management *and* their continuous exercise by the workers. There was nothing intrinsic to the old relief agreement that would allow it to be restored several months after management tore it up and workers had ceased to experience it. Collectively imposed workplace rules restraining managerial autonomy were not bargaining items that could be added or subtracted from a contract negotiation like a demand for higher wages. 'Working without a contract' was thus a particularly dangerous strategy to adopt in Chrysler plants since the implication of 'working under management's rules' meant so much more there than in GM and Ford, where management's rules already held sway.[63]

Chrysler seized the opening offered by the UAW and the market situation to transform working conditions in its plants. By October 1958 all that remained was to ensure that the national contract endorsed the new managerial control system at plant level, and to openly and publicly defeat its key local, Local 3, and thus prevent any chance of a market recovery being used to turn back the labor relations clock.

The UAW's 1958 'target' company, Ford, gave nothing away in its contract with the UAW, signed on September 17, so there was no prospect of Chrysler conceding anything additional. But the eighth Chrysler contract was not 'neutral'. Its 'benefits' were only for those leaving the company payroll (severance payments from five days' wages for up to two years' service to 150 days' wages for those with thirty years). Those still working faced two significant contractual changes that reinforced managerial authority in the workplace. First, management redrafted the 1958 contract to reflect its new policy on production standards. The 1955 agreement had allowed informal bargaining between the chief steward and the foreman, and Chrysler had agreed to give the steward 'all the data upon which the Corporation has based the standard' if the steward *verbally* requested it.[64] From 1958, however, 'all its data supporting the standard' would be made available only 'if a written grievance is filed'.[65] This deterred the worker and the steward from proceeding with borderline complaints and ensured that no compromises would be reached on the job between the steward and the foreman without the involvement of the labor relations and industrial engineering departments.

The second significant contractual change extended the degree of involvement by the international union in plant-level negotiations. Previously, if UAW rules had been adhered to and the IEB had sanctioned a strike, a local could stop work after five days of plant-level negotiations. From 1958 the negotiations had to continue 'for at least 12 days', and the *international* had to notify Chrysler 'in writing' of the strike authorization and grievances involved.[66]

The 6,000 Dodge workers called back in September and October 1958 to work on the 1959 models were more concerned with the new working conditions than with the longer-term implications for the rule-making process inherent in the 1958 contract. While the contract was ratified without marked opposition, the workforce proceeded to take a strike vote on 'rates of production, relief time and working conditions'.[67] The result was a 93% majority for a strike, but under 4,000 voted, reflecting the impact of the mass lay-offs[68] and the success of management's three-year struggle to condition its workforce to a new definition of 'legitimate' union activity.

Chrysler had three important advantages over its weakened opponent in the strike that finally took place between December 2 and December 19, 1958. It had used the new maximum of 60 days' delay between a strike vote and strike action to consolidate its new working practices at Dodge and to extract an additional two months' production from the plant. Moreover, unlike the comparable moment in 1939 when the speed-up at Dodge Main had been used by the UAW as the spark to ignite a successful struggle across all Chrysler's plants, in 1958 Dodge Local 3 was on its own. Although there were eight other Chrysler locals queuing up for IEB authorization to strike on speed-up, relief times and working conditions,[69] once the national contract was signed each was considered separately by the international. This was a recipe for a decisive management victory. The defeat marked the close of a twenty-year period in which the labor process at Dodge had been governed by workplace rules established through informal departmental and sectional level bargaining.

Although the Dodge Main two-week strike was the action of an individual plant, Chrysler generalized Local 3's defeat throughout the corporation. The 'Memorandum of Understanding on Rates of Production', signed on December 19 by Jack Conway and Doug Fraser for the UAW Chrysler Department, was given the status of a corporation-wide amendment to the national contract. The 1939 contract 'rates of production' clause had been ambiguous: 'The Management agrees that in establishing rates of production it will make studies on *the basis of fairness and equity* consistent with quality of workmanship, efficiency of operations and the reasonable working capacities of normal operators [my italic].'[70]

Instead of this commitment to studies 'on the basis of fairness and equity', the December 19, 1958 agreement laid down 'time study' itself as the impartial marker against which the studies should be judged. And it recognized total managerial autonomy over the technique chosen to make that study. The new agreement began:

> Clause 1: Time study is a generally accepted method used by management as a basis for establishing rates of production and as a basis for determining the fairness of work loads.
> Clause 2: The method of technique used by management for the establishing of rates of production is an exclusive right to management, and the Union does not have the right to challenge the method that management selects.[71]

Clauses five and six of the December 1958 agreement freed management's hands in two further respects: new man assignments could be issued whenever 'production schedules are increased or decreased on major conveyor operations'; and management could insist on workers continuing to work at their 'normal pace' when unforeseen circumstances arose that affected the original work standard. Finally, clause seven imposed a standard twenty-four minutes a day personal relief on all Chrysler's conveyor line workers.[72]

The agreement spurred Chrysler to complete its standardization of work standards and relief arrangements. In the Dodge stamping plant, it posted time standards on each individual machine.[73] By September 1959, when workers with ten years' seniority returned uneasily[74] to work on the 1960 models, the new relief procedure was in force throughout the plant. The Conant stampings plant and the foundry and core room had backed down before threats to transfer their work from Dodge Main to other plants;[75] the wire room, which did not back down, was closed.[76] The 1958 defeat was as a great a turning point as had been the 1939 victory. Six months later Quinn admitted that 'the December agreement was a "cold" one', although he still justified it since 'it paved the way for the production of the small Chrysler (car) at our plant.'[77]

'Mutuality' had finally been driven off the shopfloor at Dodge Main. The word no longer appeared in the 1958 agreements. The scope of bargaining had been deliberately restricted to the international representatives, the full-time local officers, and to the plant committee. While chief stewards were still tolerated, their numbers were soon to be reduced, and their function was changed. From being organizers of the areas which elected them in the 1930s and 1940s, they became in the 1960s mere processors of grievances. With sectional problem solving denied to them, Chrysler workers first turned to the proper 'constitutional' channels of the UAW and the company grievance procedure for answers to their problems. When these, too, appeared to fail, as they did for many black and younger workers in the late 1960s, then uncondoned wildcats, spontaneous, violent explosions and drug taking became the locus of continuing dissent.

The management victory meant workplace rules would in future be laid down unilaterally by management and subsequently only slightly amended in a consultative process that passed as contract negotiations. Chrysler's shopfloor rule-forming tradition had been 'normalized' in line with practice at GM and Ford. The result was a dramatic six-fold drop in Chrysler's strike frequency from the 1950s to the 1960s, and in a similar decline, shown in table 10, in the average annual number of hours lost in unauthorized strikes from the early 1950s to the early 1960s: GM's authorized strike loss ratio also rose significantly in 1958 when it utilized

Table 10 *Chrysler and General Motors, manhours lost and loss rates per hourly paid worker in unauthorized strikes, 1950–69*

	Chrysler		General Motors (a)	
	Unauthorized man-hrs lost	Hours lost per worker	Unauthorized man-hrs lost	Hours lost per worker
Five-yearly averages				
1950–54	1,644,510	18.6	150,264	0.42
1955–59	2,471,528	31.9	257,230	0.67
1960–64	81,394	1.28	207,670	0.65
1965–69	359,975	3.83	1,194,873	2.93
Annual average				
1940–59	1,430,089	18.21	406,525	1.40
1960–79	241,340	2.58	455,495	1.14

Source: Company data.
(a) GM data not available for 1940, 1941 and 1975. The averages 1940–59 and 1960–79 are therefore calculated on the basis of 18 and 19 years respectively.

the recession to confront fifteen GM locals over their domestic agreements. But by comparison with Chrysler, GM's unauthorized strike loss ratio remained at a very low and stable level indeed.[78] The year 1958 did not mark a decisive organizational shift in the balance of forces at GM.[79]

Edie Fox only returned from an eighteen-month lay-off in October 1959. She remembered the dramatic difference workers experienced:

> When I went back into the plant it was a whole new world. Your boss told you: 'This is your production standard. You'd better get it. This is your job. You do it!' You had the time study men there. When they felt like it they would come and time the job. After 1958 it became very dangerous to go on a wildcat.[80]

In 1959 the number of strikes in Chrysler plants fell to forty-two; in 1960, when Chrysler again produced a million cars, there were just seventeen stoppages recorded by the Corporation. From 1960 to 1965 Chrysler's yearly strike totals were less than those of GM. Labor relations in Chrysler were clearly in a 'new world'. Managerial authority had been strengthened qualitatively. *Fear* of managers, superintendents, general foremen and even foremen and of their disciplinary powers had been largely missing from Chrysler workers' subordination to management over the previous twenty years. It now returned. However, even this transformation was qualified: although 1958 saw the removal by management of most of the restraints Chrysler workers had exercised during the previous twenty years, and the structural basis of the Dodge union tradition was decisively weakened, the influence of that tradition lingered, carried by isolated individuals into the 1960s.

Part IV
Controlling resistance, 1960–1982

8   White-shirted strangers and black recruitment

This chapter focuses on the major changes that occurred at Chrysler during the early and mid 1960s. The company finally rid itself of the old 'family' management system between 1960 and 1962 and installed an outside accountant in the top job. The resulting changes in its business and operational strategies occurred in time for Chrysler to expand in the Vietnam War boom, both overseas and within the United States.

Labor relations also reflected the new climate, but in contradictory ways. The older, mainly white workers with high seniority experienced significant improvements in their living standards, in their job security and in non-wage benefits, especially in pension entitlements. The intensification of work that followed the defeat of the old sectional bargaining system did not impinge greatly on them because their seniority was moving them to the easier, off-line jobs. The steward system survived but as a pale imitation of its earlier self, while the independence of Local 3 from the international UAW was transformed into the classical dependent relationship. However, while the boom allowed Chrysler to accommodate the interests of high seniority workers and of union activists, it also required a huge recruitment drive. And the new workforce that experienced the major intensification of work in the 1960s was predominantly young and, in Detroit, black.

Section I of this chapter focuses on the managerial changes. Section II examines what happened to the local union tradition after the 1956–59 watershed. Section III outlines why the collective bargaining institutions appeared to fail Chrysler's new workers.

I. Management changes

Management was transformed following the 1958–59 recession. In April 1960, after Chrysler's market share had fallen below 14% in both 1958 and 1959, Colbert followed Walter Chrysler and K. T. Keller by moving sideways from the presidency to the position of board chairman. He chose a protégé, William C. Newberg, who had been with Chrysler since 1933, as his successor as chief executive. But the knives were still out and just two months later, when Newberg's 'unethical' major stock holdings in certain of Chrysler's suppliers became public knowledge, Colbert took back the presidency. Newberg then joined in the attack on Colbert, telling the 1961 AGM: 'We can never again have a strong Chrysler under the Czarist rule of Mr. Colbert.'[1]

The Chrysler board of directors was therefore forced to try and recruit a total outsider to take the presidency. But with the company in the doldrums and its management split by public squabbles this proved impossible. So eventually it did the next best thing. In July 1961, it appointed the company's highly effective 42-year-old accountant, Lynn Townsend, as president and, as part of the package, Colbert relinquished the chairman's seat to George Love. Townsend had only worked directly for Chrysler since 1957, although he had handled the Chrysler account at the Detroit branch of Touche, Ross and Co since 1947. So while he was not a member of the old Chrysler management family, he did know the score and had begun modernizing the company's accounting practices after he was appointed a vice-president in 1959.[2] Love was chairman of both the Pittsburgh-based Consolidation Coal Company and the Cleveland-based M. A. Hanna giant investment trust, and the idea was that his experience would balance Townsend's youth. A board member commented later: 'Love was the umbilical cord from the parent board to the child management.'[3]

Within months the whole top management team had changed. It was a crucial period. Townsend was Chrysler's youngest ever chief executive and he did not have the usual legacy of obligations to other executives. His energy and comparative youth encouraged innovation, risk taking and an air of managerial confidence. Equally, his knowledge of Ford and GM accounting and managerial practices gave him models on which to construct a more professional management system at Chrysler. While Colbert had acquired his managerial skills within the autocratic, conservative Chrysler managerial tradition, the takeover by Townsend and Love established a new breed of professional manager. As financial controller from 1957 to 1960, Townsend brought Chrysler's financial control systems into line with Ford's and GM's. He hired financial experts from Ford and introduced a cost-control program that made it possible to evaluate the impact of the new man assignments operating on the shopfloor, and a current-profit plan that allowed the daily control of costs and operations. He also introduced capital-investment and forward-cost control programs. To mark his arrival as president, Townsend drew up the company's first organizational chart, and gradually increased the proportion of white-collar workers in the Chrysler labor force from an average of 28% in 1955–59 to 33% between 1960 and 1964.[4]

Moreover, the combination of accountant and investment manager at the top greatly facilitated Chrysler's expansion. Love believed Townsend was the ideal man for the job:

> It used to be possible to control the company through personal contact. But when a company gets this big you no longer know all the people. You can't see that so-and-so is loafing, so you need a man for whom figures live. You control the company by a knowledge of figures. Townsend can spot trouble through the figures.[5]

Love's company, Consolidation Coal, quickly commissioned the industrial consultants, Loomis, Sayles and Company, to conduct a new study of Chrysler. Its report openly condemned the old 'family' management: 'In recent years, inept management has hurt the company's competitive position and adversely affected earnings.' It went on to argue that with the right top management Chrysler could get back on the tracks, and so Consolidation Coal, the industry's largest coal consortium, purchased a block of Chrysler stock. In 1962 the Rockefeller family followed suit and a director representing its interests joined the board.[6]

The extension of financial control over the company and the creation of a professional managerial hierarchy did not, however, represent the establishment of a genuine multidivisional management structure. Chrysler's old centralized 'rimless wheel' model of management actually survived: all key decisions were referred to Chrysler's operations committee, which was dominated by Townsend, who was as autocratic and as involved in day-to-day decisions as his predecessors.[7] By 1968, two years after Love had resigned as chairman, *Fortune* commented: 'So successful has Townsend been that the board of directors gives him a free hand, attributes most of Chrysler's success to him personally and regards him as almost infallible.'[8] Despite the appearance of an ordered committee structure, the reality at Chrysler was very different. There was little attempt made to encourage a separation of strategic and tactical decision making. The top seven key executives all had offices within a few feet of each other and freely wandered in and out. Townsend, meanwhile, opposed specialism in top jobs. In 1968 he boasted proudly of his vice-presidents: 'You'll see engineers selling, book-keepers in other jobs, and a lawyer as VP of finances.'[9]

It was in these circumstances that Townsend fashioned a new business strategy for Chrysler. From being a manufacturing company that produced well-engineered and often original cars and counted on customer loyalty to get them sold, it now focused on salesmanship, leaving the styling boundaries of Chrysler cars to be laid down by GM. Townsend introduced the Chrysler pentastar sign, major warranty guarantees (five years or 50,000 miles) in 1962, which forced Ford and GM to follow suit in 1966, and in 1964 he followed GM and Ford by establishing a credit company, Chrysler Financial. Townsend also encouraged diversification away from exclusive dependence on car sales. Chrysler Realty, which was originally established to assist Chrysler dealers buy well-situated sites, entered big-time land speculation. Other areas of diversification Townsend supported included a Chemical Products Group, Airtemp, the air conditioning equipment manufacturer, marine engines and boats, and the Chrysler Space Division.[10]

Townsend's two changes with the biggest knock-on effect on day-to-day operations were his decisions to follow GM and Ford into every sector of the increasingly segmented car market, and to build in advance of firm orders. The first decision meant that rather than concentrating on three or four sections of the market, Chrysler multiplied its model range and the choice of options within each model range. In 1962, before Townsend's influence began to make itself felt on Chrysler's product lines, the company offered 93 different styles; just five years later it was producing 160.[11] Since its manufacturing base was much smaller than its rivals, Chrysler's stamping plants had to produce shorter runs and change dies more often than Ford and GM, and to have many more mix changes on the assembly lines. The model proliferation made economies of scale more difficult to realize than for Chrysler's competitors and led to greater tension on the shopfloor, where shorter runs and constant changes in job descriptions aggravated underlying tensions.[12]

The second significant operational decision, to allow the build-up of sales banks rather than shut down production, was taken ostensibly to ensure a quicker delivery of cars to the dealers. In reality, it was to avoid additional rising overheads (for plant maintenance and SUB for laid-off workers) and to boost top executives' bonuses which were directly related to factory production rather than final sales volumes. In 1966 the sales bank was first allowed to grow to 60,000 units. Then it became a regular feature, swelling to 408,302 in February 1969[13] – 29% of that year's total sales. The focus on production volume rather than quality and sales, encouraged high recruitment and the intensification of work as front-line management was told to keep the line moving by sheer pressure on the workers. This, too, fuelled shopfloor combativity among the new workers just as the earlier tradition was being pronounced dead.

Townsend was convinced that expansion could solve Chrysler's problems, and he quickly released the brake on the earlier McKinsey report's advice to expand overseas. By the end of 1962, *Time* called Chrysler 'the comeback story of US business' and put Townsend's face on its front cover with the headline, 'Towards a World Market'. Chrysler's total non-US and Canada employment rose from 4,763 in 1962 to 24,046 in 1963 and by 1967 it reached 75,600, a figure equivalent to 60% of its average US employment. Between 1962 and 1967 its vehicle sales outside the US and Canada rose from 75,778 to 588,163, and its net overseas assets from $73 million to $482 million.[14] Much of this expansion was financed through increased debt. In May and August 1968 Townsend released two issues of convertible debentures at 4.75% and 5% on the growing Eurobond market. He agreed that Chrysler 'has no immediate use for most of the money' but his philosophy was to borrow it when it was a good deal so as to have it available for when it was needed.[15] Chrysler's belated overseas expansion was later criticized for diverting management's attention from pressing domestic problems, but this was not apparent in the early 1960s when the auto industry's total production rose consistently for four years from 1961 before staying at around 8.5 million cars for the next fifteen years.

The establishment of a high production plateau was a new experience for the industry. Before 1964, growth had always been associated with violent cyclical movement, but from 1965 until 1979 total production only fell below eight million cars in three years – 1967, 1974 and 1975. This expansion had a massive impact on the average hourly-paid employment of the 'Big Three':

	Chrysler	Ford	GM
1960–64	60,892	114,000	336,827
1965–69	95,170	148,000	419,230

Chrysler's manual labor force rose by 56%, Ford's by 30%, and GM's by 24% in the 1960s. Chrysler's increase reflected the increase in unit capacity from 1.2 million cars in 1963 to 2.2 million in 1969 initiated by Townsend, whose policy was described by another top executive as 'stacking cars like cans of beans on a shelf'.[16] In 1965 when Townsend opened a new assembly plant at Belvidere, about 75 miles south west of Chicago, and the new Sterling stamping plant in the outskirts of Detroit,[17] production hit a peak close to 1.5 million cars, while strike frequency hit an historic low for a boom year. His expansionary strategy appeared to work.

Townsend insisted on receiving daily shipping reports and production targets. 'If they are OK', he argued, 'the financial figures will be OK too.'[18] This was not, of course, necessarily so. Thus while Chrysler's profit rate improved in the 1960s, it was still only 4% to Ford's 5% and GM's 8% by 1968. And perhaps of greater long-term significance, the company's expansion had been achieved through allowing the debt to assets ratio to rise to 27.1% as against Ford's 7.4% and GM's 3.2%. The absence of effective board supervision had allowed Townsend a free hand to borrow large sums whenever he judged it cheap to do so. Explaining this he said: 'We have tried to take advantage of capital markets when they are good, irrespective of our building programs.'[19] By 1970 it was openly being argued that Townsend's success in the early 1960s had gone to his head, leading him to relax his managerial control and, specifically, to spend more time than he should have in 1969 as chairman of the National Alliance of Businessmen.[20] The reality, as events have shown, was that the whole 1960s expansion was based on insecure foundations. While it lasted, though, it certainly had major consequences for Dodge Main's union tradition and labor force.

II. Workers dividing

Chrysler workers lost twice as many hours on unauthorized strikes in the early 1960s as did GM workers, and Local 3's officers remained generally antagonistic to management and to the international until 1964. The formal labor relations system took longer to be fully legitimated in the eyes of the union activists than it did to implement the top-down changes of the early 1960s within management. Initially, from 1960 to 1962, the hostility of union activists to the new procedures and pressures carried the day. But the gap between the activists' rhetoric and the shopfloor reality gradually widened. The earlier tradition was upheld by the Local 3 president from 1960 to 1964, but with decreasing effectiveness, while the stewards' bargaining role gave way to a system of special pleading.

When sizable numbers of production workers were recalled to Dodge Main late in 1959, they were at first outraged by the new working conditions, especially by 'supervisors' constantly performing hourly rated workers' jobs'.[21] This complaint became a constant feature in the 1960s as Chrysler increased the numbers of foremen from a ratio of one to every seventy-five or eighty workers in the late 1950s to one for every twenty or twenty-five workers.[22] The workers' initial response was to elect the former members of the 1957 'Rank and File' caucus, Edith Fox from the trim department and Ed Liska from the body-in-white as chief stewards.[23] And one month later, Steve Pasica, the plant chairman and a founder member of the blue slate group in 1950, who had supported the veteran Pat Quinn for president in 1956 and 1958, defeated Quinn on a new militant 'Gray Slate'.[24] Pasica had been Quinn's principal lieutenant, but felt Quinn was too dependent upon Reuther and too compromised by the 1958 agreement to be able to mount a new campaign against the speed-up. After losing, Quinn made his peace with Reuther. He admitted: 'Walter offered me a job in the International; he knew damn well that if I went back in the shop, I'd stir things up . . . I'll be frank; we got bought off.'[25]

Three months after the elections the Dodge Main labor relations department unilaterally imposed a procedure to standardize discipline on unauthorized absences. A standard escalation of sanctions was imposed ranging from a verbal warning for the first offense to discharge on the seventh. Pasica urged workers to ignore it and to continue to support anyone unjustly disciplined: 'Remember it's your job and your future, so let's see if we can't correct the situation for the betterment of the entire membership.'[26] But confidence in the legitimacy of resistance had been sapped and the new procedure was soon in force.

This reassertion of managerial control over the worker's out-of-work life was echoed inside the plant by management's pressure on production standards.[27] Pasica responded with a set of recommendations for inclusion by the national UAW negotiators in the 1961 UAW–Chrysler contract. They amounted to a plea for management to surrender its recently acquired hard-won rights to change standards after the first three months of a model year, to change the method of operation of a job at any time, and to impose standards without having to bargain over them.[28] But his attempt to revive the old frontier of control through demands on the UAW's Chrysler department was a confession of weakness. If Local 3 could not insist that its own management respected these workplace rules, it had no chance of getting either Chrysler or the international UAW to take them seriously.

As if in reply to Pasica's demands, Chrysler announced it was tearing up its side of the 1959 Dodge stamping plant agreement under which the workers in the press shop had accepted the standard plant-wide relief times on condition their work would not be moved elsewhere. The Conant stamping plant was to be run down from 3,100 to just 300 workers.[29] Dodge Main had already seen its share of Chrysler's total workforce fall from 25% in the first half of the 1950s to 19% by January 1960. The implementation of management's decentralization strategy was to mean that for its last twenty years Dodge Main's role was primarily confined to building and assembling cars with a maximum employment potential of between 10,000 and 12,000 hourly-paid workers.

The onset of the 1961–62 recession ensured that the initiative remained in Dodge Main management's hands. By July 1961, when Townsend

took over from Colbert, roughly half the plant's slimmed down workforce were laid off, and most didn't get called back until the start-up of
the 1963 models. In the body-in-white those who were working were
doing so at a rate inconceivable five years earlier.[30]

	Touch-up metal finishing		Door liners	
	1956	1961	1956	1961
Jobs per hour:	40	56	40	56
Teams:	20	7	10	4
Workers:	40	14	20	8

The four-fold rise in labor productivity on these jobs was partly the result
of improved quality control and of the arrival of power (air and
electrical) tools on the lines. But these new developments were coupled
with the man assignment system and standardized sanctions backed by
the greater numbers of foremen.

The 1961 UAW–Chrysler contract, like the 1958 agreement, was
negotiated in a recessionary year. It reduced all Chrysler workers' relief
time to the standard twenty-four minutes a day established after the 1958
Dodge Main strike,[31] and in one important area it laid the basis for a
further retreat by the union from any lingering attachment to its role as a
vehicle for shopfloor bargaining. GM had operated a ratio of one
full-time committeeman to every 400 workers since 1938 while Ford had
operated on the basis of one to every 550 since 1941. In 1961, for the first
time, the Chrysler contract conceded that 'an equitable proportional
representation system' of chief stewards was needed – that is, fewer
stewards – and agreed to cut their numbers in the 1964 agreement.[32] In
the meantime, provisions were made to reduce the ratio of stewards to
members on second and third shifts.[33]

In May 1962, with the Dodge working membership as low as 5,000,
Pasica announced the merger of the blue and gray slates to fight on the
slogan 'end Gloom and Doom!'. For the first time the slate included two
blacks among its ten candidates for local office – although both were
unsuccessful. The slate's demands reflected the legacy of the 1950s:[34]

> Re-open the contract for negotiations on these key issues:
>> Shorter working week with no cut in pay,
>> Elimination of compulsory overtime, and
>> Protection against speed-up.

These demands were frequently voiced on the shopfloor during the
next fifteen years, but the tightening grip of the UAW machine and the
acceptance of the company's new definition of what constituted 'realistic'
or 'legitimate' unionism, ensured that those who campaigned for them
would not again take office in key UAW locals.[35] Indeed, Pasica's

re-election, and the election on the same slate of Edith Fox as a UAW delegate to the 1962 convention, was not a sign of any new shopfloor confidence. Rather it was a technical 'knock-out'. In the depths of the 1961–62 recession the seniority system ensured it was 'old-timers' from the 1930s and 1940s who were back working on the production lines and experiencing the new production standards. But as the 1960s boom got underway the seniority system moved them away from the hardest jobs and their anger against the company moderated.

When the first new workers were hired in 1963 they automatically went into the most exacting low seniority jobs. This procedure had been fought for by the union over many years. But in the 1960s the new workers saw the union's shopfloor representatives and their agreements in an increasingly cynical light. First, the stewards were usually of a different generation and color. But even when this changed, the gap between most workers and stewards remained huge. Several elements contributed to this: the centralization of collective bargaining within Chrysler plants away from the shopfloor; the increasing privilege associated with the chief steward position; and the transformation of bargaining into pleading with the consequence that management had increased say over which stewards appeared successful.

Townsend's labor relations staff centralized decision making in their own hands and so removed discretion from front-line supervisors. In the 1960s foremen and superintendents would refuse to take decisions. Nothing could be settled on the spot and everything went to 'Labor Relations'. At Dodge Main, five labor relations supervisors were appointed to cover different areas of the plant on the first shift, and four for the second shift. Weekly meetings enabled them to establish continuity and consistency of policy.[36] In November 1962 a steward described the effect of the transition of the steward's functions from bargaining to grievance processing:

> Remember the days when a worker or a Steward could take up and resolve a grievance with the immediate foreman?
> Now we are forced to deal with individuals who are totally removed from the realities of the job ... If a dispute of any significance arises, a parade of white-shirted strangers appear on the scene. This has a most unfortunate effect on the employees. They tend to become frightened and nervous.[37]

The hold taken by the 'white-shirted strangers' over shopfloor conditions reduced the status of both the steward and the foreman and undermined any remaining mutual respect. Shopfloor reports of 'good' foremen and 'good' stewards now became increasingly rare.

As the stewards became less effective, many workers began to see their super-seniority as more of an individual privilege than as a collective asset. In 1939 stewards had won the right to be called in when even one worker in their department was working. This was a *struggled-for* concession to help maintain collectively imposed workplace rules through periods when management might have been able to break them. It meant stewards were the last laid off and the first back. So whenever overtime was worked, they were always called in. By the 1940s, their annual wages were significantly above those of the average worker in their districts. But, in the 1940s and 1950s, this 'privilege' was accompanied by a high proportion of dismissals and an active bargaining role with long hours at the local hall after work, educating themselves, exchanging information and discussing with other stewards, and generally maintaining the sinews of an activists' organization. So most workers believed their privileges were justified.

By the early 1960s the mobilizing role of the stewards had gone and management became more accommodating to the requirements of 'union business'. In just one month at the close of the 1963 model year, excluding the seven full-time local union officers, a total of six stewards or committeemen took a whole week or more official leave of absence on 'union business', thirteen more were out of the plant for between one and three days and another twelve stewards took off for periods of between one and seven hours.[38] Many more spent time unofficially in local bars during working hours, leaving a phone number inside the plant where they could be contacted in case of trouble. They had only to ensure that a friend had clocked them in.

Management was well aware of what was taking place, and liked it. As Liska recalled, 'A steward couldn't fight management that much if management could throw him being out of the plant up at him.'[39] When it came to re-election, the incumbent would either show a burst of short-term militancy, or make enough friends in the district (fifty or seventy-five would usually be enough) through buying beers and spending time with individuals while 'walking the beat'. Management might also influence the outcome by making key concessions (or withholding them) or by encouraging canvassing (or denying it) in the period just before an election.[40]

The stewards' privileges were thus transformed from being an aspect of a struggled-for achievement of an effective shopfloor union into a gift of management. In the process, what it meant to be a steward changed. Commitment to a wider notion of *class*, of *us* against *them*, weakened. The results were seen in the stewards' falling attendances at local membership meetings or any kind of non-emergency meeting out of working hours for which they wouldn't be paid expenses and loss of earnings. And during working hours the outcome was that most stewards put up little more than a show of resistance to tighter production standards.

The 1963 model year was an important testing ground for the new Chrysler management: it was the first to reflect Townsend's personal intervention in Chrysler's styling offices, and that year's high sales and new labor intake coincided with the presence of a traditionalist Local 3 administration. Yet plant-level management held firm to its authority over the labor process. As late as half-way through the model year, a trim department chief steward reported that the time study department was still hard at work:

> The crew cuts are roaming the trim shop selecting operations that they think can be eliminated by breaking them up and dividing them among other workers.
> This is the foulest type of speed-up we have experienced. They've gotten all the meat and they are now moving in for the small pickings.[41]

The stewards had big problems in dealing with the new system. They complained: 'Elemental breakdowns on disputed jobs are slow in reaching union representatives. Labor Relations personnel seem to be the deciding factor on all disputes, even superceding the Department superintendent.'[42] And president Pasica had to plead with them to take up their workers' grievances through the procedure: 'In order to ask for Strike Action, grievances must be filed on work disputes. At this time we do not have any on file . . . Comfort for the workers on difficult jobs must be fought for and the union representatives must do their duty by writing up any jobs that are too difficult. We must build up the courage of the workers in the plant and restore their faith in the Union.'[43] But it was easier for Pasica in the local hall to talk about restoring the workers' 'faith in the Union' than it was for the stewards to deliver it. Table 11 shows that while Chrysler's manual labor force remained at its 1960 level, its productivity jumped in 1963 and 1964 to all-time highs. Little wonder, then, that in June 1964 Pasica was beaten for president by the body shop committeeman, Ed Domanski.[44] Pasica lost because his promises of action against the speed-up had proved empty.[45] Domanski's election marked the end of Local 3's ten-year spell of opposition (to Reuther) and of its traditional independence from the international. It was the start of a new era. For the next fifteen years, until Dodge Main was closed in January 1980, its president and executive board would be firm supporters of the international union leadership.

Soon after this election, the UAW targeted Chrysler in the 1964

Table 11 *Chrysler's US hourly employment and output of passenger cars per hourly paid employee, 1960–69*

Year	Hourly-paid employees (000s)	Car output per worker	Year	Hourly-paid employees (000s)	Car output per worker
1960	72.1	14.13	1965	89.8	16.35
1961	47.5	13.67	1966	93.3	15.50
1962	50.0	14.33	1967	89.0	15.32
1963	61.8	16.96	1968	101.4	15.63
1964	73.1	17.00	1969	102.4	13.60

Source: Company data; Wards *Yearbook*, Various years.

national contract negotiations. Townsend's salesmanship had pushed Chrysler back up from 10% in 1962 to a 16% share of US production, and the 1964 contract reflected this: it was the first contract in ten years to be negotiated in a non-recessionary year. It added twelve minutes a day relief time to the twenty-four minutes laid down in the 1958 Dodge strike settlement. This 'concession', restoring a little of what had been lost in the 1950s, and a $400 a month early retirement scheme for workers aged sixty with thirty years of service, were balanced by the UAW fulfilling its 1961 undertaking on the steward ratio. The UAW agreed to move towards a ratio of one steward to every 225 workers by not automatically replacing stewards as they retired. The contract left the production standards clause unchanged.[46]

A core of Dodge Main workers objected strongly. Not only did several chief stewards understand that their privileges could be jeopardized if the process of cutting away at the number of stewards continued, but many workers remembered back six years when they had between 50 and 120 minutes' relief a day and felt a little insulted that twelve of those minutes were handed back as a great concession. There was also a strong awareness that the improvement in relief time would have to be paid for by increased productivity, so the failure by the negotiators to get any improvement in the contract on production standards, created the most resentment. The Dodge ratification meeting rejected both the national and the local agreements by 419 votes to 279 – and the local's 9,500 votes were therefore cast against ratification at the Chrysler conference.

An insight into the tetchiness the UAW machine had developed after its first fifteen years of one-faction rule was given by UAW Chrysler Director Doug Fraser's angry reaction: 'Unfortunately, the thousands of Dodge Main workers who were well satisfied with the agreement did not show up to vote, thus leaving the floor to those few who were opposed. This is one of the risks you take when you run a democratic union.'[47] Allowing votes to take place at local union meetings had become a 'risk' for 'a democratic union'. The national contract was ratified by 52,031 to 10,003 with only one other tiny local voting to reject along with Local 3. Ed Domanski was even more bitter since the first local agreement he had negotiated could not be voted into effect by other plants. For him, opposition was not only anti-democratic, it was a conspiracy:

> This (rejection), I am sure, was due to the effective job done by the opposition to these agreements by distorting the facts, telling half truths and creating chaos and confusion among our members. Because they knew darn well that the Local Committee could not negotiate working conditions and standards for this plant. These demands were on the National table and only the National Negotiating Committee could negotiate these matters.[48]

To win the vote on the rejected Local 3 agreement, Domanski finally divided his opponents by having it voted on at separate unit meetings. Local 3's tradition of independence from company and international succumbed to methods characteristic of the dominant Reuther faction: manipulation replaced mobilization as the major means of exercising and maintaining the power of local union officers. In this atmosphere Chrysler's labor relations looked more peaceful than at any time since the mid 1930s. It appeared as if management had at long last discovered the formula that worked so well at GM and Ford.

The boom established around-the-year working and brought with it considerable economic rewards. Between March 1967 and February 1968 Detroit's average pay levels for office clerical workers, skilled maintenance and unskilled plant workers were 16%, 14% and 22% respectively above the US average for metropolitan areas.[49] And the 1964 pension scheme gave significant benefits to the high seniority workers who stayed with the company.

A company's power to prevent workers accumulating these benefits became an awesome threat to long-service white workers and to many black workers who had previously survived on the margins of poverty. Liska, who switched to side with the union hierarchy in the body shop in 1960, was typical of most of Dodge Main's high-seniority Polish workers in the 1960s. He believed: 'When we started, we had nothing. But once you start touching the money, you change. I changed. We all got fat. At one time you'd fight on the principle and everything else. Now? You'd just look at your paycheck.'[50]

But something dramatic happened around the mid 1960s to upset the

Table 12 *Chrysler and General Motors, man hours lost and loss rates per hourly paid worker in unauthorized strikes, 1955–79*

Five yearly averages	Chrysler		General Motors (a)	
	Unauthorized man hrs lost	Hours lost per worker	Unauthorized man hrs lost	Hours lost per worker
1960–64	81,394	1.28	207,670	0.65
1965–69	359,975	3.83	1,194,873	2.93
1970–74	308,813	3.03	269,929	0.67
1975–79	215,179	2.19	149,508	0.34

Source: Company data.
(a) GM date for 1975 not available.

more placid picture of 1960–64. To achieve the enormous expansion of the 1960s Chrysler had recruited massively and unintentionally divided its assembly division's labor force into an older high seniority group, who were largely white and usually worked the first shift, and a majority group who were young, usually black, and were concentrated on the socially-inconvenient second shift. This heavy recruitment by 1969 meant 'new' workers with less than five years in the industry made up 51% of Chrysler's labor force compared with 41% and 40% at Ford and GM respectively.[51] But the divergence of interests between the new and older workers was not identified by management or by the UAW, and from the mid 1960s on this failure increasingly upset the recently achieved institutional stability of collective bargaining. The result was that many more unauthorized strikes hit both Chrysler and GM in the second half of the 1960s (see table 12). Chrysler's wildcat loss ratio per worker more than doubled, while GM's increased nearly fivefold.[52] What changed in the second half of the 1960s was not the industry's technology or its product; nor was there a major new shift in the frontier of job control. In both companies management retained their shopfloor authority. What happened was that job and pay security increased dramatically for the older group of workers, with major consequences for the organizational traditions they maintained, while parity of conditions were denied to the new labor.

III. Black workers

At Dodge Main the 'new' workers hired in increasing numbers from 1963 were predominantly in their twenties and overwhelmingly black. They responded differently to the industry's discipline partly because the tight labor market gave them the confidence that even if they were discharged they could always get another job elsewhere, and partly because blacks in America were in the process of a major political transformation.

The relationship between the 'new' and 'old' labor force was not helped by the history of connivance by white workers in anti-black discrimination by management. In the 1930s Chrysler had employed about 2,000 blacks, half of whom were classified as unskilled janitors, common laborers and production helpers while 30% worked in the Dodge Main foundry.[53] During the war period when Chrysler recruited labor for its Tank Arsenal it ignored black production workers with seniority and by late 1941 only 170 of the 5,000 workers at the new plant were black, all of them were janitors.[54] Serious labor shortages and the federal government's Fair Employment Practices Committee established in response to the all-black March on Washington Movement in July 1941 eventually caused the auto manufacturers to recruit blacks as production workers.[55] At first, there was quite widespread white opposition. In February and June 1942 wildcat strikes occurred at Chrysler's Highland Park and Dodge Truck plants against the transfer of blacks to production work. These ended only when the international threatened the strikers to return or lose their jobs.[56] Under joint UAW and government pressure, the proportion of blacks in Chrysler's Detroit workforce rose from 2.5% in 1942 to 15% by the spring of 1945.[57]

After the war, and despite the efforts of a minority of 'red-necks',[58] the UAW's seniority agreements and Chrysler's concentration in the Detroit area ensured the proportion of blacks in Chrysler plants remained higher than at Ford and GM.[59] In 1949 the white Chrysler Kercheval workers objected for several months to the up-grading of four blacks to assembly line work,[60] but this was the last major collective act of racism by white production workers.

The absolute growth of available semiskilled jobs in the industry from 1946 to 1955 meant that both blacks and women (who were first hired on final assembly jobs at Dodge Main in 1949) were no longer seen as direct competitors for production work as they had been in the 1930s. In the 1957 boom, black employment at the four main Detroit Chrysler plants rose as high as 20.3%.[61] But while the proportion of blacks among auto industry workers as a whole rose from 3.7% in 1940, to 7.8% in 1950 and 9.1% in 1960,[62] they were still restricted to semiskilled and unskilled work. The stronger job-protection sentiment among the skilled workers and the disenchantment of many of them with the UAW led to demands for an all-white skilled union.[63] Racism went unchallenged by the auto manufacturers, who hired no more than 1% black employees out of the combined white-collar occupations.[64] To add insult to this injury, many bars in the virtually all-white mini-city of Hamtramck, in which the

Dodge Main plant was situated, refused to serve the blacks who came to work there in the 1950s, and in the 1960s some still refused to employ blacks.[65]

Although Dodge Main's final assembly plant was already 45% black in 1960, it was only in 1966 that a production worker, Charlie Brooks, was elected Local 3's first black vice-president.[66] By 1970 blacks made up 13.4% of the slightly more than one million workers in the whole US motor vehicle and motor vehicle equipment industry. And of these, four out of every five black males were in the front-line of the production process, the three lowest blue-collar occupational categories.[67] In Detroit, which employed nine out of every twenty blacks in the industry,[68] black militancy from the civil rights movement and black nationalist politics began to have a dramatic effect on the shopfloor.

The pattern of grievances began to reveal a major disciplinary problem. In 1966 while production standards were the most common grievance handled by Local 3 officers, the total number of dismissals challenged through the procedure reached 222 – about one in fifty of the total labor force. The most discharges were for falsifying applications, followed by 'insubordination, walking off jobs', 'excessive absenteeism' and for being 'under the influence of intoxicants'.[69] They showed young workers responding as individuals to the harsh working conditions and discipline of Dodge Main. A retired UAW member told one observer in 1970: 'The younger generation is not going to take the crap that we had to take.'[70] They lied about their job histories and abused the foreman. And many dealt in or used drugs in the plant. It was a very large and potentially profitable market of well-paid workers, away from the prying eyes of the police. By 1968 most of the younger black and white workers smoked marijuana on the job to ease the monotony – and management didn't worry too much. Liska recalled:

> They took pills, they were shooting up their veins . . . and no-one knew how to stop it. Management condoned it. There were supervisors selling it, stewards selling it. But they didn't try to stop it. The fear was there. It was big business, and the pushers inside the plant had an organization outside.
>
> Management didn't fire too much on these things. If you didn't do the job, that was one thing. But if you were shooting up they didn't care about you. Everybody closed their eyes on it.[71]

With large sums of money changing hands, and certain workers taking drugs on credit and then finding they owed their pay check to the pusher, the atmosphere inside became more charged. Many workers began carrying weapons to work, some even took in handguns. Even so management didn't bother too much as long as production wasn't affected.

What was also quite different from the 1940s and 1950s was that management refused to let the period of labor shortage weaken its shopfloor authority over the labor process. Management's dogged pursuance of its 'right to manage', even at the height of the new boom, provoked large numbers of complaints:

> *The Foreman has only one goal, 'Get the production out – the hell with the workers' problems.'
> *The production helper classification is being abused. Many times workers are taken off this classification to higher paid operations and then they are not paid for this work.
> *Time Study men interfering with workers. This should be done by Supervisors, NOT Time Study Men.
> *Standards are changed at foreman's whims.
> *Supervisors take off seniority workers and allowing lesser seniority men to stay on operations, saying 'I can take you off anytime I please as long as I pay you,' etc.
> *Doctor Skowron is not doing the job he was hired to do. A worker injured his back and had to wait one and a half hours in the medical department to be serviced and then told to go back to his job ... The Union charges Dr Skowron of being too arrogant.[72]

The grievances were the same as ten and twenty years earlier. But there were no longer any fixed points of self-evidently 'fair' conduct or worker-influenced workplace rules by which management was constrained to operate. So Local 3 president Domanski could only appeal to management to stop ignoring the workers' problems. And pleading was pretty ineffectual. Brooks, the black Local 3 vice-president, protested: 'Supervisors are ignoring the Union completely.'[73]

Shopfloor *bargaining* had ceased. The formal procedures took time, were liable to managerial obstruction, and were rarely successful. So local officers and plant committeemen increasingly turned to informal deals with management.[74] Ed Liska, who served on Local 3's EB from 1962 until 1972, believed the domination of the case-book grievance procedure effectively forced local officers to replace 'bargaining by threat' with 'pleading a case'. 'If the steward don't win it at the first step,' he recalled, 'you're going to have a hard time.' The only way for the officers to show any results, then, was to plead for leniency and to seek 'trade-offs' with personnel and labor relations managers.[75] Management, by giving or withholding small concessions on grievances or penalties, was thus able to influence the apparent effectiveness of particular union representatives in the eyes of their members, particularly in the run-up to election periods.[76]

The plea-bargaining system appeared increasingly unjust when the racial composition of those doing the pleading and those dispensing 'justice' came to differ substantially from those receiving the penalties. There is no agreement on the exact date Dodge Main employed a majority of black workers. But by 1967, the year of the Detroit 'Rebellion', the lowest seniority jobs in Dodge Main on the main conveyor line jobs in the body shop and trim department were overwhelmingly black, while the whole final assembly plant was 60% black by 1970.[77]

By the late 1960s, the inability of the existing union organizations to articulate workers' grievances and effect any significant change in working conditions, had led many of the 'new' workers to shun the UAW. Dodge Main's black workers were not uniformly black nationalist, into drugs and violence or all Uncle Toms – as the various stereotypes depicted at the time. But the concept of 'collectivity', of workers' ability to influence the work situation lying in the exercise of their collective strength, was clearly in tension with the feeling that you were on your own.

Two tendencies among the black workers, however, stood out against individualism: those influenced by the black nationalist and socialist politics of the Black Power movement, and those blacks who had entered the local UAW machine. The first sign of their presence surfaced in August 1965 when four power house workers wrote to the *Dodge Main News* complaining that blacks were discriminated against for promotion.[78] The local's recording secretary, the former 'rank and file' caucus supporter, Ed Liska, was assigned to reply. His answer reeked of self-congratulation:

> The 12,000 workers in the Dodge Plant have various problems with management, but the most stirring scene going unmentioned is that Whites and Coloreds work together, eat together, discuss family problems, discuss sports, Union problems, Human, Personal Problems, and Political Problems with no sign of animosity displayed by either party . . .
> The UAW Union has done more for Equal Rights than any other organization in the Nation. The seniority and ability to do a job is the key in our Contract. This Agreement is all that the Civil Rights Movement is really seeking, the right for equal opportunity for a better way of life.[79]

The local officers' complacency was unacceptable to many hundreds of Dodge Main's black workers whose outside political experiences were teaching them to stop requesting civil rights and to start fighting. Despite the rapid transformation of the main production areas of the plant to a majority of black workers, the number of black foremen could be counted on one hand and the plea-bargaining process that was supposed to protect them from managerial excesses was run by a clique which was predominantly white. Out of these frustrations came the election in 1968 of four blacks to the ten-strong Local 3 executive board and, simultaneously, the emergence of the Dodge Revolutionary Union Movement, DRUM. The futures of these two tendencies were determined in small part by the energy of the individuals who comprised their leaderships, but primarily by the wider configuration of international union and national politics.

9 DRUM beats ... and is beaten: 1967–1973

A mythology has developed that suggests the Dodge Revolutionary Union Movement (DRUM) and the labor revolt of the late 1960s and early 1970s appeared out of nowhere.[1] But more detailed study suggests the strike issues were similar to those which aroused protests ten, twenty and even thirty-five years before. What was new was the organizational and ideological momentum of the resurgence of combativity. A 'new' labor force influenced by 'new' views of what was 'fair' attempted to challenge the 'old' dictates of unilateral management.

The situation paralleled the 1930s: an 'unfair' working environment for many production workers persuaded a small minority to act, while many more gave passive support to their actions to improve working conditions. Handfuls of organized socialists and communists (in the 1930s) and black revolutionaries (in the 1960s), thus appeared to exert an influence disproportionate to their numbers. In the 1960s, however, the new militants had to contend with the UAW as well as with management. The auto plants were already 100% union shops and the UAW was legitimized by management and in law. A 1930s level of discontent or of organizing among autoworkers was no longer enough to effect permanent change. Strike action stood little chance of success and strikers faced great risks of identification and procedural discharge.[2] Much of the conflict that occurred in the late 1960s therefore took non-strike forms. The slight rise in strike frequency between 1967 and 1973 above the levels before and after was the tip of a sunken iceberg of continuing resistance to unilateral managerial authority.

Section I traces the origins of DRUM to traditional autoworkers' protests, and shows how management's inept reaction gave the protest enough legitimacy to allow a small group of radicals to generalize from the grievance of 'unfair' penalties to the 'unfairness' of racialism and unilateral managerial control. Section II considers the nature of

DRUM's demands, and suggests how the movement temporarily affected the frontier of control.[3] Section III demonstrates how Chrysler and the international union ultimately defeated DRUM by breathing new life into the plea-bargaining relationship and by encouraging the take-over of Local 3 by a friendly black administration.

I. 1967–68: DRUM starts to beat

The six-day Detroit 'Rebellion' of July 1967 took place when Dodge Main was shut down for the annual model change-over. There was no opportunity for the members to protest against Local 3's EB agreeing to allow between fifty and a hundred national guardsmen to use Local 3's hall to guard the plant, about three miles from the scene of greatest destruction.[4] The biggest of the series of 'ghetto uprisings' that had begun in Watts, Los Angeles, in 1964, the 'Rebellion' led to the deaths of nine whites and thirty-four blacks. There were 3,800 arrests, 2,700 buildings looted and more than $500 million of damages. A subsequent statistical analysis concluded: 'While an important segment of the black community either participated in or supported the events of the insurrection, actual participation was disproportionately clustered among the more deprived segments of the black working class (i.e. the segment of the black working class that had less stable employment).'[5]

The significance of the 1967 rebellion for most of Dodge Main's black workers was not that they participated – though a body shop worker was killed and an inspector was shot in the leg[6] – but that they *sympathized*. The distinction between participation and support was not grasped by Local 3's leaders, neither white nor black. Recording secretary Liska immediately blamed 'the Communists', while Brooks, the only black EB member, argued that 'the shameful tragedy in our city during the week of July 24 ... could not be considered in any way a part of any civil rights struggle'.[7] However, Ford and Chrysler were more perceptive. They responded to this 'bargaining by riot' by announcing they would open special hiring offices in the ghetto. Moreover, the rebellion also stimulated a political rethink in Detroit's black community which, by the fall of 1967, was rife with political ferment.[8]

In this atmosphere UAW president Reuther chose Ford as the target company in contract negotiations, and struck it for two months in September and October 1967 before winning improved lay-off pay of nearly 95% of earnings for up to a year.[9] In solidarity with Ford, Chrysler and GM refused to renew their contracts with the UAW and stopped deducting UAW members' dues payments.[10] This release from the no strike provisions of the contract intersected with the growing political radicalization of the mid 1960s to give the Dodge Main trim department workers the confidence to stage a three-day wildcat protest against tight work standards. Chief Steward Fox reported:

> They told me, 'Edie: one o'clock we're walking out.' And they did. They stopped and the whole trim shop shut down. Everyone was waiting and then Stanley Flint shouted, 'What the hell we're waiting for? Let's go!' And everyone walked out.
> Workers went to the Local hall, made their own signs. For many of the young blacks it was their first strike. They made fires and manned the picket for three days. The whole plant supported them.
> It needed to be done. It was the feeling.[11]

Fox helped personally 'legitimize' the wildcat by walking out too, and the Dodge tradition of the 1950s reasserted itself as the whole plant honored the picket line.

After three days, however, a group of strikers who belonged to a new black caucus called 'Concerned Members for a Better Union' started to argue to go back, and the strike ended.[12] But it did so, significantly, without the firings that had become customary after strikes within the contract period. The solidarity of the November 1967 strike fired the imagination and hopes of many new workers. The interaction of the old tradition of sectional problem solving with the new combativity had brought strike action back into the vocabulary of the Dodge Main shopfloor.[13]

The failure of the local and international union leaderships to harness the militancy of the younger workers created growing resentment in 1968 as Chrysler kept raising production targets. In January one woman protested: 'We haven't gained much on the working conditions which we have been fighting for several years. Our brothers and sisters are working harder than ever. As a matter of fact, they are working harder now than before our Union was organized.'[14] On March 2 and March 22 body shop workers staged further protests on work standards and management disciplined forty-two of them. Worried by a possible growing trend the personnel manager, Leonard Nawrocki, called in Local 3 president Domanski and the plant committee to warn them that if any more 'illegal walkouts' took place then 'severe discipline will result'.[15] In return for what he took was an assurance that the local would stop further walkouts, Nawrocki then suspended the penalties on the body shop workers.[16]

However, Nawrocki's 'compassion',[17] as he later described it, helped to legitimize the walkouts. On April 22 management raised its production schedule again and hired an extra 600 workers. Yet, during the next four days as management increased the line speed in stages up from forty-nine cars an hour to fifty-six, half of these new hires either left in disgust or were fired.[18] The result was an intense speed-up in several areas of the plant, where, as Domanski protested, 'management shorted the manpower about 30 or 40'.[19] A rash of grievances was immediately filed:[20]

Trim Department	18
Final Assembly	11
Paint Shop	7
Car conditioning	2
	38

Workers were quite aware that this was a major speed-up because they had already been fully manned up to work at fifty-six cars an hour in 1967,[21] and on Saturday 27 April when the line speed finally hit fifty-six cars an hour again with less labor, the women who worked in the fender assembly area staged a fourteen minute protest sit-down.[22] To cope with the 14% increase in line speed the final assembly had received just 7% more labor.[23]

The dispute festered on, with workers still under acute physical pressure, until the following Thursday when rumors spread that those who had stopped the previous Saturday would face heavy penalties. A second ingredient was now present: the 'unjust' penalty. It didn't matter that the superintendent added two workers temporarily to the group of women fixing fenders to the cars. The women knew the additional workers would be taken away as soon as they had made up lost production. An hour or so later the third recurrent element in such wildcats appeared: the workers' pay checks were handed out.[24]

As usual, large numbers of second shift workers who had staged the sit-down the previous week left the plant at their 10 p.m. lunch period. When they came back at about 10.25 p.m., a group of six women and two men formed a picket at the main gate and persuaded the others not to go in.[25] The strike was on. The next afternoon, at the suggestion of management, Liska, the new president elect, went to the warehouse gate to try and persuade the four women and one man picketing there to leave. He noted in his diary that night: 'The girls kept saying that they are tired of the speed-ups and nothing is being done to help them. They refused to come to the Local Hall and kept on picketing.'[26] The strikers believed their only remedy was direct action. The experience of these white women workers in their late twenties and early thirties with several years' seniority was that the grievance procedure was a waste of time.

It was a textbook conflict. Management's pressure for cars led it to speed up the line and rely upon disciplinary procedures to keep production rolling when they couldn't hire fresh labor quickly enough. The job got tougher. One striker explained: 'I work on the steering column job and when I get home I am too tired to do anything. The work is getting harder and harder and nothing is being done about it.' And another added: 'I work on the bumper job and I can't keep up. More work is asked and I have to use sleeping pills when I get home.'[27]

Management had legitimated this return to bargaining through industrial action in two ways: by acknowledging that the workers' grievance was a 'fair' one, when it added the temporary workers to the work group, and by its 'fair' treatment of the earlier wildcats. Moreover, the plant's other workers sympathized with the strikers: a handful of pickets at the two main gates were enough to stop the vast majority of production workers from entering on Friday and Saturday.

Chrysler got a court injunction issued against twenty workers for illegal picketing on the Saturday and when, on Sunday afternoon, nine of the pickets turned up to meet the local officers, they 'agreed not to picket and go back to work'. Significantly, though, Liska's diary also records that 'the Officers promised to do everything possible to fight for them'.[28] Work resumed on the following Monday morning and as part of the informal understanding reached between the union and plant management, two workers who had already been discharged were reinstated.[29]

Top management at Highland Park took several days to decide how to respond. They felt a few workers had to be fired to avoid allowing wildcat strikes to re-emerge as an established practice at Dodge Main. But they knew there were risks attached to discharging too many workers, particularly the longer-service white women. 'Unfair' dismissals could easily provoke a further strike and still greater losses of production. So they initiated a course of action designed to be hard but with the risks reduced by the old stratagem of 'divide and rule'. They would select a quiet time to penalize the workers and when they did they would hit the younger black workers who had organized solidarity more severely than the white women workers who had initiated the strike.

The company waited until the next Saturday night, May 11, when it would be most difficult to organize a protest stoppage. Then the final assembly superintendent, Dodge Main's labor relations director and a Highland Park representative worked from 11 p.m. until 2 a.m. calling workers into the office one by one to hear their penalties. Five were discharged (two more workers joined them on Monday day shift), nine were given thirty-day penalties, four given five-day penalties, two three days and four just one day each.[30] The black participants in the picketing were hit disproportionately and to reduce still further the risk of further protests, the front-line supervisors were ordered to mount a major disciplinary crackdown against the entire workforce.

Forty-eight hours later, Liska noted:

> The most alarming facts reveal that the Dodge management is hell bent on penalizing everyone in the plant for any and all violations. Reports throughout the day are coming in that labor relations and supervisors are threatening everyone and are spying on workers who leave the plant for lunch, etc. Cameras are being used in all parts of the plant.
>
> The workers are in a fighting mood and are demanding action against the management.[31]

But while management's response successfully intimidated workers from taking any immediate action, it had two longer-term consequences. First, the general crackdown alienated the whole membership, but particularly the executive board who then publicly excused the wildcat and condemned the penalties. Second, it underlined the local's ineffectiveness before an aggressive management. Neither pleading nor following procedure were allowed to achieve results.

Inadvertently, management's actions had highlighted the need for more effective organization at the moment when black Detroit was mourning the assassination of Martin Luther King (shot one month earlier) and was searching for new ways of getting results. In this failure of institutions, the leadership of the protest passed to a network of black militants that included a core of workers at Dodge Main and a small group of Trotskyist-influenced black students who had been putting out the radical monthly *Inner City Voice* newspaper since the 'Rebellion'.[32] They were able to connect the specific injustice of the discharged black workers to the growing resentment against continuing racial discrimination felt by most black workers.

Both black and white workers had joined in the wildcats between November 1967 and May 1968, although the activists were few in number beside the 12,000 Dodge Main workers. However, the immediate circle of local officers, stewards and hangers-on was also small. It involved only between 100 and 150 persons,[33] a figure that is on a par with the 300 workers who were riled up enough to go to the local hall on Tuesday May 14 to protest the intensification of discipline in the plant,[34] and with the 135 who attended a Sunday special membership meeting and voted to hold a strike ballot.[35] While on June 3 only 491 workers bothered to vote (388 in favor, 103 against),[36] the threat posed by this group of new militants to the old local union leaders and the more moderate blacks who were working with them was real.

The personality who linked the May 1968 wildcat to the establishment of DRUM was a final assembly worker, General Gordon Baker. But the issue was the feeling of most blacks in the plant that Chrysler had singled out *black* participants in the wildcat for punishment. Baker was twenty-six years old and he had worked at Dodge since October 1964. He was in the same informal group as the editors of the *Inner City Voice* and he was one of the two men who joined the women's picket line on May 2 in a gesture of solidarity for which he was fired.[37] Less than two weeks after Baker was frog-marched out of Dodge Main, Brooks reported 'that a leaflet titled DRUM is being circulated around the Plant and it is a slanderous and mud-slinging leaflet'.[38]

II. DRUM demands

DRUM began its existence as a poorly printed bulletin written and distributed by Baker and a group of about nine Dodge workers, helped by others on the *Inner City Voice*. The first DRUM bulletin accused management of treating blacks unfairly:

> Referring to the above discharges and disciplinary action taken against the pickets, the overall administration of punishment was overwhelmingly applied to the Black workers who were held responsible for the walk-out which was directly caused by company indifference towards working conditions.
> Three Black workers were fired outright. They were given 30 days off, and numerous others were given from one to five days off.
> Why must the Black worker continue to be utilized and exploited beyond humane reasoning and judged by double standards? It is time for Black workers to concern themselves with malicious tactics used by the White Power structure in its attempt to demoralize the integrity of the Black individual . . . You have but one life, live it with dignity.[39]

It struck a chord. Many workers knew the strike had been initiated by a group of Polish women around Helen Demski and others in the same Rosary Society.[40] But the bulletin didn't stop there. It argued that the immediate injustice was only part of a wider problem:

> Black brothers and sisters comprise 60% of the production workers at Hamtramck Assembly, yet the percentage of Black supervisors and shop stewards are too low to mention . . .
> While Chrysler is going into the ghetto for common labor, they go to the suburbs for supervision and skilled workers. The Black worker who tries for supervision is told that his attitude isn't right, which means that he thinks BLACK. The black worker who tries out for skilled trades is given a test [for] practising journeymen to pass. Where the white worker may not be given a test at all. This situation must be stopped

now. We as black men and women looking for equal opportunity to employment cannot tolerate this. The time to put a stop to this is now.[41]

Brooks, too, had to endorse the charge of racism against Chrysler. In his regular *Dodge Main News* column the following month he wrote: 'We get a little more than our share in Vietnam . . . I, therefore, must once again call upon the Hamtramck Assembly Management and the Huber Foundry Management to call a halt to the underhanded discrimination practised by some of your supervision.'[42] But while Brooks had no immediate answer, DRUM did. It called for individual and collective action against management.

In July DRUM staged its first major display of strength by organizing a two-day community picket on the Dodge gates after a march of 150 workers to the union hall. Around 70% of the black workers refused to cross, along with a handful of whites. The wildcat was against – 'Racism, Discrimination and Intimidation; Bigotry and Abuse from Supervisors; Indiscriminate discharge of black workers'. It was considered highly successful since no one was fired, and DRUM's influence increased and its tone became more strident.[43]

Management had stirred resentment among black workers, but in the polarization that occurred white workers also resorted to shopfloor protest. The plant committeemen for the skilled workers in the renamed Hamtramck Assembly plant and Huber Foundry had been highly critical of Domanski for not immediately denouncing the production worker wildcatters.[44] Their fear that black workers were getting special treatment was fueled by DRUM's biting attacks on white racism. Partly in response to DRUM's July wildcat a group of white skilled workers staged a one-day racist strike a week later. This occurred when management wished to pay a black worker the skilled pay rate for cleaning the Huber Foundry sewers. The Huber Foundry skilled trades didn't want to do the work themselves, but objected to blacks doing a classified 'skilled' job. They put up a picket in their cars at some distance from the plant and none of them turned up to work. Management seized upon this strike to mete out a bit of 'racial equality' and they fired the Huber Foundry skilled trades chief steward, Cy Van Fleteren.[45]

This disciplinary action, however, had the opposite effect to that intended. It left the Local 3 officers with two sets of discharges which appeared similar but in fact were very different. There were the May 2 strikers, against whom the company had cast-iron cases, including photographs and several statements from supervisors. Their cases could not be won through the grievance procedure. To secure the reinstatement of all seven would require a management climb-down or the whole plant to stage a successful strike. But, as Liska and Brooks put on the record at the special Local 3 membership meeting on May 26, 'according to Contractual procedures, discharge cases are not strike-able'.[46] Then there was a white chief steward against whom there was no evidence except his failure, along with the rest of his members, to appear at work on July 18. The Van Fleteren case could be fought and won *within* the procedure. What superficially appeared to be two similar cases were not and as it turned out different treatment was finally meted out in October 1968: Van Fleteren was reinstated while General Baker and Bennie Tate, both black, remained discharged.[47]

DRUM had not been marking time. It had organized an effective boycott of two local bars which refused to hire blacks, and had run a candidate, Ron March, in a special election for Local 3 Trustee. He headed the first ballot, with 521 votes, but lost the October 3 run-off by 1,386 votes to the Liska faction white candidate's 2,091.[48] The numbers supporting DRUM were growing and DRUM's claim that the election was stolen was widely believed.[49] Its reputation also spread beyond Hamtramck and 'revolutionary union movement' groups were established at Ford's Rouge plant and at Chrysler's Eldon Avenue gear and axle plant, where twenty-six workers were fired in January 1969 as a result of a wildcat protest against penalties imposed on workers returning late from an ELRUM meeting.[50]

The emergence of DRUM reflected the dovetailing of the wider civil rights movement with shopfloor workers' demands for restraint over the exercise of managerial authority. When DRUM listed fourteen demands, the first eight were straightforward demands for 'fair' treatment:

1. 50 black foremen.
2. 10 black general foremen immediately.
3. 3 black superintendents.
4. A black plant manager.
5. That the majority of the employment office personnel be black.
6. All black doctors and 50% black nurses in the medical centers at this plant.
7. That the medical policy at this plant be changed entirely.
8. 50% of all plant protection guards be black and that every time a black worker is removed from plant premises that he be led by a black brother.[51]

None of these demands *directly* challenged Chrysler's capacity to control the labor process, and most, if not all, were implemented during the next five years.[52]

Two other groups of demands raised by DRUM did, however, directly threaten managerial control. In language borrowed from the traditional

·Dodge left, DRUM raised demands for a new grievance system, job safety, a fight against the speed up, the four-day week and a doubling of production workers' wages.[53] And it also threw in several 'transitional' demands that were supposed to build bridges to wider black nationalist politics but which it never tried to act upon:

9. DRUM demands that all black workers immediately stop paying union dues.
10. DRUM demands that the two hours' pay that goes into union dues be levied to the black community to aid in self determination for black people.
11. DRUM demands that the double standard be eliminated and that a committee of the black rank and file be set up to investigate all grievances against the corporation, to find out what type of discipline is to be taken against corporation, and also to find out what type of discipline is to be taken against Chrysler Corporation employees.
12. DRUM demands that all black workers who have been fired on trumped up racist charges be brought back with all lost pay.
13. DRUM demands that our fellow black brothers in South Africa working for Chrysler Corp. and its subsidiaries, be paid at an equal scale as white racist co-workers.
14. DRUM also demands that a black brother be appointed as head of the board of directors of Chrysler Corp.[54]

Unlike the demands for an end to racial discrimination and for new shopfloor restraints on managerial authority, these last demands were irreconcilable with managerial power. They could win support from a highly political few, but unless a much deeper radicalization took place in America, they would not mobilize anyone else.

DRUM's impact on the frontier of control is not quantifiable. There was a marked fall in car output per manual employee from 1968 to 1970, but this was primarily because production targets were lowered faster than workers were laid off. Yet it would be surprising if the barrage of publicity given by DRUM to individual cases of foremen harassing black and women workers, and the regular resort of angry workers to physical protest, did not have some effect. A new wave of primarily *defensive* struggles broke out in which workers collectively protested against 'unjust' discipline and against working in excessive heat in the summer. Liska's diary entry for Tuesday, February 25, 1969 carries a typical report of these recurrent short stoppages and threats of picketing:

Trim Shop Problem

Thursday, Feb. 20:
Work stoppage due to a worker being penalized three days. After work stoppage management reduced the penalty and workers went back.

Friday, Feb. 21:
About 15 members from this same group (Fox district) did not report to work. They came to the pay office and demanded their pay checks. The checks were in the department office. The group went to the department and after creating a scene, swearing, drinking, calling other workers names for working, etc, they got their checks and left.
Monday, Feb. 24:
After an all day investigation by management, they, at the end of the day meted out several penalties for the Friday incident. One fellow was discharged, four were given penalties up to five days off.
Tuesday:
Three of the five workers penalized reported to work. One actually went on the line and started to work. Supervisors notified them of their penalties, etc. A work stoppage of about 12 minutes occurred before others went to work and the three men left the plant. The three men told management that Edith Fox told them to come in. She denied it.
After the first break, again a work stoppage occurred. About 12 minutes were involved and the lines started out again.
During the rest of the day, Chuck Walters (Committeeman) and Edith Fox met with the management to discuss the penalties. The discharge case was reduced to five days.
After the meeting, about 3 p.m., Edith Fox went along the lines in the group and told everyone to go to the local hall for a meeting.[55]

The issue that provoked the first short solidarity stoppage was an 'unjust' penalty. Further penalties against the group who were celebrating their initial victory and who only entered the plant to collect their pay checks caused the second.

The thrust of the group's anger against the company was, however, restrained. The lines were only stopped for brief periods and the three who at first defied management by coming in to work in spite of their penalties, soon went home. They knew there was a limit beyond which further 'illegal' acts would bring about an escalation by management. Instead, the full force of their frustration was directed against a target which was not a real threat: the white left-wing chief steward, the black committeeman and Local 3's president. Liska's diary entry concluded:

About 50 persons were in the Executive Board room. Chuck Walters tried to explain what happened at the meeting. They would not listen. Edith Fox tried to explain about the problems. They shouted her down. Ed Liska tried to talk about procedures that must be followed. Deaf ears. Joe Gordon attempted to talk. He was shouted down and called names. The group was totally unreachable. Few did not know the rules. Some from the extreme militant group. Others just came along to hear and see. Swearing, dirty talk and just plain arrogance prevailed at the meeting. They say, 'send telegrams to the five people who were penalized, get them back to work and get rid of the general foreman, etc' ... Simple as that.

They said that they will picket the plant on Wednesday.

Liska cautioned them that they will be fired and that injunctions will clear them off the gates, etc. They ignored the plea.

The meeting ended up with shouts, yells, confusions. No one knew exactly what will happen, except that there is a total breakdown in that trim group.[56]

While car production remained at high levels, and before the longer-term changes Chrysler was planning were fully implemented, labor relations at Dodge Main remained literally on a knife's edge. Liska, who was president from 1968 to 1972, later explained his problem with taking up many discharge cases: 'A lot of guys didn't think hitting a foreman or stabbing him is doing anything wrong. So they say they're innocent.'[57]

In another incident in February 1969, a spotwelder was suspended by a black labor relations supervisor without explanation and denied the right to collect his possessions. While his steward was arguing his case, Rushie Forge, the DRUM activist involved, 'suddenly turned around and hit Young with his fist, then he reached inside of his shirt and pulled out a dagger, lunged at Young and struck him twice in the back'.[58] To protect themselves some foremen started to carry guns, which became so common in the plant that in 1969 management posted notices prohibiting them.[59] Workers were still being dismissed for being in possession of guns or for firing them inside the plant in 1970 and 1971.[60]

In the 1940s and 1950s similar workplace unrest was often viewed as an opportunity by the full-time local officers to increase their bargaining leverage with management. But by the late 1960s they viewed it as a destabilizing, hostile element. To the sheltered UAW officials of Solidarity House, who had marched behind Walter Reuther and Martin Luther King in the quarter of a million-strong Freedom parade down Detroit's Woodward Avenue in 1963 on the twentieth anniversary of the Detroit race riots, the movement was doubly shocking. It challenged their ostensible liberalism and disturbed their comfortable relationship with the auto companies.

Once the UAW realized DRUM had survived the first highly charged weeks after the May wildcat, it fell back on Reuther's traditional weapon against dissent, red-baiting. The July 1968 issue of the UAW's official magazine, *Battleline*, charged:

Black Power advocates are claiming that 'white racist foremen' are 'harassing, insulting, driving and snapping the whip over the backs of thousands of black workers at the Dodge plant.'

Using these lies as their base for creating discontent they have formed the '*Dodge Revolutionary Union Movement*' (DRUM). The theory behind the movement is pure marxism (divide and conquer), and they even quote from the works of a noted communist, W. E. B. Dubois, in their newsletter (DRUM).

It appears to us that the communist-inspired black power movement has shifted from looting and burning to leading campus revolts and attempting to bring the black workers into the revolution.

It was exactly this combination of events which the Reds used – almost successfully – to bring the iron curtain down on France recently. With only a handful they spearheaded the student strike while communist goons kept the French workers from returning to their jobs.

We know the communists look upon Detroit's automobile plants as the economic bellwether of the country. And to bring their production to a screeching halt through internal revolution would better serve the enemy's purpose than if they were bombed out by enemy aircraft.[61]

In Local 3, Liska dropped his earlier sympathetic approach and headed off trouble by relying on the old tactic of denying the militants a platform at general membership meetings: 'I learned that too, being a local officer,' he admitted. 'Only the politicians who want to stick you with something showed up to regular membership meetings, so you told your guys to stay away or go to the bar next door in case we need you.'[62] This tactic enabled the EB to settle the 1968 wildcat grievances without having to put the settlement before the membership. It also bought time to get more blacks involved in the UAW machine locally and nationally.

The UAW's red-baiting further antagonized DRUM's supporters. In the March 1970 Local 3 elections Fox ran on a militant opposition platform, the United National Caucus.[63] DRUM attacked her as a 'liberal', while Liska, running again for president, was accused of having 'almost dead racist old pollocks standing in line for two and three hours trying to vote for some already dead pollocks'.[64] But DRUM had already passed its peak and while its verbal rhetoric got more vitriolic, its capacity to mount real industrial protests waned. Liska, although opposed by Ron March and another black candidate, secured an overall majority and was re-elected without the need for a run-off, while his 'United Membership' slate of four blacks and six whites won all ten executive board positions.

The ease with which Liska won the 1970 election surprised both Liska and DRUM. Liska had asked Reuther to send physical assistance, and a dozen armed international staff workers from the regional office had spent election day at the local hall.[65] DRUM complained bitterly after the election that 'Liska won at the point of a gun',[66] and didn't run again in any further Local 3 elections. But DRUM's defeat was real. It followed an internal faction fight within the League of Revolutionary Black Workers[67] and a 20% cut in production in February 1969. *Fortune* saw this contractions as 'the end of Chrysler's hard-fought recovery from the dark days of 1961'.[68] It undoubtedly ensured the lay-off of most of Dodge Main's DRUM-supporting low seniority workers. Yet DRUM's defeat was also planned: Chrysler had worked hard to bring more blacks into supervisory and management jobs and to enhance the prestige of moderate blacks within Local 3.

III. Beating DRUM

Chrysler's more measured response to the DRUM challenge was to develop a new 'liberal' image. Corporate labor relations policy consciously abandoned its defense of racist practices. Instead it sought to remove 'genuine' racial injustice while continuing to act vigorously against the revolutionaries who wished to challenge its power. That this change was a cosmetic forced on the company is confirmed by Lee Iacocca's suggestion of continuing racial prejudice in the boardrooms of the Big Three some twelve years later.[69] But at the time the change was quite dramatic. Dick Clancy, the personnel manager who was moved to Dodge Main in 1969 with the brief of 'integrating' the plant, boasted later: 'Within a year I had DRUM beaten.'[70] Significant numbers of former black union activists, and even some who had come close to DRUM, were promoted to foreman.[71] And with the room for racial conflict on the job reduced, DRUM's ability to generalize from a particular production standard grievance or particular piece of harassment on the basis of 'white against black' became more limited.

Chrysler also encouraged the emergence of 'responsible' black local union leaders whom it accepted would have to represent a majority black plant.[72] But this carried a price: management had to show a willingness to allow certain up and coming local activists to 'win' a few victories. Top management had been fairly contemptuous of the 'responsible' local leadership after 1958. But the return of industrial unrest revived their interest in having an effective union help keep the lid on the kettle. So management consciously built up individual stewards and officers as a force through which changes (albeit of a minor character) could take place. This explains why Liska's recollection, 'We won almost everything we went in for',[73] accompanied the evidence of harsh discipline, a high turnover and, in 1973, renewed spontaneous revolt in several of Chrysler's Detroit plants. The policy was generally successful. By restoring some credibility to a new layer of union activists it persuaded several articulate individuals, who might otherwise have remained in opposition, to work within the local structure.

Clancy understood he had to win the hearts and minds of the local's activists as well as to re-educate and integrate the Dodge Main supervision. He calculated that joint work by management and Local 3 activists for the United Foundation charity could bring managers and Local 3's officers together. First he held a fund-raising dinner in the Dodge Main canteen. Then he wrote a bleeding heart letter to Ed Liska:

> I do not want to believe that our leadership at Hamtramck is any less socially aware, or has any less will to ask our people to give of themselves to help others; yet, the record says so.
>
> Last year (1969), your local and this plant had to suffer the ignominy and embarrassment of raising the fewest dollars per employee of any plant in Chrysler Corporation for the care and cure of the blinded, the lame, the bedridden, the incurably sick, and the mentally and emotionally retarded persons who cannot help themselves.
>
> Ed, I am addressing myself to the pride of your stewards and committeemen who are the leadership of Local 3. They have been selected as leaders. Leadership has its obligations. One of the most important is to raise the sights of those they serve. It is no less true in our plant community than in our national community: people are hungry for good leadership. They will respond to good and sound leadership that will challenge them in terms of their human spirit to rise above pessimism, negativeness, fault finding. The leadership, Ed, that this country lost to the assassin's bullet in the 1960's can only be replaced by the people themselves. We can work together for peace and harmony at Hamtramck in the 1970's for a better plant community. Let this be a beginning – to show this community that we can arise above our differences in service to the common good.[74]

This secured him an invitation to a return dinner in the Local 3 hall. For many of Dodge's managers and supervision it was the first time they had ever been inside the union building only yards from the plant. Having established informal contact over this broader, humanitarian issue, Clancy subsequently encouraged it over problems inside the plant.[75] Within a year Clancy's 'working together' approach was rewarded in the highly successful 1970 United Foundation drive, which won support from 96% of Dodge Main's workers.[76] It was also tested in more tangible ways.

The first test of the new relationship came when a group of second-shift workers stormed out of the plant at midnight in September 1970. As other workers continued to work, a few of the strikers got drunk and attacked some cars in the Joseph Campau parking lot. When exaggerated accounts of the damage were reported inside the plant, many of those still working stormed out and attacked the group in the parking lot who had intended to stay through the night and picket the day shift. After quite a battle the pickets were dispersed and the strike threat disappeared.[77] The company had been able to mobilize anti-strike and anti-militant sentiment among the majority of workers as a result of the misdirected anger of a few.[78]

The following June an incident at the gate led to a walkout by the second shift in the assembly plant and to four chief stewards and eight other workers being fired. It was the biggest potential explosion Dodge Main had experienced since 1968, but the EB was able to prevent any further walkouts and to secure the reinstatement of all four. The test was passed with flying colors. Liska pointed the lesson out to the workforce: 'The membership helped greatly by not having additional walkouts which would only result in more penalties and hamper the negotiations for the stewards and others who were already discharged.'[79] The new labor relations strategy had given the old collective bargaining institutions and relationships between the local officers and management the kiss of life, while DRUM, dying in its ugly internal political split, had lost its representative character.[80] DRUM had taken the blame for attacking workers' cars and its supporters could no longer point to the total ineffectiveness of 'going by the rules'.

The removal of many racist foremen was not accompanied by a less harsh regime or loss of control of the labor process. Discipline remained severe over lateness, absenteeism and production standards. One man who had worked at Dodge Main for nearly five years was suspended for five days in 1971 after coming to work late because he had been picked up for questioning – and then released without charge – by the police.[81] He had telephoned the foreman explaining the situation, but it hadn't helped. Informing the foreman in advance wasn't good enough either for a trim department worker who told her foreman she would be late because she had to take her baby to the doctor. She 'did not come at all due to baby crying all afternoon',[82] and was also given a five day penalty lay-off. One worker with twenty years' seniority was sent home by the company doctor because a boil on his stomach had burst. But when he returned to work two days later he was suspended because he 'did not bring in any substantiation' for his absence.[83] In another grievance, a worker complained that when his wife telephoned the plant to ask him to take her to hospital at 6 p.m. his foreman had refused to release him. When he finally did agree to let him go, at 11 p.m., the worker returned home to find his wife had had a miscarriage.[84] Leaving without permission for any reason was bound to lead to the severest of penalties – occasionally a thirty-day suspension and usually a discharge.

Workers were also forced to accept work standards and, after the major quality complaints received in 1969, to do their job without any of the customary short cuts. One supervisor, for example, suspended a worker with a complaint about his job for five days for 'insubordination' when the worker said, 'I won't go to work until I see my steward'.[85] Disciplinary action for poor work was very common: typical cases were ones where a man was suspended for a day for 'failing to follow instructions' by not pulling the dip stick on *every* car to check that the transmission was filled,[86] or where a man with a 'long bad record' was finally discharged for not spraying glue on the roof of a car about to be fitted with a vynl top.[87] Less common was the case of the worker given a five-day penalty for faulty work on a car weeks after it left the plant. Liska noted:

> Car in California found without oil in axle. Management gave McLaughlin, seniority 1964, five day penalty for failing to check axle. How in the hell can they track the car several weeks later and 2,000 miles away as checked by this man?[88]

As with most grievances discussed between the local UAW officers, plant committee and the labor relations managers, this penalty was passed on to the 'next step'. Even if the penalized axle oil worker ever won the grievance and got paid the five days' money he had lost, the penalty reflected the extent of managerial authority. Unlike systems of natural justice, the procedure accepted by the UAW involved workers first carrying out the sentence imposed by the supervisor and only being given an appeal afterwards. In the next boom quality would again take second place to getting the cars out,[89] but the disciplinary system kept workers in a state of insecurity, whether management wanted better quality or more cars.

By the Dodge Main elections of May 1972 DRUM was totally marginalized. All it could do was to advise workers to vote for the more militant of the non-DRUM black candidates.[90] DRUM's active support, perhaps 200–300 workers at its peak in October 1968, was down to below 100 before the 1970 election defeat and then fell away to a handful.[91] Even twenty to thirty committed workers could have constituted a viable UAW local caucus, as the smaller UNC group around Edie Fox did.[92] But DRUM did not have a consistent strategy of using the organizational framework of the local to advance policies or individuals. Primarily a political organization, its strength depended on the extent to which its generalizations of grievances struck home. As Dodge Main's black workers experienced less obvious discrimination in the early 1970s, so the diminishing cadre's activity was reduced to mere propaganda.

The elections saw Andy Hardy defeat Liska by a few hundred votes. Hardy, Liska's vice-president from 1970 to 1972, thus became Dodge Main's first black president and another black worker, 'Big John' Smith, became vice-president. Blacks took six of the ten Local 3 EB positions.[93] Hardy, whom DRUM had categorized in its 1968 'Tom Chart' as an 'out of sight' plant level 'Uncle Tom',[94] brought 'Black Power' to Dodge Main in a completely different manner from that envisaged four years earlier by those who triggered the movement inside the plant.

The new black Local 3 officers had been groomed by the international under heavy fire from the black nationalists. The tradition they acquired was a blend of the official Reutherite history of the UAW, complemented by detailed knowledge of the UAW–Chrysler contract and an instinct for the factional politics of the place-seekers active in Local 3. When the opposition claimed continuity with the early militant struggles of the UAW, Joe Gordon, Local 3's first black recording secretary, did not disagree:

> You may not know it, but this Union had a communist beginning. It was not intended to be a unifying focus for the working classes, but a disruptive force designed to bring about a class struggle between labor and management. The end results would enable them to make inroads into key industries, disrupt the economic stability of this nation and destroy capitalism.
> The scheme backfired. Its grip was broken by men and women armed with the unity, strategy and commitment that spelled better things for working people. The Union has been a God-send to the workers and especially the Black Workers.[95]

With this view of union history as progress away from 'class struggle', and embittered by the years of abuse from DRUM, the new administration showed fewer doubts about breaking picket lines or surrendering plant autonomy to the international than had Liska.[96] Hardy and a group of Local 3 officers and stewards were quite ready to respond in August 1973 to UAW Chrysler vice-president Fraser's call for assistance to help defeat a wildcat at the Mack Avenue plant. Hardy boasted: 'The days of early unionism were remarked by many of us who manned those gates on Thursday and Friday August 16 and 17, 1973 in a show of strength on behalf of the UAW.' And he went on, 'We urge that you also refuse to accept smart literature from those outside agitators who are trying to overthrow not only your UNION, but the US Government as well.'[97] The Hardy–Smith administration in Dodge Main was totally loyal to Solidarity House and got on very well with Clancy, the personnel manager.[98]

This close relationship between the international and the company, was demonstrated in April 1973 when the EB rounded on the trim department after eleven workers were discharged for trying to mount a lunchtime picket to support a worker given a five-day penalty:

> Some say the President made them lose their jobs. THIS IS UNTRUE. I was at the Plant the day before the 11 people got discharged ... and the President asked them to 'Go back to work and nothing would happen'. But the next day, after they refused to *listen* and were *discharged*, they found out that they did have a family at home and *no jobs*.[99]

Despite the renewed production boom, shopfloor bargaining by industrial action at Dodge Main received neither *informal* legitimacy from sympathetic local officers, nor *political* legitimacy as a response to new acts of managerial racism. DRUM had been beaten. It could neither establish an alternative institutional framework nor take over the UAW and so win the recognition from management it required for direct bargaining. This was clearly demonstrated in the contrast between the passivity at Dodge Main later that year, and three wildcat strikes at other Chrysler Detroit plants.

The 1973 wildcats were stimulated by the highest-ever employment total reached by Chrysler, the intensity of the drive for production and a summer heat wave in a contract year.[100] Yet Dodge Main was relatively quiet, only stopping half a shift earlier than the national strike call issued when the contract expired in September.[101] Dodge management and the UAW had achieved much. They had altered the color of the existing collective bargaining institutions, and allowed black stewards and plant committee members marginally more influence in pleading for their members. The system had been given a new credibility.[102] In these ways the growth in combativity triggered by a sense of racial injustice was turned around. Aware of the change, management took to gently tapping the stewards over the fingers if their closer relationship with management caused them to provoke unnecessary friction with their members. Thus the labor relations manager complained about 'the recent work stoppages where employees refused to work because of lack of proper union representation (namely, unannounced stewards and alternate stewards' absences)',[103] and warned the local officers not to let things go too far.

This balance of forces survived until 1980 when Dodge Main was closed. After 1973 neither an 'outside' politics nor the presence of an 'inside' tradition existed to give ideological justification to an independent shopfloor struggle against management. 'Good labor relations' in the plant were seldom interrupted by wildcats.[104] The early 1970s saw management successfully reassert its authority over the intensity of work. Chrysler's subsequent crises in the mid and late 1970s cannot be blamed on the militancy of its workers: they must be laid squarely on the shoulders of management.

10 Crisis, closure and concessions: 1974–1982

The most recent past often defies sober analysis. At Chrysler the usual problem of a ten-year rule protecting the Local 3 archives, closed company records and sparse but biased press coverage, have been aggravated by the company's life and death drama. As it careered towards bankruptcy Chrysler twice changed its top management and then appeared to undergo a miraculous recovery in 1983 and 1984. The media had little difficulty in naming one man responsible: Lee Iacocca, after all, had put his name and face on the line in an unprecedented advertising campaign. At least five books on the fall and rise of Chrysler have now appeared all making the same point.[1] But if Iacocca takes the plaudits for the most drastic managerial reorganization at Chrysler since its foundation, there are also other explanations for the new labor relations climate that go deeper than a change in personalities.

By the mid 1970s new trends in Chrysler's labor relations had already emerged and it was these that were strengthened by the subsequent crisis and managerial reorganization. Far from the last ten years leading to a genuine reconciliation of the interests of management and managed and an 'end of Fordism' and its system of drive control and adversarial bargaining,[2] there has been a continuity with the post-war labor settlement in the mass production industries. Nor has the 'disciplinary effect of higher unemployment rates and the growing threat of layoffs and plant shutdowns'[3] been the only reason for declining strike activity in the second half of the 1970s.

Sectional collective bargaining, the moral assertion of workers' rights and a union tradition of resistance were the three factors underlying shopfloor struggle at Chrysler over the preceding forty years. But in recent times they were all emasculated, and their absence resulted in fewer restraints being imposed on the exercise of managerial authority in Chrysler than at any time since the 1930s. This is not, of course, to argue that the 1980s have witnessed the rebirth of arbitrary dictatorial management. Rather, the argument is that within its own perceptions of labor problems and available solutions, management could exercise almost entirely unrestrained choice as to which strategy to implement. It opened up its possibility of strategic choice. Thus in 1979–82, when management decided to exercise its authority in new ways, the locals had neither the will nor the power to object, while the international officers had no reason to do so.

Section I of this chapter begins with a discussion of the longer-term trends that began to change labor relations. What happened in the mid 1970s to the underlying factors that had previously sustained resistance? How did the union tradition change? Section II considers the impact of the 1973 oil embargo on Chrysler management and the subsequent turn to Iacocca and Ford business methods that led in 1980 to the closure of Dodge Main. Finally, section III considers the evolution of the international union's relationship with management and the emergence of concession bargaining after Chrysler approached bankruptcy in 1979.

I. New trends

In the 1970s two developments coincided to discourage shopfloor resistance at Dodge Main: in the wider world outside, blacks gained more political recognition, while inside the plant, management and UAW greater 'race awareness' reformed the bargaining system to limit the possibilities of generalizing specific grievances. In 1973 Coleman Young, a black Democrat and former 1940s UAW opponent of Reuther, was elected mayor of Detroit. This election and that of increasing numbers of blacks to UAW local executive boards appeared to endorse the view that rights could be won gradually through due process rather than through struggle. The case for action outside union channels became more difficult to argue and on the shopfloor the minority ready to take it became more isolated. Simultaneously, as conflict was reabsorbed into institutional procedures, the sense of moral outrage that triggered wildcats became increasingly limited to situations where management broke its own rules.

The summer wildcats at Chrysler plants in 1973 have been interpreted as indicators of a rising momentum of struggle.[4] But very small numbers of workers were directly involved in them and the issue involved in the first, successful, action was quite different from those in the two subsequent defeats. The first thirteen-hour act of resistance, in July 1973 at the Chrysler Jefferson Avenue assembly plant, was initiated by just two workers who occupied a cage containing the power switch. Their action was successful in achieving the removal of a racist foreman, something that would have been inconceivable five years earlier. But this did not represent a major inroad on managerial authority since open racism was no longer within the rules laid down by Chrysler management.

Aware, however, that a dangerous precedent might have been set, both Chrysler and the UAW stamped hard on the two August walkouts that followed. These wildcats, on the issues of speed-up and production standards, were initiated by very small groups and were followed by widescale dismissals. The new relationship between the company and the international was demonstrated by the UAW mobilizing 1,000 plant committeemen from locals all over the Detroit area to turn up at dawn, two mornings in succession, to help break the Mack Avenue stamping plant strike. After several years in which the UAW had been constrained by the need to re-establish some credibility with its largely new and young black labor force, it was confident enough to confront members who broke management's rules.

The implications of this mobilization were not lost on Chrysler labor relations managers. Chrysler management saw this as the green light for escalation. During the June 1974 Warren Truck plant wildcat strike against the firing of a chief steward and three other body shop workers for leading a 'sick-in' ten days earlier, management not only secured injunctions against illegal picketing but brought a judge to the plant to order the arrests of thirty defiant pickets.[5]

By the mid 1970s when management broke rules that had originally depended on workers' combativity (like proper seniority or foremen being stopped from working), the option of industrial action was no longer considered, and the grievances that were written up went into procedure. In procedure, the inflexible written rules and a rigid case law of umpire decisions effectively established the frontier of shopfloor control wherever management wanted it. Groups of workers only believed it was legitimate to take action outside the procedure when management broke its own rules by, for example, insisting workers remain at their jobs in temperatures it had previously agreed were unacceptable. By August 1979, the definition of management's rights was so clearly established that Chrysler got seven Trenton, Michigan engine plant strikers sent to prison for a week when they refused to obey injunctions to stop picketing after a strike caused by the extreme summer heat. As recently as 1977 heat walkouts had still been regarded by management as natural under extreme weather conditions and the company's 1979 response confirmed a stiffening of managerial authority on the eve of the bail-out request to Congress.

Accompanying the more restricted definition of a 'legitimate' wildcat came a narrowing of the potential appeal of unauthorized action. At Chrysler in the 1940s and 1950s a section or department picket would not generally be crossed by other production workers. By the 1960s such solidarity was exceptional, and by the 1970s collective resistance increasingly became limited to the shift, department or work group *first* affected, and to minimize the risk of further retaliation picket lines would rarely be set up. In-plant actions took over from open confrontations as they had done in GM and Ford plants since the 1940s: stoppages lasting only a few minutes, 'sick-ins', refusals to work overtime, and the slow execution of orders became the dominant tactics.[6] The collective character of worker resistance dissolved into the individual forms of protest that had always existed: lateness, absenteeism, poor quality work, restriction of output and occasional moments of sabotage.

This individualization of shopfloor struggle could only have recrystallized into a new collective movement if the next ten years had both repeated the 1960s boom, and continued to deny black workers substantial political and economic progress. The trend away from collectivism was, however, reinforced by two major economic crises which led to the lay-offs in 1974 and in 1979 of big sections of the 'new' labor force.

These various factors working against independent shopfloor activity were accompanied by the consolidation of a different tradition among the group of blacks who ran Local 3 and, after Reuther's death, in the international union. From 1950 until 1970 the UAW under Reuther had a fairly 'civilized relationship' with the auto companies.[7] The relationship was based on the international not supporting local resistance to managerial authority, in return for which the UAW extracted the maximum price for its members' labor. In bargaining to extract this high price Reuther was also prepared to allow the controlled explosion of bottled-up plant-level conflict. Thus underlying the 'civilized relationship' was an assumption of conflict of interests between collective labor and capital. However, by the early 1980s the UAW had distanced itself from that assumption. Bargaining became essentially 'consultative' and 'non-adversarial', and was about the *mutual* problems American labor and capital faced in a contracting world economy. The new assumption was that large areas of the United States were threatened by deindustrialization, a threat to both management and managed alike. Both the local and international UAW ceased to operate as organizations whose dynamic was provided by the need to mobilize *against* management.

The change in attitude was accelerated by the 1979 crisis, but had already been signalled in Dodge Main and in international policy from the mid 1970s. In September 1973 the Chrysler contract only scraped through in the Local 3 ratification vote as several hundred workers remained unconvinced by the propaganda barrage in favor of the 'historic' contract and believed more could have been won and less conceded. The production workers endorsed it by 613 to 528 and the skilled tradesmen by 25 to 23 in a turnout of just 13% of the plant's 9,000 workers.[8] As the oil embargo bit into Chrysler's sales in 1974, however, it was the 'young militant workers', as the *Dodge Main News* termed the opponents of local president Hardy, who were laid off first.[9] Hamtramck's 8,000 workforce was virtually cut in half by the lay-off of the whole of the second shift. In May 1974 Hardy stood down to take a staff job with the international union and Joe Davis was elected Dodge Main's youngest-ever president, with 'Big John' Smith as his vice-president.[10] They immediately launched a campaign to change the period of office for all plant and local positions from two- to three-year terms.[11]

The Local 3 campaign to implement the rule changes passed at the 1973 UAW Los Angeles convention reflected the incumbents' confidence that the laid off militants wouldn't bother to return to Hamtramck to vote. The high seniority workers who held their jobs in Dodge Main despite the thousands of dismissals between 1965 and 1973 were those Davis appealed to for support for the three-year term:

> The membership of this local union should not be confused by the drive being put on in the Hamtramck Assembly Plant against the three year term. The only reason this drive is being put on is to allow those individuals who are passing the petitions to run for elective office in 1976 rather than 1977 . . .
> It is only good common sense to have all elections at the same time in order to save money . . .
> It is my honest feeling that activities such as a Christmas Party for the children of our members and a family picnic each year are a must. We cannot hold these things unless we find ways and means to collect the money to pay for same. By holding three year elections, these programs can become a reality.
> Do not be fooled by propaganda that the 2-year term will give you better representation. Remember, a divided leadership never work together to the full extent that they can help the membership.[12]

The language of confrontation and mobilization had vanished from the lips of Local 3 officers. Instead of an argument, Davis called on workers to vote for a kids' Christmas party and a summer picnic – and won by a three to one majority.[13] Local 3's first summer picnic since the 1940s eventually took place on August 1, 1976 – in time to be remembered in the 1977 elections.[14]

In August 1975 Hamtramck Assembly called back 2,000 of the lower seniority workers on the second shift to work on the 1976 models.[15] After a year's lay-off they found the workplace atmosphere significantly different from that of 1973. Independent black politics in Detroit and in the nation had collapsed, or entered into the Democratic Party. While, in the plants, returning workers found the workplace union organization was more remote than ever. A joint Local 3–Chrysler labor relations redistricting exercise had been held at the all-time employment low of February 1975.[16] The number of chief stewards had remained at around ninety for as long as the plant had 12,000 workers. It had fallen naturally to about sixty when employment was cut back to 8,000 in 1970 and 1971 and stayed there when employment rose to 12,000 again in 1973. But when 75% of the plant's workers were laid off during the 1975 model year, the number of chief stewards was finally cut to under forty.[17]

The redistricting exercise coincided with the extension of the surviving chief stewards' terms of office from two to three years. Together the changes made the re-establishment of an opposition network very difficult, especially since the 1967–73 'young militants' were dispersed throughout the plant when they were called back. The work groups which, by the late 1960s, had established sufficient trust and confidence to create collective sectional loyalties against unfair management actions were split up – partly by design and partly through automatic 'bumping' in lay-off and recall procedures.[18] Individual black militants who returned were more isolated than ever and were also faced by many black supervisors and an overwhelming majority of black stewards and local officers.[19]

Moreover, Local 3 had changed more deeply than in color as the retirement or isolation of those who carried the earlier independent tradition from the 1950s into the 1960s assisted a shift to more dependence upon the international. The Pasicas, Liskas and Foxes, and even the Domanskis of the 1960s generation of Local 3 officers, had all acquired their union experience leading and participating in the wildcat strikes of the 1940s and 1950s. And it was their generation who used the thirty-and-out contract retirement provisions to quit auto work in the late 1960s and early 1970s. In contrast, the last three Dodge Main presidents, Andy Hardy, Joe Davis and John Smith, and virtually their entire executive boards and plant committees, were hired into Dodge Main in the 'quiet' early 1960s.

The international union also changed. Under Reuther the assessment of the UAW as 'a right-of-center union with a left-of-center reputation' was close to the mark.[20] Reuther wielded immense power cloaked in a very limited formal democracy. His strength meant the international might have sat out the demand for more black representation. In 1970 the position was that while 30% of UAW members were black only 13%

of staffers were.[21] But when a very surprised Leonard Woodcock assumed the presidency of the UAW after Reuther's aircrash death in 1970, it opened up the possibility of change.

Woodcock, an ex-Socialist Party survivor from Reuther's distant radical past, was elevated to the presidency by the closest possible vote on the international executive board: thirteen votes to twelve against the man Reuther had been grooming as his successor, Chrysler department vice-president, Doug Fraser.[22] To stay at the top of the UAW since 1947, when he was first elected on the Reuther slate to the IEB (after just six months' work in an auto plant), Woodcock had long since abandoned his early radicalism and had learned a great deal about survival. His narrow selection led him to try and strengthen his base by courting popularity with the membership in the 1970 strike against GM. This was the first time GM had been struck since Reuther's epic name-making struggle in 1945–46.

A second way Woodcock strengthened his personal power base was through pushing blacks forward at international level. Dodge Main's new black leadership was a convenient source of black recruits to the international staff: in 1970, Charlie Brooks, Local 3's first black vice-president, in 1974, Andy Hardy, Local 3's first black president, and in 1978 his successor, Joe Davis, all went onto the international payroll.

The international union, originally staffed by activists who had risen to prominence through their capacities in organizing rank and file struggle against the corporations (or through their friendships with those who had), also underwent a transformation in the early 1970s. A generation of 'pork-choppers' replaced the generation of former activists and agitators. The end of the Reuther era and the rise to high office of a second generation of union bureaucrats who were more experienced in suppressing rank and file militancy than in mobilizing it, was widely welcomed by management. Clancy, Dodge Main's personnel manager throughout the 1970s, recalled:

> Relationships changed remarkably in the 1970s between us and the UAW. It required statesmanship of a high order by a lot of people. There had to be a philosophical thrust on the part of the international union towards harmony and to provide the opportunity to effect harmony . . .
> I'm thinking of occasions when their people got out of line and went undisciplined and anarchistic, and they would take disciplinary action and say – 'Get the hell into the main stream of the labor movement or get the hell out.'[23]

The 'philosophical thrust' to greater cooperation, Clancy suggests, was provided by Fraser during his period as the UAW's Chrysler vice-president:

The international union kept a close eye on their own people. Fraser ran a pretty professional shop. Of course, he had to be assured we had someone there who would sort things out on our side. But when he was, if I had a problem I'd call Chrysler Corporate Headquarters and they'd contact Fraser or someone else in the international who would help our problem.[24]

Fraser, in this respect, was doing no more than bringing Chrysler's labor relations into line with the pattern of problem solving at GM and Ford, where behind-the-scene contacts between the union department and corporate headquarters had been a way of life since the 1950s. But the impact of *change* is always more marked than the impact of consistency. Even before he became UAW president in 1977 Fraser had become identified with pressure for industry-wide cooperation.

The argument is not that shopfloor grievances disappeared as the UAW and the company grew closer together. Chrysler's relationship to the car market virtually ensured an organization of work that encouraged conflict. It still manipulated production levels primarily through lay-offs and rehires, so employment in its plants was significantly less stable than at Ford and GM.[25] Also by maintaining a presence in all sectors of the market it was forced to run more models on its lines, giving workers a less stable job situation. The potential for conflict was demonstrated in the mini-boom of 1976–77, when Chrysler rehired 24,000 workers and unauthorized strikes erupted in 1977 over working in freezing conditions in an extreme winter and in ovenlike conditions in the summer heat-wave that followed. However, the seventy-six unauthorized strikes in 1977 were a warning to management not to breach its own rules on proper working temperatures, they were not strikes to impose new restraints.

Fraser's closer relationship with Chrysler encouraged local officers to reach similar accommodations with their opposite numbers. Local agreements were already largely ritualized consultations about a limited range of working conditions and job classifications in the 1960s. But the occasional combativity of national bargaining had ensured that the local bargaining relationship also recognized conflicting interests. So arguments about the number of pay phones near the lines at Dodge Main reflected both the *national* balance of forces and whether the international was seeking conflict, as well as the tradition, politics and personalities of the two local teams of negotiators. In the 1970s, as conflict got put on national bargaining's back burner, so this also happened at local level.

Local 3's negotiations on its 1976 agreement illustrate this tendency of bargaining to shift from an adversarial arena to a consultative one. Talks began in July 1976 and quickly 'broke down', leading to a strike vote in

Table 13 *Dodge Main: an analysis of the plant-wide and trim department demands raised in the 1976–77 Chrysler–Local 3 contract negotiations*

Demand negotiated	Plant-wide restraints			Demand negotiated	Trim department restraints		
	Social	Efficiency	Worker		Social	Efficiency	Worker
Health and safety: roof leaks, lighting, fans water fountains, etc.	3	9		Fans for extracting fumes and cooling		5	
Meals and vending facilities	1	8		New smoking rooms	2		
Availability of lockers	4			New lunch area, pop and coffee machines		2	
Parking lot problems			3	More lockers	2		
Elevator service			2	Extra time clock		1	
				Elevator service		2	
				Extra pay phones	2		
				Heating complaints	2		
				Clean 6th floor of trim shop daily		1	
				Supply new hog ring guns, metal plates for body pushers		2	
				Extra coveralls	1		
Plant environment	8	22			9	13	
Pay discrepancies			5				
Medical department: passes, proper treatment	2	1	1				
Insurance and compensation office hours	1						
Notification of PQX cases	1						
Operational rules	4	6	1				
Shift transfer request book: proper receipts			1	Notification to UAW of all job changes	1		
Notice of lay-offs, callbacks etc: in writing			1	Equalization of overtime hours			1
Attendance penalties: issued quickly and record clean after two months		1	2				
Seniority workers to be offered overtime before probationary workers			1				
New wording for emergency call-out of workers from the plant			2				
Managerial rules		1	7		1		1
Insistence on spelling out in full 'failed to follow a direct order' offense			1	'Environmental relief' for job where workers jump in and out of every car			1
Foremen working			1				
Managerial authority			2				1
Total	12	29	10		10	13	2

Source: Dodge Main News, January 22, 1977.

August. Nothing much was then expected to happen until after the national contract was signed on November 5, 1976. Despite this, regular meetings of Hamtramck Assembly labor relations and personnel staff with the local's ten-person negotiating committee continued. They cemented closer relationships between management and the four local officers, five plant committee members, and an international rep. from Region One. Negotiations began in earnest only in November and continued for two months until the final agreement was reached on January 7, 1977. The whole bargaining process over just one agreement had lasted seven months.[26] Even if the issues being negotiated had been dominated by questions of managerial authority and struggled-for restraints, the negotiating process alone would have defused and demobilized any potential resistance.

Many aspects of the work environment were discussed, but neither the demands tabled by Local 3 nor the final local agreement significantly challenged managerial authority on the shopfloor. Table 13 breaks down in two ways, the plant-wide and trim department demands raised in Local 3 in 1976, during the height of the last big boom in Chrysler sales and production. First it classifies the demands or potential restraints on management into the four general issue areas: the plant environment, operational rules, managerial rules and managerial authority. Then it assesses the content of these demands, whether they are social restraints required to comply with the law or common working practices elsewhere, or efficiency restraints that would improve the efficiency of labor, or worker-imposed restraints. The demands that made the list submitted to management had been distilled through unit and plant committees into a 'bargainable' shape, but what they show of the bargainers' expectations is revealing.

The most frequent issue raised was the plant environment: improvements to it made up 88% of trim department demands and 59% of the plant-wide demands. Moreover, most of these environmental restraints could be justified by the bargaining committee in terms of increasing the efficiency of the plant. The second largest issue raised concerned improvements in the operational rules governing the administration of the plant's payment and sickness procedures. More overtly job-linked managerial rule improvements came third in frequency. These were for written restraints on management to humanize its existing job rules. The issue of direct managerial authority, of management's shopfloor prerogatives, barely surfaced.

Taking the two 'managerial' categories of table 13 together, another observation can be made. Workers felt least legitimacy in raising managerial issues at the department level. When they were raised, demands related to labor control issues would be raised at plant level, and even then overwhelmingly in a procedural context: seven of the ten demands for restraints on managerial prerogatives were to improve existing rules. The union negotiators appeared confident enough only to make demands that management exercise its plant-wide authority 'fairly' within its own rules. Demands for stricter limits to that authority, especially at departmental level, were almost non-existent.

The evidence of few demands for restraints on managerial authority is confirmed by the actual agreement. President Joe Davis summarized its 'highlights':

> Some of the highlights of the Agreement are as follows:
> A Vending Service for our food which would give us completely enclosed air conditioned cafeteria with hot food and a menu approved by the Local Union. Breakfast will be served prior to the start of the shift each day that the plant operates.
> Many of the problems experienced by the members regarding pay shortages and checks not available for an employee when the week's work is finished have been settled. We have firm language that will take care of this problem in the future.[27]

The few challenges to managerial authority or its rules that had been made were brushed aside. The demand that foremen who continued to 'work on hourly-rated jobs after being counselled by the union be given time off as a disciplinary penalty, up to and including discharge' was dropped. In return Hamtramck Assembly labor relations agreed to circulate copies of Chrysler's letter to union negotiators stating it was not policy to have foremen do hourly-paid work that had been included in the national contract. At the same time the plant-wide demand for the elimination of 'failed to follow a direct order' as a reason for disciplinary action was settled by management agreeing 'that the reason for discipline will be specifically stated'. The other demands for managerial rule changes were given similar treatment.

The only progress was where management could see efficiency gains or was under legislative pressure. As it did on the Chrysler works council of the pre-UAW days, management could easily 'assure the union that roof leaks will be repaired on a continuing basis' and even give a priority list of roof leaks 'for completion as weather permits'.[28] Workers' expectations were not dashed – they were never raised in the first place. Consultative bargaining was a process that bore little connection to shopfloor frustrations. In contrast with the 1930s, however, it was not the workplace which precipitated the next major move in labor relations, but management.

II. Management in crisis

By the mid 1970s Chrysler's profits were too low to finance its massive debt, its international pretensions and investments in new products. Something had to give. Chrysler's downfall resulted from an accumulation of poor management decisions that left Chrysler wide open to the 1973 oil embargo, the introduction of federal fuel economy and safety standards, and to the massive penetration of the US market by Japanese

Table 14 *US new car registrations, import penetration and Chrysler car production, 1960–79*

Five-year average	Total US new car registrations (millions)	Imported car registrations (a) (millions)	Imports (%)	Chrysler US production (millions)
1960–64	6.998	0.417	6.02	0.935
1965–69	9.106	0.811	8.9	1.451
1970–74	9.752	1.467	15.04	1.337
1975–79	10.024	1.842	18.38	1.105

Source: Ward's *Automotive Yearbook, 1980*, 152.
(a) All Volkswagen registrations were still counted as imports in 1979 although large numbers were then being produced at Volkswagen's New Stanton plant, purchased from Chrysler in 1977.

cars. For the weakest major American auto maker, floating on debt, and already suffering the consequences of the virtual standstill in new investment in the 1970–71 recession, the second half of the 1970s were disastrous. Chrysler's share of US production held up at 16% in 1973 and 1974 but was down to 10% by 1980.

The four-month embargo on Middle East oil sales to the United States that began in October 1973 increased fuel costs and pushed buyers towards more fuel efficient cars. GM already had a long-term strategy for 'down-sizing' each of its basic model lines. Not to be deflected by the recession, it increased its capital investment from $2.1 billion in 1973 to $2.5 billion in 1974. At Chrysler, by contrast, where there had been no forward planning on fuel efficiency, the recession and the company's non-existent credit rating forced cuts in investment on plant, tools and equipment from $629 million in 1973 to $466 million in 1974.[29]

The oil embargo also stimulated the federal agencies responsible for the 1970 Clean Air requirements to push ahead faster than industry wished. The details are not significant here, what is important is that the smaller manufacturers, Chrysler and American Motors, were adversely affected by the need to raise standards of fuel efficiency and safety. The larger manufacturers could defray the costs of research and design over basic model lines that included usually four or five car types, while Chrysler had at most only two car types operating in a particular market segment. These additional costs were a convenient explanation of Chrysler's poor returns in 1974–75 and again in 1978, and John Riccardo, president from 1975–79, certainly earned his nickname as the bad-tempered 'Flamethrower' in blaming them.[30] What was needed, however, was the reallocation of resources to cope with the new market situation, and where Chrysler management failed, others didn't.

Imported cars began to take a large share of the American market in the early 1970s: by the second half of the 1970s, as table 14 shows, imported cars were even more important. Imports, particularly Volkswagens, increased steadily in the 1960s, but the cars that tipped the balance against Chrysler in the 1970s were Japanese models.

In 1968 and 1969, when the Japanese challenge began, VWs still accounted for 55% of all cars and trucks imported into the US. Toyota and Datsun's share was just 16%. But between 1975 and 1979 the share of all car and truck imports taken by the big five Japanese firms, Toyota, Datsun, Honda, Mazda and Subaru, rose from 48% to 66%. The competition was fiercest in the growing compact and subcompact market segments where profit margins had always been lower. There was massive substitution of imported Japanese cars for American cars in the 1974–75 recession and at the onset of the 1979 slump. Between 1974 and 1975, when Chrysler's share of the declining total of car registrations fell by 2%, the share held by imports rose by 2.5%; and when recession struck again in 1979 and Chrysler's market share fell 1%, imported cars took nearly an extra 5%.[31] The availability of Japanese cars meant there was no room for Chrysler to raise prices to establish profit levels high enough to meet its debts. Unlike GM and Ford, it had neither massive resources nor a profitable international empire to fall back on. To stay in business, Chrysler had to take still more debt on board, and to reorganize its management.

Chrysler chairman Lynn Townsend reacted swiftly to the first sign of crisis in 1970. Company president Virgil Boyd was sacrificed after a new line of full-size cars coincided with a recession and a market shift to smaller cars. In his place Townsend appointed a former fellow accountant from Touche, Ross, the same Detroit firm he himself had worked for, John Riccardo.[32] The cosmetic effect of this management reshuffle wore off as losses rose from $52 million in 1974 to $259.5 million in 1975, following the launch of a full-size passenger car line at the same time as the oil embargo. For the first time since 1933, no dividends were paid.

At fifty-six, after fourteen years in Chrysler's top job, and having made himself an extremely wealthy man, Townsend's own card was finally marked. *Fortune* later described him as 'more like an old-style Hollywood film star than a midwestern auto company chief', and added bitterly: 'he never really seemed to understand the fundamental business of his company'.[33] Townsend named Riccardo as his successor as chairman and another protégé, Gene Cafiero, as Chrysler president, and retired.[34] Townsend defended their lack of experience, saying: 'At this level of management it doesn't make a difference what your background is.'[35] The idea, Riccardo's successor commented later, 'was that a guy with talent could climb any mountain. After a few years of being shuffled around, everybody at Chrysler was doing something he wasn't trained for'.[36] The lack of specialism among what had swollen over twenty years to thirty-five vice-presidents led to a lack of confidence and attitudes alternating between bravado, buck-passing and indecision. Townsend's last legacy was to place into the top jobs two men who didn't like each other and who had different ideas as to how to rescue the company.[37]

The change at the top did not immediately affect the company's business strategy. Chrysler continued to compete in all segments of the market and to maintain instant product availability (and high executive bonuses) through production for the sales bank rather than production for sales. Quality, too, took second place to output. The 1975 models had been rushed through by Riccardo and were launched with major engineering faults, while cuts in the number of quality-control staff in 1975 were not reversed in the mini-boom of 1976–77. Poor quality showed when the new cars went out on the road; by 1978 research on early customer complaints showed Chrysler quality some 30% worse than Ford or GM.[38]

Chrysler's reputation as a company run by sound financial men was maintained by Riccardo, who agreed with fellow former accountant Townsend that he could manage without specialized internal financial controls.[39] Riccardo kept in close touch with the banks on whose credit Chrysler was now trading. In the mid 1970s he was forced to make two world trips to prominent foreign banks to enlist their cooperation. These trips paid off. As long as Chrysler kept up its interest payments and repayments of principal, its very size as America's tenth largest corporation was its guarantee. Banks from all over the world wanted to lend it money. As late as November 1978 the international banking world was ready to give still more credit. An assistant vice-president of Barclays Bank International said, 'None of the bankers seriously thought that this major corporation was going to flop on its belly.'[40] Few questions were asked, even by the strong financial interests on the Chrysler board. In 1971 twelve of Chrysler's twenty-three board members were also directors or trustees of major banks or financial institutions and this was true through the whole decade. By 1979 ten of Chrysler's thirteen outside directors had interlocking directorships in banks and other financial companies. They remained quiet as long as the mounting debt burden didn't interfere with dividends. As a controlling mechanism, overlooking the running of the company, the board was totally ineffective.

Where Riccardo differed from Townsend was in his readiness to cut his international losses. He had not personally built Chrysler's worldwide empire and it was easier for him to signal the retreat than it was for

Townsend. In the 1975 crisis Townsend's earlier international expansion, through the acquisition of minor loss-making overseas subsidiaries, was a millstone around the parent company's neck.[41] Chrysler had neither the managerial capacity nor the resources to restore these subsidiaries to profitability. If anything, the diversion of managerial capacity to the overseas holdings was even more damaging than the diversion of financial resources. A Chrysler treasurer commented later: 'The parent was hurt more by the attention required of high-level management overseas than by investments.'[42] But the estimated $200 million lost by Chrysler US in attempts to keep Chrysler UK afloat didn't help.[43]

Within days of becoming president, Riccardo flew to London and got the British government to underwrite future losses incurred by Chrysler UK. And within a year, Riccardo was considering the sale of the whole Chrysler European operation. The sale eventually came in August 1978 after nearly two years of on–off discussions. Riccardo and Peugeot president Jean-Paul Payrare signed the deal on British soil (where tax advantages for Peugeot would be enormous). In exchange for 25% of its world-wide capacity Chrysler got $230 million in cash to pump into its domestic product program and a 15% share of Peugeot stock worth a further $200 million.[44]

Despite Riccardo's international pruning, Chrysler's market share was down to 11.8% by 1978 and in that year its operating losses slumped back to the level of 1975.[45]

Chrysler's net profit or losses ($m)	
1974	− 52
1975	− 282
1976	+ 423
1977	+ 163
1978	− 205
1979	−1,097
1980	−1,710

Riccardo had hired Harold Sperlich, Ford's key product design executive, and initiated a rescue plan that would provide a new model in 1980, but in the short term he had run out of answers.[46] In August 1978, less than a month after Henry Ford II had fired his company president, Lee Iacocca, both Riccardo and the Chrysler director who was manager of the Rockefeller family fortune asked him to head up Chrysler. Three months later, the 54-year-old Iacocca got Cafiero's job as president, with the understanding he would take over Riccardo's job as chief operating officer a year later.

The appointment was more than another change in top personnel. By making an executive with thirty-two years' experience at Ford its top man, Chrysler was buying (for $1.5 million down and an annual salary of $360,000) more than one individual: it was buying the Ford system, and it was replacing the accountants who had headed the company since 1961 with a car salesman, the architect of the supremely successful Ford Mustang sales drive of the 1960s. Approaching catastrophe was the catalyst and Iacocca happened to be available.[47]

Iacocca quickly hired several other current or retired Ford managers and even poached Ford's advertising agency to run Chrysler's account. The Ford executives were contemptuous of the old Chrysler managerial tradition. Iacocca argued that 'the Townsends of this world . . . wrecked this industry' and found it incomprehensible 'that in 1978 a large company could still be run like a small grocery store'.[48] When *Time* magazine gave Iacocca the accolade of a front cover and the title 'Detroit's comeback kid' in 1983, pre-Iacocca top management had virtually disappeared. The 'bunch of mini-empires' that had survived since the 1930s were welded together in an accountable committee system, and those who didn't like it were fired. Thirty-three of the thirty-five vice-presidents were fired within three years and the four most senior officers left were all ex-Ford. Only one of the restructured nine-member top operations committee survived the first two years.[49]

Chrysler's shake-up was not just in personnel as in Townsend's purge seventeen years earlier, but also in work organization and labor relations. A new quality control system and new financial controls directly affected day-to-day operations. Quality control was re-established as a separate management function. This encouraged front-line supervisors to report recurring manufacturing faults rather than deal with poor quality by the standard tactic of increasing the pressure on the workers doing the job. This change filtered point-of-production conflict back to the engineering and design departments where they could more easily be resolved.

The new financial control system let Chrysler accurately identify the cost and profitability, or absence of it, of individual components or processes. This directly encouraged product standardization. Since the early 1960s Chrysler had been providing a mass of options in its attempt to spread its narrow model range across all segments of the market. At the Warren truck plant, for example, seven shades of white were offered to customers, and these were now cut to two.[50] This standardization had a big impact on the labor process: changes in the 'mix' of work were involved in many assembly line disputes. Even though no actual increase in work was involved, if a job sequence was suddenly changed, the anaesthetic effect of a steady work routine would be disturbed. By cutting the variety of options coming down the line, and by ensuring longer runs on the presses and in the machine shop, the new management was able to reduce the potential number of points of shopfloor conflict.

Iacocca also established clearer channels of managerial responsibility and information and introduced the standard Ford practice of management-by-objectives. The quarterly listing of individual managers and executives' objectives, for checking against performance, stimulated an on-going review of managerial efficiency in all departments. The policy quickly pinpointed the weakness of building cars for the sales bank rather than in response to customers' orders.

Chrysler's large cars were again swelling the sales bank and working capital was falling rapidly. Iacocca moved rapidly to phase out the sales bank by cutting production and laid off 15,000 workers in January 1979 and a further 5,000 by early June. But this strategic shift away from a sales bank was overtaken by events. Iacocca had only been Chrysler president for two months when the Iranian revolution overthrew the Shah and triggered the doubling of oil prices. In 1979 Americans turned again to smaller cars and Chrysler was left with a growing bank of unsold cars as its market share tumbled. Almost in desperation the new ex-Ford top management team scanned the books for cost savings. A 32-year-old trim plant in Lyons, Michigan headed the list and 'Chrysler's flagship' plant, Dodge Main, followed.

The decision to close Hamtramck Assembly was not surprising. Dodge Main's eight-storey structure meant its plant overheads were exceptionally high when production was low, while stock movement around the plant was always more complicated (and hence more costly) than in the single storey plants of the 1950s and 1960s. So when one of its four production lines was taken off in January 1979, and the labor force of about 8,500 cut by 25%, it became what the jargon called 'overfacilitated' – too much investment and too many overheads producing too little output.[51] What was a surprise was the ease with which this once militant plant was closed. This was a mark of the weakness of workplace unionism in Chrysler by the late 1970s, and an encouragement to Iacocca to pursue the rest of his rationalization program still more quickly.[52]

Chrysler's labor relations department planned the shut-down carefully to avoid creating unnecessary problems with the UAW or the remaining workers. Management announced on May 30, 1979 that the plant would close in June 1980. The aim was for the closure to gradually become legitimate and inevitable. Under the plan the UAW could go through all the motions of heated opposition but by the time the actual closure was imminent the will to resist would be gone. The long notice doubled as a gesture towards long-term consultation with the international and an uncharacteristically astute piece of forward-planning by the labor relations department. It ensured that the 'Save Dodge Main' campaign was doomed from the start. While 3,000 people turned out on the first Saturday demonstrations, there was no immediate urgency to strike the plant or prevent work being transferred elsewhere.[53] Militant speeches were translated into lobbying Congressmen, and the campaign rapidly lost momentum, despite widespread support from the people of Hamtramck.

The original closure time scale was, however, overtaken by the sharpening of the crisis. Chrysler's 1979 losses were rising to $1 billion, a record for any American company. In August 1979 workers on two more of Dodge Main's lines were laid off and from September 1979 only the first shift on one line was still working. The seniority system, then worked, operated with a vengeance for the 2,300 remaining workers. None of them had under ten years' seniority, and many had started there, like Edie Fox, in the 1940s when they were in their late teens or early twenties. They clung to full-time employment by 'bumping' younger workers – and so were forced to move from their previous easier jobs in material handling, the stores and sub-assemblies back on direct production. 'It was terrible,' recalled Edie Fox, 'seeing all those workers in their fifties back working on the line, jumping in and out of cars like they had last done twenty years earlier.'[54]

Finally, these workers joined management in wanting the closure to happen quickly – to end the agony of exhaustion on the line and to enable them to collect severance and early retirement benefits. They had had enough. Between 1,500 and 2,000 of these Dodge Main veterans retired rather than move to the jobs on the second shift at the Jefferson Avenue assembly plant they were entitled to.[55] When management announced on December 9 it was bringing the closure forward to January 1980 there was no resistance left. Clancy was still worried, but only about the quality of the remaining cars: 'The only real worry I had was that the last four weeks of production would be bad – but this was the best quality we had built there for years, that last month.'[56] Even this was taken care of. Chrysler gave the supervisors a commitment that if they went 'out of here pridefully' they too would all be guaranteed jobs on the second shift at the Jefferson Avenue assembly plant, building the new K-car scheduled to be launched in August.[57] So the last cars produced at Dodge Main were built with surplus supervisors literally all over the place.[58]

The closure was unstoppable. Clancy's view was that 'You'd have to have had leadership to do anything different'.[59] But a leadership capable of mobilizing resistance had not existed since DRUM's defeat in the early 1970s. Neither the organizational nor the ideological basis for collective resistance remained. The only 'legitimate' collective form of expression had become the UAW local and national apparatus. Elsewhere, Chrysler workers exercised their frustration by throwing out half the incumbents in forty local officer elections in 1978 and 1979.[60] But the anger remained unstructured and the new administrations operated within the same rules as their immediate predecessors.

At Dodge Main, 'Big John' Smith, who had taken over the Local 3 presidency in January 1978 when Joe Davis took a job with the international, was certainly not going to lead any fight. Even the remotest chance of such an eventuality had been ruled out by the UAW campaign to win Congressional backing for a federal government bail-out. Smith spent the last weeks deep in paperwork ensuring that as many of Dodge Main's 8,500 on-roll workers 'bumped' other workers in other plants – a possibility established in the special Detroit-wide transfer agreement negotiated by the international as a supplement to the 1979 contract. Two and a half years after the closure, and a year after the plant was physically demolished, nearly 5,000 of these workers had been offered jobs elsewhere.[61]

The seven-month closure process, as Clancy proudly said, 'didn't affect production'.[62] On January 4, 1980 the last car went through the final assembly department and the conveyor stopped. The remaining workers cleaned up and went home. The plant that had produced cars continuously since November 1914 was shut. One hundred and fifty yards away down Joseph Campau, the UAW Local 3 hall closed a few weeks later.

III. Labor relations in the early 1980s

The death of Dodge Main's local union, like its birth, was symbolic of the arrival of a new period in management–labor relations, for it was brought forward, and the small possibility of resistance finally eliminated, after UAW president Doug Fraser agreed to treat Chrysler as a 'special case' in the 1979 contract negotiations. The smooth closure helped the emergence of a 'non-adversarial relationship' between the UAW and the auto companies that legitimated two major new developments: contract concessions and quality circles.

In 1977 Woodcock retired and the 60-year-old Fraser was finally allowed the reins of power. In one way he was like his predecessor, another stop-gap president chosen more because of his length of service and the proximity of his retirement than because of exceptional talent. But, as the last of the old 1940s Reuther caucus, Fraser was particularly capable of dressing up management–union cooperation in radical rheto ric. When, like Woodcock, he felt he had to open his presidency with a gesture of defiance, he attacked the Carter administration's failure to implement its promised pro-labor measures, and slammed GM for failing to support the 'fragile, unwritten compact' between labor and management. GM, he charged, had not countered the backwoodsmen–employer propaganda that 'labor power' was a growing menace. Business leaders were forcing the UAW to return to the struggle perspective of the 1930s:

> I believe leaders of the business community, with few exceptions, have chosen to wage a one-sided class war today in this country – a war against working people, the unemployed, the poor, the minorities, the very young and the very old, and even many in the middle class of our society. The leaders of industry, commerce and finance in the United States have broken and discarded the fragile, unwritten compact previously existing during a past period of growth and progress . . .
>
> I cannot sit there seeking unity with the leaders of American industry, while they try to destroy us and ruin the lives of the people I represent. I would rather sit with the rural poor, the desperate children of urban blight, the victims of racism, and the working people seeking a better life . . .
>
> We in the UAW intend to reforge the links with those who believe in struggle: the kind of people who sat down in the factories in the 1930s and who marched in Selma in the 1960s.
>
> I cannot assure you that we will be successful in making new alliances and forming new coalitions to help our nation find its way. But I can assure you that we will try.[63]

Fraser was actually doing two things in this speech. He was warning the auto industry against pursuing an open shop (non-union) policy as it relocated in the sunbelt states;[64] and he was fuming against GM for its seeming ignorance of the danger to the industry posed by high fuel prices and the Japanese challenge.

The 1978 rhetoric of a 'one-sided class war' soon changed to full cooperation with the new Iacocca management under the dual impact of the 1979 recession combined with a Japanese challenge that threatened the survival of large parts of the domestic US auto industry. Moreover, Iacocca's unprecedented managerial and labor shake-out had removed any middle ground. Iacocca's public attacks on previous mismanagement at Chrysler gave Fraser one argument to use within the UAW in support of UAW concessions, while the context of unprecedented losses gave him another.

Once Fraser allowed financial losses to determine a new bargaining pattern with Iacocca, it would only take poor results at Ford and GM in 1981 and 1982 to win similar concessions. Fraser's experience with

Chrysler prepared him to lead the whole UAW into acceptance of quality circles, employee involvement, plant closures and, in 1982, into concessions at Ford and GM. The 1978 rhetoric of class war had concealed a clear desire for class peace. This is why, less than a year after quitting Carter's Labor Management Group, the 'new coalition' rhetorically demanded by Fraser in 1978 took the form of a joint UAW–company delegation to Washington to plead for federal funds to bail out Chrysler.

Chrysler moved towards total collapse in 1979 as the overthrow of the Shah of Iran led rapidly to a new rise in oil prices and another major customer shift to fuel-efficient cars, and triggered a world recession. The domestic car market fell for four consecutive years from its 1978 peak, and despite Chrysler's management changes in 1970, 1975 and 1978, the unthinkable nearly happened: America's tenth biggest company almost went to the wall. In August 1979 Riccardo begged the federal government for a $1 billion tax concession. But in a pre-election year the Carter administration was unwilling to be seen handing over such sums on a plate. The request for tax relief to be offset against projected profits for 1981 and 1982 was rejected and government agencies began to estimate the impact of the largest-ever corporate bankruptcy in US history. Congressional hearings then began on another option – a federal loan guarantee. This was far from Riccardo's liking. It involved providing Congress with an unprecedented amount of confidential company information on profits and product plans, and the establishment of an emergency loan-guarantee board with powers to administer the loan. So in September Riccardo announced he was stepping down immediately in favor of Iacocca.[65]

Immediately Fraser was informed of the depth of Chrysler's problems he agreed to use UAW influence in Washington for the bail-out, and, to show good faith, he allowed the 1976 contract to expire in early September 1979 without any 'working without a contract' disputes. Negotiations continued smoothly until agreement was reached six weeks later on October 25. In the new contract Fraser broke the big three bargaining pattern to give Chrysler concessions that added up to $203 million below Ford and GM's costs. The concessions delayed a rise in the basic wage by six months and put back to 1981 the introduction of eight workers' paid personal holidays. Improvements in Chrysler workers' pensions in January 1980 were cut to only 70% of the increases to be paid at Ford and GM.[66] The international's wholehearted support led Iacocca to agree to much greater involvement by international officers in all levels of company–union relationships, and he offered Fraser a seat on the Chrysler board from the next AGM in May 1980.[67] It was also agreed that in future, international reps could sit in on the last stage of plant-level discussion of grievances. The greater participation of international officers who were more remote from the shopfloor helped smooth the way for the introduction of new technology, labor savings and tighter lateness and absence procedures.

In October 1979, Fraser and director of the UAW's Chrysler department, vice-president Mark Stepp, stressed to their own members that while concessions were the only alternative to total closure, they were only temporary:

> There is no way your bargaining committee would allow any deviation from the pattern if we were not convinced that Chrysler was 'on the brink' and that concessions are necessary to save the jobs of Chrysler workers . . .
> Despite the concessions, in the third year Chrysler workers will reach the pattern achieved at GM and Ford.[68]

'Full parity' with GM and Ford was promised by May 1982 and the concessions were approved. Confident that ratification would be recommended by the 256-member Chrysler Bargaining Council meeting in Kansas City, Fraser and Stepp flew to Washington on October 31 to hear Carter ask Congress to approve a $1.5 billion loan guarantee conditional on Chrysler matching it with another $1.5 billion.

Fraser's promise of a return to parity was quickly blown off course when Congress imposed 'take-backs' as a condition for agreeing the federal loan guarantee. On December 19, 1979, when it finally passed the loan, the Senate added a condition that the workforce forfeit 'unrecoverable' concessions worth $259 million. After two weeks of intensive activity the UAW's negotiating committee delivered the goods – on the day Dodge Main was closed. Fraser and Stepp presented the second round of concessions to their members with a similar argument to that used three months earlier:

> The additional contract concessions occurred for one simple reason: the *alternative was an immediate Chrysler bankruptcy and a massive loss of jobs for Chrysler workers* . . .
> Despite the necessity of making those additional sacrifices to save our jobs, the UAW Negotiating Committee succeeded in getting Chrysler to agree to modified contracts that achieve three crucial goals:
> (1) The new contract fully protects the complete cost-of-living allowance;
> (2) The pact provides the full health and fringe benefit package and all of the pension improvements negotiated in October; and,
> (3) Chrysler workers still will receive GM and Ford pattern wages, benefits and pensions by the end of this agreement.[69]

It was a classic stick and carrot package – the threat of bankruptcy and the pledge that the concessions would be recovered 'by the end of this agreement'.

The new concessions froze wages for a year and ruled out individuals taking any extra days' leave throughout the year (paid personal holidays) during the whole term of the agreement. This contract modification was the first actual 'take-back', although even here it was a retreat on promises rather than on existing conditions. A novel element in the package encouraged workers to identify still more closely with Chrysler. Shares worth $162.5 million, or about one-sixth of the then virtually worthless Chrysler stock, were allocated to a special trust under an Employee Stock Ownership Plan (ESOP). And another new clause was designed to appease the Canadian section of the Chrysler workforce: Canadian Chrysler workers would be allowed to ratify the agreement separately and to negotiate their own contract in 1982.[70] Without an alternative, the depleted workforce voted a second overwhelming ratification to these changes.

During 1980, cooperation between the UAW and Chrysler continued. In June management–worker quality committees were established in Chrysler plants along the lines of GM's quality of work life groups and Ford's employee involvement program. Yet in his autobiography Iacocca is more enthusiastic about the impact on improving the quality of Chrysler cars made by his four senior quality control managers.[71] The impression of tokenism in Chrysler's quality circles experiment is confirmed by the experience of the Sterling Heights stamping plant in the summer of 1982. There, two years after the quality circle program had been initiated, only twenty workers of the 2,700 working regularly attended the meetings and in three months only ten improvements had been submitted by workers in the new suggestion boxes.[72] Iacocca also argues that 'we got the union to side with us on absenteeism . . . to put some teeth into the rules to penalize the chronic offenders.'[73] But the constant fall in absenteeism, from an absenteeism rate of 7.9% in 1977 to 5.1% in the first half of 1982, probably owed more to the heavy toll of closures and lay-offs on the younger workforce than to union support for management.[74]

The argument here is not that the non-adversarial relationship established with the international officers was unimportant, but rather that on the shopfloor the non-adversarial policy was not as important as the experience of the recession in disciplining the workforce. The tension between remote international officers and shopfloor Chrysler workers was highlighted in the 1982 negotiations. Fraser's first contract was rejected by a two-to-one vote. The *New York Times* described this as 'the first time a major contract in the auto industry had been defeated by the rank and file . . . a serious repudiation of the union leadership.' Yet when workers were then asked to strike, they voted by a similar margin to resume talks.[75] Shopfloor resentment qualified by a feeling of powerlessness was the background to the progress of non-adversarial bargaining.

In August 1980 Iacocca launched the new Chrysler K-car at Detroit's Jefferson Avenue plant. But as the world recession deepened and Carter tried to control inflation by raising interest rates, Chrysler sales continued to slump. The result was a $1.7 billion loss in 1980. This led Iacocca to demand an extra $600 million in concessions from the UAW, a call backed by the Treasurer in Carter's outgoing administration, William Miller, who warned that without them there would be no more funds available from the Loan Guarantee Board.[76]

The UAW let out a howl of rage. Fraser immediately released a letter to Iacocca objecting to his tactic of negotiating in public: 'Given Chrysler's difficulties, our hope is you will devote full time to handling the company's problems and will stop attempting to be the self-appointed spokesperson for the auto industry and corporate America on labor–management relations.'[77] But in a statement issued by the UAW's Chrysler Council two days later the UAW swallowed hard and agreed for the second time to reopen negotiations on the 1979 contract:

> Thus, while it may be necessary for extraordinary steps to be taken regarding the Chrysler–UAW collective bargaining agreements, these are a response to the requirements of the government decision makers rather than the demands of management . . .
>
> UAW members will do what is necessary to meet the requirements of the Loan Guarantee Act, but we must know what is true necessity rather than merely a management goal, and we must be assured that others will do their fair share.[78]

The fiction that the UAW would be allowed to distinguish between concessions based on 'true necessity' and those which were 'a management goal' did not last long. Iacocca records he made one of his shortest-ever speeches to the UAW negotiating committee, something like: 'You've got until morning to make a decision. If you don't help me out, I'm going to blow your brains out. I'll declare bankruptcy in the morning and you'll all be out of work. You've got eight hours to make up your minds. It's up to you.'[79]

The January 14, 1981 agreement gave the company a further $622 million cost advantage over the national contract pattern, everything Iacocca had originally demanded. It implemented a virtual wage freeze for the last twenty months of the contract, allowing only one more topping up of the cost-of-living allowance and stopping the two further scheduled increases in the base rate; it delayed the next scheduled pension increase for five months and stopped the others; and it withdrew the proposal to give three shift workers a rise in paid lunch time from fifteen minutes to twenty minutes a day.[80]

Two letters attached to the new contract provided 'sweeteners'. One was a promise to negotiate a profit-sharing agreement to give workers 'no less than 15% (of the) profits in excess of 10% of net worth'.[81] The other agreed to 'formalize a non-adversary procedure in which committees will be formed at the national and local level' so UAW officers could be 'given the opportunity to constructively input ideas into the decision-making process prior to implementation of decisions which might adversely affect their job security'. Yet this offer of consultation on the steady stream of closures – by early 1983 sixteen plants had been closed out of fifty-two since Iacocca took over – did not mean a loss of managerial authority. The letter added: 'the Corporation cannot agree to any limitation on the responsibility for the final decision', and 'the work of the committee is and must remain confidential'.[82]

Fraser's recession bargaining differed from the UAW's traditional post-war brand of business unionism only by the degree of its support for managerial objectives. Clancy, who was transferred to Chrysler's corporate labor relations headquarters after the closure of Dodge Main, recalled how the basis for the close collaboration between Fraser and Chrysler management in the early 1980s had been established earlier: 'In the 1970s when we had to get deviations from the Union and required them to bend in the interests of productivity, I found that if the issue was sufficiently vital they'd (the Union officers) use a great deal of commensense and go along with you.'[83]

By 1981 it was clear the international union would no longer place other than consultative restraints on company-wide managerial authority. Significant resistance to shopfloor managerial authority had long since ceased. Weak workplace organization of the mid 1970s had been weakened further and transformed by Chrysler's crisis to the point where union locals ceased to voice workers' collective aspirations. Fraser was aware of the change taking place and defended it. He told critics of his taking the directorship on Chrysler's board, 'Maybe the adversary relationship is precisely what's wrong with the American labor movement.'[84] The UAW was now in a junior partnership relationship with Chrysler management. It shared the same goal as Iacocca – the economic survival of the company – and was committed to cooperation to attain it. Crucially, the union no longer had a distinct *raison d'être* as an organizer of collective resistance to management. 'The union in Chrysler,' an international officer said confidentially in the summer of 1982, 'no longer exists in the plants in any recognizable form.'[85]

The impact of concession bargaining at Chrysler was felt far beyond the auto industry. Once the argument that domestic labor costs were a major part of Chrysler's crisis was accepted by the UAW, then when Ford and GM also moved into loss situations, the logical step was to extend the same accommodations to them. Late in 1981 the UAW agreed to early negotiations with Ford and GM on the 1982 contracts, and 'take away' contracts were signed at both companies in the spring of 1982. Within three years of the first Chrysler concessions, its concession–bargaining pattern had become the 'norm' in both public and private sectors of American industry. The UAW's agreement to lower the price of Chrysler labor became a signal to employers everywhere to demand similar sacrifices.

The lowering of the price of UAW members' labor reflected a shift in the balance of class forces in the US in favor of managerial power. The shift occurred as managements exploited opportunities created by the recession, by the falling costs of high technology and by the longer-term decline in the density of unionization among the American labor force. The 'sweeteners' provided to the UAW in exchange for the concessions – Fraser's seat on the Chrysler Board, ESOP, profit sharing, joint consultation on closures and joint labor–management quality circles – were presented to UAW members as a step forward by labor. Yet in the context of the overall shift in balance of power they have a different significance. Had they been worker-imposed restraints on managerial authority, they might have had a different role. But, negotiated from a position of weakness, they obscured labor's independent interests. At best, they merely weakened workers' collective representation. At worst, they could help destroy it and provide unrestrained managerial authority with still greater workplace legitimacy in the guise of a cooperative Taylorism.[86]

In 1954 Clark Kerr had observed: 'Conflict is essential to survival. The union which is in constant and complete agreement with management has ceased to be a union.'[87] If the 1980s develop into a decade in which highly centralized union organizations increasingly participate in 'non-adversary' relationships with management, then the quiet closure of Dodge Main in the first week of 1980 may have heralded more than rationalization of a large core company in face of a severe economic crisis. It might signal the end of unionism as American workers have known it for the last fifty years.

Part V
Conclusion

11 Power and exceptionalism

In this study of fifty years of shopfloor labor relations at Chrysler it has been argued that it is impossible to explain developments simply in terms of technological change in the labor process or of far-sighted managerial strategy. Although labor relations can only be understood in the context of an unremitting struggle between capital and labor, the outcomes were often unintended, and the actors were often unaware of likely results. Thus the labor–capital conflict took a different shape in different auto companies and gave rise to a different labor experience at Chrysler than at GM or Ford. Explaining the different pattern of labor relations in auto companies operating on a similar scale in the same market has been the main aim of the book. The explanation has concentrated on the complex interaction of factors that shape management's frontier of control over the labor process. These include the strength or weakness of managerial economic power, management's role in shaping the form, politics and traditions of workplace employee organization, the countervailing impact of the presence or absence of independent working class politics in wider society, and the changing role of international union organization.

The discussion of Chrysler in relation to GM and Ford allows powerful comparisons. Here is an industry in which technology can be treated as constant; where each firm's labor market, although not identical, was situated largely in the same area of the United States; where plant size – if GM's Flint Chevrolet division is seen as an extended River Rouge or Dodge Main – was roughly comparable; and in which managements dealt with just one international union. Yet there were major differences between these firms in the level of open conflict, especially in unauthorized strikes.

The argument began with evidence that the greater strength of shopfloor organization in Chrysler developed primarily as an unintended consequence of management action. At Chrysler a more militant shop-floor organization developed through the establishment of a different tradition of legitimate workplace action. In Chrysler traditions developed that condoned sectional industrial action; these traditions were then sustained by labor in specific circumstances which were either fostered misguidedly by deliberate management policy, or were generated through management's failure to execute another policy. Because there were not the same consistent lapses in GM and Ford management, local traditions of active restraint on managerial authority in their plants did not long survive the initial boost given them by the achievement of worker-imposed union recognition in 1937 and 1941.

This study does not seek, however, to present a thesis of managerial determinism as an alternative to either a Braverman-type technological determinism or the labor historians' traditional treatment of unionism as an independent variable. The independent activity of groups of workers was crucial in whether such management lapses were taken advantage of or not.[1] The extent of this independent activity was, moreover, closely related to four major shifts in workers' political beliefs over the fifty years: to the election of a reform President in the 1930s; to the strengthening of US nationalism during World War II and the subsequent dominance of anti-communism within the labor movement; to the rise of the civil rights movement and a new upsurge of radicalism in the late 1950s and 1960s; and, most recently, to the conservative revival of the late 1970s and early 1980s.

Yet while the momentum to independent organization was fueled by wider political developments the opportunities arose as a result of management actions. The exceptional wildcat strike frequency, retention of a higher steward density and existence of more effective restraints over managerial authority in Chrysler than in GM and Ford for most of these fifty years was at root a reflection of differences in their top managements. GM had adopted a multi-divisional structure by the mid 1920s, and could apply its management-by-policy tradition to industrial relations by the mid 1930s. In its dealings with the UAW thereafter it had the capacity to consider the consequences of particular methods of opposing union encroachment on its managerial rights before trying them out.

GM's capacity to learn lessons from its experience does not mean its strategy consistently aimed to *incorporate* union organization. Instead the flexibility of its management structure was used to test out a range of different methods of *combating* the threat of unionism.[2] The argument here is that GM's anti-unionism was, consequently, consistently more cost-effective than Chrysler's. Ford adopted GM's management struc-

ture in the late 1940s, although as a family-controlled company it
retained a powerful idiosyncratic flavor. Chrysler, however, reproduced
the Ford-type management structure effectively only in 1979, and aspects
of its traditional autocratic, intuitive, one-man-rule structure still survive
today. Chrysler managers were allowed little room for experimentation
and virtually none for systematic reflection. Often, even if they had
wished to do so, the weakness of their centrally-operated accounting
system made it very difficult to establish much more than superficial
'scientific management' practices. The company's weak economic performance meant managers were either under pressure to maintain
production at any price or were forced to drastically cut back both
production and manpower. Faced with the mixture of aggression and
opportunity provided by rapidly changing management policies, Chrysler workers constructed their own autonomous traditions.

This argument underlines the importance of providing reasonably
similar subjects if the purpose of a comparison is to develop a theory that
explains differences. Comparing Chrysler with IBM, Sears & Roebuck
or IT&T, companies whose 1978 net sales were all within a few million
dollars of Chrysler, would not have thrown as much light on essential
differences as has this comparison with GM and Ford whose net sales
were four times and three times respectively greater than Chrysler's.[3]

Chrysler has been shown to have been an exception within the US
auto industry but the presence of its consistently high levels of open
conflict throw doubts on the American 'exceptionalism' argument, that
the US *working class* was very different from working classes elsewhere. Typically, the exceptionalists present a catalogue of descriptions
of ethnic and racial divisions, geographical dispersal (the impact of the
frontier), economic prosperity and social mobility to explain American
labor's 'lack' of class consciousness and class solidarity.[4] Yet this
approach is flawed by the failure to make explicit the ideal model of
consciousness and solidarity with which American workers are being
compared. If it is *British* labor with whom American labor is being
compared, then this study of shopfloor unionism at Chrysler disputes
the extent of American exceptionalism. At Dodge Main there was an
enduring sense of class identity and also occasional demonstrations of
common purpose with other workers, neither of which was significantly
different from that observed in the similarly sized Austin Rover (Longbridge) plant in Britain in a parallel historical study conducted by the
author.[5] To have validity, assertions of 'peculiarity' must be rooted in
firm comparisons.

Moreover, even a cursory examination of 'strong' American class
consciousness and solidarity presented in several radical histories sug-

gests that several of the elements most frequently listed as causing 'weak' class consciousness, such as the geographical dispersal and ethnicity of labor, have in certain circumstances produced its opposite.[6] If these factors work to defuse consciousness at some times and to consolidate it at others, they are not on their own useful explanatory variables.

What is needed are comparative studies which can identify differences and similarities both in patterns of working class behavior between different American firms (and industries) and between the American labor experience and the experience of other labor movements.

The importance of comparing like with like is why it is also helpful to offer a brief survey of industrial relations in the British auto industry. For while there are many obvious differences between the American and the British industrial relations systems,[7] there are also many shared social and legal traditions, a common history of 'voluntarism' in industrial relations and a similar emphasis on collective bargaining as the key means of industrial problem solving.[8] In comparing the Chrysler labor experience with that of British labor in the auto industry, important similarities appear which support the argument that management, its power resources and its flexibility of access to those resources, is the major structural factor shaping differences in levels of open conflict.

In the 1930s union membership in British auto plants was concentrated primarily among skilled workers and union density fluctuated between 10% and 20% of the workforce.[9] With the conversion to war production and under the protection of the Essential Works Order during World War II, union membership rose temporarily to around 80%. But in most auto plants renewed managerial antagonism in the slack post-war labor market reduced union density to about 40%, from which point it rose slowly between the late 1940s and mid 1950s in contrast to the more rapid rise in auto production.[10] In the late 1950s and early 1960s, however, as pay insecurity returned with gathering price inflation, and as job insecurity reappeared in the sharper 'stop–go' economic cycles, union membership in most UK auto plants rose quickly to 90% or higher.[11]

Unlike the situation in America, continued management hostility to 'outside' unions interfering with the 'right to manage' meant that despite the achievement of union shops, no single union was granted negotiating rights for all workers. So multi-unionism flourished and the number of shop stewards continued to rise in order to represent the growing ranks of union members, encouraging a shift in the balance of power within the British unions from the national officers to the shopfloor.[12] Sectional stewards not only served as dues collectors, but in piecework areas management bargained directly with them over pay, and in day-rate areas and plants management had to contend with them over manning levels, job timings and the mobility of labor.[13] By their refusal to legitimize the bargaining role of the unions' full-time national officers, British managers had inadvertently legitimized a collective bargaining system that could challenge each and every aspect of management's shopfloor authority.

In the tighter labor market of the 1960s, and as the loss of formerly guaranteed overseas Empire and Commonwealth sales and the lowering of tariff barriers against European imports stimulated fierce competition in the UK home market,[14] most UK managements reluctantly accepted significant restraints over their unilateral exercise of control of the labor process in return for short-term cooperation in achieving production targets. When, in the mid and late 1960s it became clear that this policy was failing to sustain the domestic market let alone the international one, a major restructuring of the UK industry took place. This was accompanied in British Leyland and Chrysler UK by attempts to raise labor productivity and reduce labor costs by moving from piecework to measured day work,[15] and in Ford by moving from its historic day work system to a more intensive MDW system.[16] By the mid 1970s it was clear that this attempt to restore managerial authority in BL and Chrysler UK had largely failed.[17] BL was nationalized and Chrysler UK had to be bailed out by the British government in 1976 before being sold to the French company Peugeot in 1978. What had effectively sealed the fate of the two firms was their inability to compete in product range, age, quality and value with imports into the UK from Europe and Japan, where labor productivity was significantly higher than in Britain.[18]

In the 1979–83 recession managements in Leyland, Peugeot–Talbot, Ford and Vauxhall (GM) implemented a wave of plant closures and job reductions,[19] and in Leyland top management orchestrated a deliberate confrontation with its shop steward organization to remove accumulated restraints over its shopfloor authority.[20] Within the last two or three years managements in most British car plants re-established the control over the labor process that it effectively ceded from the late 1950s to the mid 1970s. By 1985 the industrial relations director of Austin Rover argued that sectional shop stewards no longer had any real bargaining power left and that sectional stoppages had entirely disappeared.[21]

Strong shopfloor union organization arrived in Britain much later than has been suggested in recent American accounts.[22] But when it did, roughly between 1965 and 1977, it succeeded in imposing very real restraints on managerial control over the labor process. In Chrysler UK's Linwood plant, for example, hourly paid press shop workers in these years completely controlled their own pace of work, organized extended relief periods of an average of fifteen minutes in the hour, held shop meetings that customarily extended into working time and were attended by all stamping plant workers, and controlled the allocation of overtime in such a way that management was frequently obliged to offer overtime to large numbers of workers it did not require to get particular jobs completed. No workers were successfully disciplined by management for exercising any or all of these restraints on management's frontier of control.[23] These informal, shopfloor restraints were much more significant in limiting managerial authority than were the formal grievance procedures and job classifications introduced in American plants during the 1940s, because in Britain they were consistently backed by sectional industrial action.[24]

How does this brief outline of unionization in the UK auto industry help our understanding of American labor relations? At this point it is necessary to return to the concept of managerial power and power resources. The major differences between the two industries in the period after 1933 were that the American auto industry was significantly larger, more concentrated and more vertically integrated than the British which, for example, retained an independent body-building sector until the late 1960s. Another difference was that in Britain too many producers produced too many models, establishing the parallel with Chrysler's American experience, that they gained only limited benefits from possible economies of scale. As has been argued before about Chrysler, an unintended consequence of a business strategy involving the multiplication of model lines is a high number of changes in model mix and hence of potential points of conflict over job standards. In British plants, where sectional industrial action played a central part in bargaining over standards, the large numbers of models and the annual model changes that occurred until the 1970s thus contributed significantly to the level of open shopfloor conflict.

Another important difference is in the scale of the two industries. The contrasting levels of economic power can be simply identified in the gross profits accumulated in the 1960s and 1970s. Between 1960 and 1978, GM earned $37.6 billion and Ford earned $13.8 billion profits. In contrast, from 1960 to 1977, British Leyland earned profits of just £324.2 million, Vauxhall/GM earned £88.6 million and Rootes/Chrysler UK accumulated losses of £113.5 million. Ford UK returned American-level profits of £791.4 million, while Chrysler US's $524 million profits were in the same league as British Leyland's.[25]

Top British managers shared with Chrysler US significantly smaller power resources and less room in which to maneuver against union organization than at GM and Ford. The outcome of this economic weakness is apparent in a comparison of national strike trends in Britain and in America. For while strike frequency in the two countries from 1931 to 1979 tended to move in opposite directions, falling in the US and rising in the UK, another relationship has been more constant: except for World War II, the proportion of short strikes in Britain lasting under a week was consistently twice the proportion in the US. The most likely explanation of this trend is that British strikes tended to be shorter because the smaller power resources available to British managers led them to settle strikes more quickly.[26]

Not only were the power resources of GM and Ford huge, and supported by significant pieces of federal legislation in 1947 and 1959, but their multi-divisional and management-by-policy organizational structures enabled the top management to easily make use of these resources. In Britain management not only had smaller power resources with which to withstand union pressure, but was poorly educated in management skills and maintained organizational structures that impeded strategic decision making. It was only during World War II, as a result of government action, that personnel officers were appointed in most large UK factories, while 34% of American plants employing over 250 workers already had functioning personnel departments by 1929.[27] After World War II the British auto firms continued to be dominated by the old pre-war top management personnel, with their neo-paternalism and individual idiosyncracies,[28] and who caused deep aggravation when the merger process that had been completed nearly thirty years earlier in America resumed in the 1950s and 1960s. Pre-war management structure, style and pattern of ownership remained virtually intact in Britain until the late 1960s.[29]

British workers seized the opportunities made available to them by managements anxious for short-term peace to establish widespread restraints on managerial authority. British management lacked the foresight and consistency to be able to conduct a restructuring similar to that undertaken at Chrysler in the late 1950s. Only when economic crisis had gripped the industry for over ten years did it respond. British Leyland, in this respect also similar to Chrysler US, ultimately undertook such a restructuring only when it was totally reliant on state finance and intervention and was effectively bankrupt, and when the disciplinary impact of recession helped guarantee adherence to a new managerial regime.

This interpretation of the British experience clearly supports the thesis that the excercise of strategic choice by employers, despite the continuity of worker resistance to managerial control, goes a long way to explaining the distinctive features of that resistance.[30] In this light both the more open conflict in Chrysler than in the two other major American auto makers, and the greater institutionalization of conflict in post-war America than in Britain, appear less exceptional. Differences there certainly were and are. But they are not the result of some peculiar weakness exhibited by American workers.

This study of Dodge Main suggests that American workers, like those elsewhere, have struggled and continue to struggle to impose restraints over their managements. But they have done so within a balance of forces determined by their own politics, traditions and struggles and by the history and strength of management. It has not been the absence of American workers' combativity that has given American labor its distinctive organizational and political form, but the greater strength of American management in general compared to British. And the organizational and economic weaknesses of Chrysler management compared to GM and Ford, rather than any generic peculiarities of Chrysler workers, led to its long record of bitter labor relations conflict.

Notes

Preface

1 Large strike data, 1937–58 in Bureau of Labor Statistics (BLS), Report 148 (October 1959), Table 3, 5–11, and Report 574 (September 1979), Table 2, 6–12. General Motors unauthorized strike data, letter to author, September 15, 1982; Chrysler Corporation unauthorized strike data, letter to author, October 26, 1981.

2 This is the 'decay of homogenization', followed by the 'segmentation of labor' and by the 'decay of segmentation' presented in David Gordon, Richard Edwards and Michael Reich, *Segmented Work, Divided Workers: The Historical Transformation of Labor in the United States* (New York: Cambridge University Press, 1982), 12–16.

3 Assumptions of a complete contrast between the US and UK shopfloor experience are contained in David Brody, *Workers in Industrial America: Essays on the 20th Century Struggle* (New York: Oxford University Press, 1981), 206; and in Nelson Lichtenstein, 'Auto Worker Militancy and the Structure of Factory Life, 1937–1955', *Journal of American History* (September 1980), 348.

4 Allan Flanders, *Management and Unions: The Theory and Reform of Industrial Relations* (London: Faber & Faber, 1975), 167.

1. Management, managed and control

1 Two exceptions are: Robert Ozanne, *A Century of Labor–Management Relations at McCormick and International Harvester* (Madison: University of Wisconsin, 1967); and Ron Schatz, 'American Electrical Workers: Work, Struggle, Aspirations, 1930–1950' (Ph.D. thesis, University of Pittsburgh, 1977).

2 Nelson Lichtenstein, *Labor's War at Home: The CIO in World War II* (New York: Cambridge University Press, 1982), 2.

3 Craig Zabala, 'Collective Bargaining at UAW Local 645, General Motors Assembly Division, Van Nuys, California, 1976–1982' (Ph.D. thesis, University of California, Los Angeles, 1983), 1.

4 The BLS data is 'based on all work stoppages involving six workers or more and lasting at least a full day or shift'. Since strikes are largely illegal during the term of the contract, this cut-off point of workers being out for a whole day only counts strikes during the term of a contract when workers are ready to defy the law. It misses the high proportion of 'quickies' that last for minutes or for part of a shift. The BLS insensitivity to inter-firm differences is highlighted in its breakdown by name of firm of large strikes involving 10,000 workers or more. This raises the strike frequency of General Motors whose labor force is more than four times the size, for example, of Chrysler. The reality according to the companies' own data is very different. Thus while between 1959 and 1978 the annual average large-strike frequency rate of Chrysler and GM as measured by the BLS was both 0.03 strikes per 1,000 hourly paid workers, the all-strike frequency rates kept by the companies showed Chrysler at 0.46, nearly four times greater than GM's annual average frequency of 0.12 strikes per 1,000 workers. Company data: Chrysler and GM Labor Relations Departments; BLS data: BLS, *Collective Bargaining in the Motor Vehicle and Equipment Industry*, Report 574, September 1979.

5 Sumner H. Slichter, *Union Policies and Industrial Management* (Washington DC: Brookings Institution, 1941), 578.

6 Sumner H. Slichter, James E. Healy and E. Robert Livernash, *The Impact of Collective Bargaining on Management* (Washington DC: Brookings Institution, 1960), 6.

7 Lichtenstein (1982) *op. cit.*, 4.

8 Richard Polenberg, *One Nation Divisible: Class, Race and Ethnicity in the United States since 1938* (New York: Viking, 1980), 225.

9 As Craig Littler has pointed out, they look for 'a total solution ... a conceptual search in order to pin-point the magic strategy that successfully stabilized capital/labor relations': *The Development of the Labor Process in Capitalist Societies* (London: Heinemann, 1982), 3; Stephen Wood argues that Andrew Friedman and Richard Edwards both present 'management as omniscient, conspiratorial and able, at least for a certain period of time, to get its own way – that is, to solve successfully its problem of control': *The Degradation of Work? Skill, Deskilling and the Labour Process* (London: Hutchinson, 1982), 16.

10 Harry Braverman, *Labor and Monopoly Capital: The Degradation of Work in the Twentieth Century* (New York: Monthly Review, 1974), 27. In Braverman's terms it is not possible to separate the study of 'a class *in itself*' from 'a class *for itself*'.

11 William Lazonick, 'Industrial Relations and Technical Change: The Case of the Self-acting Mule', *Cambridge Journal of Economics*, 3 (1979), 238, 259.

12 Andrew L. Friedman, *Industry and Labor: Class Struggle at Work and Monopoly Capitalism* (London: Macmillan, 1977), 80–2. This criticism by Friedman of Braverman is endorsed; but it does not follow that the only choice facing management is 'direct control' or 'responsible autonomy'; part of the argument below is that pursuance of the former strategy by Chrysler management helped create space for the emergence of the latter.

13 Stephen A. Marglin, 'What do Bosses do? The Origins and Functions of Hierarchy in Capitalist Production', in *The Division of Labour: The Labour Process and Class Struggle in Modern Capitalism*, Andre Gorz (ed.) (Hassocks, Sussex: Harvester, 1978), 17.

14 Gordon *et al.* (1982) *op. cit.*, 3.

15 *Ibid.*, 185–239.

16 Michael Burawoy describes his aim as 'to demonstrate how consent is produced at the point of production – independent of schooling, family life, mass media, the state and so forth': *Manufacturing Consent: Changes in the Labor Process under Monopoly Capitalism* (Chicago: University Press, 1979), xii.

17 In this omission the study is strikingly similar to the classic study by Charles R. Walker and Robert H. Guest, *The Man on the Assembly Line* (Cambridge, Massachusetts: Harvard University Press, 1952), 123–34, whose discussion of 'The Worker and the Union' does not refer to committeemen, chief stewards, blue button stewards or how workers resisted the production standards and managerial discipline which came out top on the list of grievances.

18 Richard Hyman, *Industrial Relations: A Marxist Introduction* (London: Macmillan, 1975), 42.

19 John Child, *British Managerial Thought* (London: Allen & Unwin, 1969), 201–2.

20 In a more recent work Michael Burawoy appears to acknowledge the wider influences over what he calls 'the politics of production'; 'Between the Labor Process and the State: The Changing Face of Factory Regimes under Advanced Capitalism', *American Sociological Review*, 48 (October 1983), 587.

21 Robert M. MacDonald, *Collective Bargaining in the Automobile Industry: A Study of Wage Structures and Competitive Relations* (New Haven: Yale University Press, 1963), 396–7, 400.

22 Eighty-four per cent of the 33.5 million manhours lost in Chrysler's unauthorized strikes over all four decades were lost between 1940 and 1958. So were 85.9% of the total 81 million manhours lost in authorized strikes, reflecting the massive losses in the strikes of 1948 and 1950.

23 National contract negotiations took place annually from 1939 to 1947 when the first two-year term was agreed, only to be renegotiated in 1948. Subsequently, long-term contracts were agreed in 1950, 1955, 1958, 1961, 1964, 1967, 1970, 1973, 1976, 1979, 1982 (the 1982 contract was only signed in January 1983 after a strike by Canadian Chrysler workers) and 1985. Before 1958 the UAW only authorized non-contract-year strikes twice, in 1952 and 1957. But between 1959 and 1980, while authorized strikes took place in all seven contract years (losing 6.5 million manhours), the UAW also authorized strikes in a further eleven non-contract years (causing Chrysler to lose 21.1 million manhours). In 1982 the UAW reluctantly authorized the Canadian strike – its reluctance leading to the breakaway of the Canadian autoworkers in December 1984; and in 1985 it authorized an eight day strike to regain wage parity with GM and Ford. This was conceded for the third year of a deal which expires one year after GM and Ford renegotiate, in 1987.

24 BLS, *148* (October 1959), Table 3, 5–11; BLS, *574* (September 1979), Table 2, 6–12.
25 There is a danger in overreliance on large strike data since Chrysler and Ford concentrated production at Dodge Main and the River Rouge from the 1930s to the 1950s. This raised their propensity to record large strikes since small departmental or sectional strikes had a speedier multiplier effect on lay-offs (the numbers directly and indirectly involved are not segregated in the BLS statistics) than in the smaller and more geographically dispersed GM plants. The frequency rates are also not strictly comparable since a higher proportion of Chrysler and Ford hourly paid workers were exclusively employed in automobile assembly than was the case in GM. They can therefore only be relied upon to provide a trend.
26 See James W. Kuhn, *Bargaining in Grievance Settlement: The Power of Industrial Work Groups* (New York: Columbia University Press, 1961); E. Batstone, I. Boraston and S. Fenkel, *Shop Stewards in Action: The Organization of Workplace Conflict and Accommodation* (Oxford: Blackwell, 1977); Hugh Beynon, *Working for Ford* (Wakefield: EP Publishing, 1975).
27 John Humphrey, *Capitalist Control and Workers' Struggles in the Brazilian Auto Industry* (Princeton, New Jersey: Princeton University Press, 1982), 8–9.
28 *Ibid.*
29 Ian Maitland, *The Causes of Industrial Disorders: A Comparison of a British and a German Factory* (London: Routledge, Kegan and Paul, 1983), 108, 111.
30 P. Friedlander, *The Emergence of a UAW Local, 1936–1939: A Study in Class and Culture* (Pittsburg: University of Pittsburg Press, 1975), 111.
31 Child (1969) *op. cit.*, 13.
32 William Brown, *Piecework Bargaining* (London: Heinemann, 1973), 98–9. The development of 'managerial discretion' within an organization, when the expansion of a centralized unitary–form company to a level of complexity beyond the physical capacity of an individual chief executive, has been identified by Chandler and Williamson in terms of a loss of financial control; A. Chandler, *Strategy and Structure* (New York: Doubleday, 1966), 282–3; O. E. Williamson, *Markets and Hierarchies: Analysis and Antitrust Legislation* (New York: Free Press, 1975), 135.
33 Keith Thurley and Stephen Wood, *Industrial Relations and Management Strategy* (London: Cambridge University Press, 1983), 3.
34 Hyman (1975) *op. cit.*, 64. The terms 'power' and 'authority' are not used in a Weberian way because, as Stephen Hill points out: 'It became clear to several observers in the mid-1970s that the apparently agreed frameworks of rules which used to guide conflict resolution and the apparent consensus on the basic details of the organization of industry were based largely on worker acquiescence in the face of superior managerial power, rather than on any institutionalization and legitimization of norms and customary procedures'; *Competition and Control at Work* (London: Heinemann, 1981), 149.
35 Alan Fox, 'Industrial Sociology and Industrial Relations', Royal Commission on Trade Unions and Employers Associations, Research Paper 3 (London: HMSO, 1966), 6.

36 Richard Hyman and Robert H. Fryer, 'Trade Unions: Sociology and Political Economy', in *Trade Unions under Capitalism*, Tom Clarke and Laurie Clements (eds.) (London: Fontana, 1977), 152.
37 Carter L. Goodrich, *The Frontier of Control* (London: Pluto, 1975, 1st edn 1920), 27.
38 Goodrich accepted 'discipline and management . . . are convenient terms for the frontier of control', but insisted 'that frontier must be looked for as a shifting line in a great mass of regulations'; *ibid.*, 62.
39 *Ibid.*, 253.
40 William Brown, Robert Ebsworth and Michael Terry, 'Factors Shaping Shop Steward Organization in Britain', *British Journal of Industrial Relations*, XVI, no. 2 (1978), 148.
41 Richard Herding, *Job Control and Union Structure* (Rotterdam: University Press, 1972). Part 1 sets out to demonstrate how the 'real interests' of workers are obscured by the 'collective-bargaining ideologies' (p. 16) that pretend to be advancing the 'humanization' of the workplace but instead are promoting 'hierarchization' and 'rationalization' (p. 21). But Herding none the less overstates his point by virtually denying that 'job control devices' operate to any significant extent to restrain arbitrary management.
42 Richard Price, *Masters, Unions and Men: Work Control in Building and the Rise of Labour, 1830–1914* (Cambridge: Cambridge University Press, 1980), 9.
43 Price defines 'craft control' as 'control that was overlain by support systems of tradition or genuine skill'; *ibid.*, 11.
44 Hyman (1975) defines 'workers' control . . . in *collective* terms: the determination by the whole labour force of the nature, methods and indeed purpose of production'; *op. cit.*, 180.
45 Hyman describes this workplace legitimacy as: 'a shifting set of traditions and understandings which are never identical in any two work situations . . . governing workers' relations with one another and with management'; *ibid.*, 25.
46 Brown (1973) *op. cit.*, 168.
47 P. J. Armstrong, J. F. B. Goodman and J. D. Hyman, *Ideology and Shopfloor Industrial Relations* (London: Croom Helm, 1981), 39–49.
48 Price, *op. cit.*, 7, writes: 'When workers sell their labour power, they implicitly recognize a certain degree of subordination to the orders and mandates of the employers . . . But it is precisely from this subordination that many of the problems of industry derive. For employers' authority is never total nor is it ever unambiguously accepted by workers. There is a constant and unremitting resistance and challenge to employers' authority that assumes many different shapes and forms.'
49 W. Baldamus, *Efficiency and Effort: An Analysis of Industrial Administration* (London: Tavistock, 1961), 125.
50 Alvin W. Gouldner, *Wildcat Strike* (Yellow Springs, Ohio: Antioch, 1954), 59, 18.
51 Armstrong *et al.* (1981) *op. cit.*, 15.
52 Hyman (1975) *op. cit.*, 197.

53 Thus Henry Ford openly defied the Wagner Act in the 1930s; GM and Chrysler did so covertly.
54 Littler (1982) *op. cit.*, 42.
55 Many studies of particular plants have demonstrated this; see, Friedlander (1975) *op. cit.*; John G. Kruchko, *The Birth of a Union Local: The History of UAW Local 674, Norwood, Ohio, 1933–1940* (New York: Cornell University School of Industrial and Labor Relations, 1972). In the British auto industry: Beynon (1975) *op. cit.*; Henry Friedman and Sander Meredeen, *The Dynamics of Industrial Conflict: Lessons from Ford* (London: Croom Helm, 1980); Batstone *et al.* (1977) who posit the development of a crucial quasi-elite group among a vehicle plant's shop stewards.
56 Stanley Aronowitz, *False Promises: The Shaping of American Working Class Consciousness* (New York: McGraw Hill, 1973), 409.

2. Fifty years of labor politics, unions and the UAW

1 Daniel Guerin, *100 Years of Labor in the USA* (London: Ink Links, 1979), 113.
2 Art Preis, *Labor's Giant Step: Twenty Years of the CIO* (New York: Pathfinder, 1972), 63.
3 Gordon *et al.* (1982) *op. cit.*, 177, who are citing Irving Bernstein, *Turbulent Years: A History of the American Worker, 1933–1941* (Boston: Houghton Mifflin, 1969), 500.
4 Irving Bernstein, *The Lean Years: A History of the American Worker, 1920–1933* (Boston: Houghton Mifflin, 1960), 47–82, demonstrates that the benefits of the undoubted economic growth of the 1920s largely missed American workers.
5 George Bain and Robert Price, *Profiles of Union Growth: A Comparative Statistical Portrait of Eight Countries* (Oxford: Blackwell, 1980), 88. Union membership quoted here is that calculated by the National Bureau of Economic Research.
6 P. K. Edwards, *Strikes in the United States, 1881–1974* (Oxford: Blackwell, 1981), 254.
7 Bernstein (1960) *op. cit.*, 77–80.
8 *Ibid.*, 47–50, 63–5, 76–7; Samuel Lubell, 'Revolt of the City', in *Electoral Change and Stability in American Political History*, Jerome M. Clubb and Howard W. Allen (eds.) (New York: Free Press, 1971), 9–16.
9 Bernstein (1960) *op. cit.*, 508–11.
10 Bernstein (1969) *op. cit.*, 338–41; Bernstein (1960) *op. cit.*, 66–70.
11 Bernstein (1969) *op. cit.*, 363, 218–98.
12 William McPherson, *Labor Relations in the Automobile Industry* (Washington, DC: Brookings Institution, 1940), 13–14.
13 Bernstein (1969) *op. cit.*, 184–5.
14 *Ibid.*, 328–49, 515.
15 Roger Keeran, *The Communist Party and the Auto Workers Unions* (Bloomington: Indiana University Press, 1980), 136.

16 Bernstein (1969) *op. cit.*, 386–400. The UAW's appeal was lost by 125 votes to 104.

17 *Ibid.*, 457.

18 Alan Brinkley, *Voices of Protest: Huey Long, Father Coughlin, and the Great Depression* (New York: Alfred A. Knopf, 1982), 44–5, 107–8; Bernstein (1960) *op. cit.*, 445.

19 Bernstein (1969) *op. cit.*, 504–9.

20 *Ibid.*, 449.

21 Sidney Fine, *Sit-down: The GM Strike of 1936–1937* (Ann Arbor, Michigan: University of Michigan, 1969), 96.

22 Lichtenstein (1982) *op. cit.*, 12.

23 David Montgomery, 'Spontaneity and Organization: Some Comments', *Radical America*, 7, no. 6 (Nov.–Dec. 1973), 73.

24 Interview by author with Gertrude Nalezty, Detroit, August 10, 1982.

25 The semiskilled unionization movement of 1889–91 in Britain also faced hostility from the government, employers and craft unions, but it triggered the formation of independent labor political organizations.

26 Brody (1981) *op. cit.*, 142.

27 More realistic estimates of UAW membership and levels of actual participation in the auto industry sit-down movement are available: Bert Cochran, *Labor and Communism: The Conflict that Shaped American Unions* (Princeton: Princeton University Press, 1977), 114–18, suggests there were only 200 UAW members out of the 4,500 workforce at Kelsey-Hayes before the December 1936 sit-down there; he estimates the climb in UAW membership in Flint as going from 150 in October 1936 to 4,500 in December out of a total GM workforce in the city of 47,000; Fine (1969) *op. cit.*, 251, reports 208 Cadillac sit-downers, 49 Fleetwood Fisher Body sit-downers and 96 Guide Lamp sit-downers. These were plants where management kept control of the gates and so workers who left the sit-down could not return or be replaced. In fact, the Fleetwood figure Fine uses was the number who originally voted to sit-down, and the number who actually stayed in was less than that; J. W. Anderson and S. Jefferys, 'Enlisted in the Suitcase Brigade: The Life of an Autoworker who Stayed in the Shop' (Unpublished MS, 1983), chapter 6; Fine (1969) *op cit.*, 142–4, suggests only about 10% of the Cleveland Fisher Body workforce of 7,200 were UAW members when its sit-down began in December 1936, and GM testified that only 259 workers actually disobeyed its order to leave the plant; he also reports the Flint Fisher Body No. 2 sit-down beginning with 'not more than 50 workers on the body line'. Fine, *ibid.*, 168, cites recollections of sit-downers on numbers in the No 1 plant varying from over 'one thousand on some days . . . to a low of 90 on one occasion', and the Michigan National Guard report listing 450 in the No. 2 plant on January 5 falling to 17 on January 26, 1937.

28 Fine, *ibid.*, 94.

29 Hyman (1975) *op. cit.*, 71–2.

30 Cochran (1977) *op. cit.*, 143.

31 Martin Glaberman, *Wartime Strikes: The Struggle Against the No-strike*

Pledge in the UAW during World War II (Detroit: Bewick, 1980), 133–4, counterposes a 'political' resistance by wartime strikers to the rapid growth and bureaucratization of the UAW, but marries the two in a bureaucratic victory explained by 'sufficient concessions' and the 'quick incorporation of the accumulated militancy'. But how 'political' was the wartime wildcat resistance if it could be so easily and rapidly overcome?

32 Keeran (1980) *op. cit.*, 235–6; Nelson Lichtenstein, 'Industrial Unionism under the No Strike Pledge: A Study of the CIO during the Second World War' (PhD thesis, University of California, Berkeley, 1974), 334.

33 Brody (1981) *op. cit.*, 174.

34 Bain and Price (1980) *loc. cit.*

35 P. K. Edwards (1981) *op. cit.*, 254.

36 P. K. Edwards, 'The Exceptionalism of the American Labour Movement: The Neglected Role of Workplace Struggle', SSRC Industrial Relations Research Unit paper (Coventry: University of Warwick, February 1983), Table 2, 7.

37 Lichtenstein (1982) *op. cit.*, 38–41, 51–3.

38 P. K. Edwards (1983a) *op. cit.*, 7, shows that the number of workers involved in reported strikes outside the coal industry rose 23% from 33.8 per 1,000 employees from 1937 to 1941 to 41.6 per 1,000 from 1942 to 1945.

39 Lichtenstein (1962) *op. cit.*, 126.

40 *Ibid.*, 51, 72–81.

41 P. K. Edwards (1981) *op. cit.*, 173; Lichtenstein (1982) *op. cit.*, 113.

42 P. K. Edwards (1981) *op. cit.*, 254.

43 Preis (1972) *op. cit.*, 281, is clearly wrong to refer to the 18½ cents agreed at GM after a three month strike in 1945–46 as 'a proud victory'. Anderson and Jefferys (1983) *op. cit.*, chapter 8, suggest the failure to win more than Chrysler and Ford, where the same settlement was reached without strike action, had a demoralizing effect among shopfloor workers.

44 Mike Davis, 'The Barren Marriage of American Labour and the Democratic Party', *New Left Review*, 124 (Nov.–Dec. 1980), 74, is right to point out the significance of 'the rise of wartime nationalism' on the subsequent course of labor history. But he oversteps the evidence in arguing that this 'ultimately created the basis for a new cultural cohesion within the postwar American working-class'. Not only is that 'cultural cohesion' problematic, but 'wartime nationalism' does not in itself explain the 1940s rightward shift of American politics. In Britain, for example, it did not prevent the election of the Attlee Labour Government. Wartime nationalism was important – but as one of a complex of factors that included the post-war strength of American capitalism, American management's own history and dynamics, and the serious weakening of independent (from the employers and the state) working class organizations.

45 Lichtenstein (1982) *op. cit.*, 19. Ford and Chrysler joined GM in securing a 'no strike' security clause in their contracts in 1946 after the national no strike pledge had lapsed.

46 David Caute, *The Great Fear: The Anti-Communist Purge under Truman and*

Eisenhower (London: Secker & Warburg, 1978), 27. The CIO's Political Action Committees were formed in 1944 to campaign for the re-election of Roosevelt in response to the poor Democratic performance – especially in the CIO strongholds of the Midwest – in the 1942 elections; M. Davis (1980) *op. cit.*, 70.

47 Angus Campbell, 'A Classification of Presidential Elections', in Chubb and Allen (eds.) *op. cit.*, 107–9. Harry Truman was elected vice-president of the United States on the Roosevelt ticket in 1944 and assumed the presidency on Roosevelt's sudden death in April 1945.

48 McCarthy chaired its Sub-Committee on Investigations; Caute (1978) *op. cit.*, 85, 106.

49 Christopher Lasch, *The Agony of the American Left: One Hundred Years of Radicalism* (London: Penguin, 1973), 66–7.

50 Caute (1978) *op. cit.*, 356.

51 Caute cites an estimate that in 1958 about 13.5 million Americans came within the scope of the loyalty program; to this total he adds another 4.5 million who worked in the private sector in defense related industries and in companies where the employer or the union had inspired a security program. He concludes that about one in every five working people in the mid 1950s had to take an oath or receive clearance as a condition of employment; *ibid.*, 269–70.

52 Herbert Irvine's contemporary study of shop stewards and UAW democracy. 'The UAW–CIO Shop Steward. A Consideration of his Role as a Force for Democracy' (MA thesis, University of Buffalo, February 1951), 86, argued: 'The leadership has established a thoroughgoing control in the realm of collective bargaining and strikes, greatly limiting the initiative of secondary leaders and the rank and file itself in these matters.'

53 Irving Howe and B. J. Widick, *The UAW and Walter Reuther* (New York: Random, 1949), 182; F. Marquart, *An Autoworkers' Journal* (University Park, PA: Pennsylvania University Press, 1975), 109–110.

54 Gordon *et al.* (1982) *op. cit.*, 216–19; Jeremy Brecher, *Strike!* (Greenwich, Connecticut: Fawcett, 1972), 342.

55 MacDonald (1963) *op. cit.*, 400.

56 Jack Stieber, *Governing the UAW* (New York: Wiley and Sons, 1962), 132, 35–6.

57 Harvey Swados, 'The UAW – Over the Top or Over the Hill?', *Dissent*, X, no. 4 (Autumn 1963), 330.

58 Cochran (1977) *op. cit.*, 259, 279; Anderson and Jefferys (1983) *op. cit.*, chapter 7; Marquart (1975) *op. cit.*, 139; Stieber (1962) *op. cit.*, 92–4.

59 Hyman (1975) *op. cit.*, 116, argued: 'The ability to negotiate with the employer(s) over a significant range of issues represents a source of power within trade unionism: centralized bargaining over the main substantive conditions of employment normally consolidates the control of the central negotiators over the union membership.'

60 Howe and Widick (1949) *op. cit.*, 239–40.

61 *Fortune*, July 1950.

62 Gordon *et al.* (1982) *op. cit.*, 219–20.
63 See the discussion of 'labor revolts' in R. Herding (1972) *op. cit.*, 255–319. Paul Edwards recently explained this 1970s' 'over emphasis on the radical possibilities of rank and file action and a corresponding lack of concern with its limits and the resilience of the institutionalized system' as a 'reaction against the complacency' of the 1950s and early 1960s; P. K. Edwards (1981) *op. cit.*, 217.
64 Company data.
65 Edward Greer, *Big Steel: Black Politics and Corporate Power in Gary, Indiana* (New York: Monthly Review, 1979), 33, draws a parallel between the victory of the 1967 black coalition in Gary, Indiana, and the victory of the multi-ethnic New Deal coalition in 1934.
66 In an important critique of Brecher's *Strike*, David Montgomery agrees that for many American workers, 'nothing corrupts like powerlessness'; but he argues equally that others have a different experience and that 'For the last century the union, even in some of its worst forms, has provided a shield behind which workers of no more than average aggressiveness have found both emancipation from the bonds of subservience to the bourgeois order and a link between themselves and their more forceful shopmates': Montgomery (1973) *op. cit.*, 71.
67 James R. Green, *The World of the Worker: Labor in Twentieth Century America* (New York: Hill and Wang, 1980), 234. Federal and municipal employees made up most of the increase in union members.
68 Bain and Price (1980) *op. cit.*, 89. The percentages in both NBER and BLS series quoted are of 'potential union membership', the civilian non-agricultural labor force.
69 George Ruben, 'Organized Labor in 1981: A Shifting of Priorities', *Monthly Labor Review* (January 1982), 26.
70 Quoted in 1972 by Kim Moody and Jim Woodward, *Battle Lines: The Coal Strike of '78* (Detroit: Sun, 1978), 110.
71 Staughton Lynd, 'Workers' Control in a Time of Diminished Workers' Rights', *Radical America*, 10, no. 5 (September–October 1976), 7–9, lists ten areas in which court decisions limited the already narrow definition of workers' rights created by the Taft–Hartley Act of 1947.
72 August Meier and Elliott Rudwick, *Black Detroit and the Rise of the UAW* (New York: Oxford University Press, 1979), 213.
73 James A. Geschwender, *Class, Race and Worker Insurgency: The League of Revolutionary Black Workers* (New York: Cambridge University Press, 1977), 41.
74 B. J. Widick, 'Black Workers: Double Discontent', in *Auto Work and its Discontents*, B. J. Widick (ed.) (Baltimore: Johns Hopkins University Press, 1976), 56.
75 This is discussed in three articles by Frank C. Pierson, H. R. Northrup and Jack Barbash in *Industrial Relations*, 1, no. 1 (October 1961).
76 Leonard R. Sayles and George Srauss, *The Local Union* (New York: Harcourt, Brace, 1967), 161.

77 Geschwender (1977) *op. cit.*, 40.

78 *Ibid.*, 48.

79 Quoted in Philip Foner, *Organized Labor and the Black Worker, 1619–1973* (New York: International Publishers, 1976), 334.

80 *Ibid.*, 335.

81 Polenberg (1980) *op. cit.*, 168, 181–90.

82 Green (1980) *op. cit.*, 234; Sidney Lens, *Radicalism in America* (New York: Cromwell, 1969), 369–74.

83 Detroit Free Press, *Blacks in Detroit* (Detroit Free Press reprint, December 1980), 44.

84 Green (1980) *op. cit.*, 240–5.

85 Quoted in Studs Terkel, *Working* (New York: Avon, 1975), 262.

86 Interview by author with several Detroit autoworkers, summer 1973.

87 Polenberg (1980) argues that 'the years after 1963 witnessed the most powerful surge of social reform since the New Deal', detailing 'legislation in the fields of medical care, education, housing, civil rights, poverty and immigration', *op. cit.*, 173, 181–207.

88 *Ibid.*, 276–8.

89 Michigan Department of Social Services, 'Monthly Trend Report of Key DSS Statistics: May 1982' (Detroit: Data Reporting Section, June 25, 1982), Table 1a.

90 Quoted in Moody and Woodward (1978) *op. cit.*, 123.

91 Company data, *Detroit Free Press*, August 9, 1982.

92 Moody and Woodward (1978) *op. cit.*, 58–9, describe how in Detroit several auto union locals started to organize collections in mid February 1978 – to be followed two weeks later by Fraser announcing a national donation from the UAW to the UMW.

93 Zabala (1983) *op. cit.*, 125.

94 D. Quinn Mills, 'Reforming the United States System of Collective Bargaining', *Monthly Labor Review* (March 1983), 19–21.

95 Interview by author with Ernie Savoie, Director, Labor Relations, Ford Motor Company, Detroit, June 30, 1982.

96 Interview by author with Fred G. Haubold, Director, International Labor Relations, General Motors, Detroit, June 29, 1982.

97 Slichter (1941) *op. cit.*, 561.

98 Jack Stieber, 'Unauthorized Strikes under the American and British Industrial Relations Systems', *British Journal of Industrial Relations*, 6, no. 2 (July 1968), 235–7.

99 Company data.

100 In 1973, for example, the international informally encouraged action by seven Chrysler plants (including a half shift strike at Dodge Main instigated by president Andy Hardy) on the expiry of the 1970 contract. Woodcock, still in negotiations, then called an official strike but did not break off talks with management. This maneuver allowed him to release the pressure building up in the rank and file, while keeping tight control of the strike movement and giving himself time to finalize agreement with the corpor-

ation just one week later. Interview by author with Dick Clancy, Chrysler Corporation Labor Relations Executive and Personnel Manager at Hamtramck Assembly, 1969–80, Detroit, July 28, 1982.

101 Company data.

102 Gordon *et al.* (1982) *op. cit.*, 219; Jonathan Zeitlin argues similarly for the UK, 'Workplace Organization in the British Car Industry: A Review', *History Workshop*, 10 (Autumn 1980), and is challenged by Dave Lyddon, 'Workplace Organization in the British Car Industry: A Critique of Jonathan Zeitlin', *History Workshop*, 15 (Spring 1983).

103 Slichter, Healey and Livernash (1960) *op. cit.*, 663.

104 J. R. Norsworthy and Craig A. Zabala, 'Worker Attitude, Worker Performance, and Productivity', (Washington, DC: Bureau of the Census, Sept. 1983, mimeographed), 19–20.

105 Charles F. Sabel, *Work and Politics: The Division of Labor in Industry* (New York: Cambridge University Press, 1982), 194–227.

106 Goodrich (1920) *op. cit.*, 54.

107 Hill (1981) *op. cit.*, 169–73.

108 Gordon *et al.* (1982) *op. cit.*, 215.

3. From company picnics to Coughlin

1 Bernstein (1960) *op. cit.*, 7.

2 Charles K. Hyde, *History of the Dodge Brothers Motor Car Company Plant 1910–1980* (Detroit: Wayne State University, 1981, mimeographed), 17; Harold Katz, *The Decline of the Competition in the Automobile Industry, 1920–1940* (New York: Arno, 1977), 159.

3 Donald F. Davies, 'The Price of Conspicuous Production: The Detroit Elite and the Automobile Industry, 1900–1933', *Journal of Social History* (Fall 1982), 24.

4 Reginald Stuart, *Bailout* (South Bend, IN: And Books, 1980), 39–51.

5 Sidney Fine, *The Automobile under the Blue Eagle* (Ann Arbor: University of Michigan, 1963), 18.

6 Katz (1977) *op. cit.*, 111.

7 See table 1 in A. D. Chandler, *Giant Enterprise* (New York: Harcourt, Brace & World, 1964), 3.

8 Katz (1977) *op. cit.*, 164.

9 Top executives used to leave their work to meet him at the Detroit train station on his return from frequent business trips to New York City as they fought over the succession; Stuart (1980) *op. cit.*, 50; Howell John Harris, *The Right to Manage: Industrial Relations Policies of American Business in the 1940s* (Madison: University of Wisconsin, 1982), 27, cites Clarence J. Hicks, *My Life in Industrial Relations: Fifty Years in the Growth of a Profession* (New York: Harper, 1941), 111: 'In no area . . . is the character and personality of the controlling executive or group more clearly reflected than in policies dealing with labor relations.'

10 Robert W. Dunn, *Labor and Automobiles*, (New York: International Publishers, 1929), 153.

11 *Ibid.*, 103.
12 *Ibid.*, 146.
13 Anderson and Jefferys (1983) *op. cit.*, chapter 3.
14 Stanley B. Mathewson, *Restriction of Output among Unorganized Workers*, (New York: Viking Press, 1931), 40.
15 *Ibid.*, 45.
16 Fine (1963) *op. cit.*, 20.
17 Zaremba oral history, August–October 1961; transcription in Oral History Archive, Walter Reuther Library, Wayne State University [archive abbreviated to WSU in future references], 4.
18 Anderson and Jefferys (1983) *op. cit.*, chapter 3. Anderson was known subsequently as 'Little John' Anderson to distinguish him from a leading CP member 'Big John' Anderson.
19 Ross collection, Box 3, Report dated December 11, 1933. Document collections of Walter Reuther Library, Wayne State University [collections abbreviated to WRL in future references].
20 Anderson and Jefferys (1983) *op. cit.*, chapter 2; Greer (1979) *op. cit.*, 89.
21 Ross oral history [WSU], 3.
22 Bannon oral history [WSU], 1.
23 Nalezty interview. The wire room was a show department because it was a relatively clean department situated on the first floor near the main entrance to Dodge Main and the predominantly women workers were issued with blue overalls with the Dodge motif on them. Zaremba recalled conditions in the heat treatment department: 'It was a cardinal sin to speak during working to your fellow workers'; [WSU], 3.
24 Chrysler Corporation, *Financial and General Fact Book* (Detroit: Chrysler 1973), 81: new Plymouth registrations rose from 64,301 in 1930 to 249,667 in 1933.
25 Cited in Bernstein (1969) *op. cit.*, 2.
26 P. K. Edwards (1980) *op. cit.*, table 4A, 258.
27 Anderson and Jefferys (1983) *op. cit.*, chapter 3; for a complementary account of the 1933 Briggs strike see Keeran (1980) *op. cit.*, chapter 4.
28 Keeran (1980) *op. cit.*, 95.
29 Marquart collection [WRL], Box 3.
30 Zaremba oral history [WSU], 3.
31 Bernstein (1969) *op. cit.*, 95.
32 National Recovery Administration, *Code of Fair Competition*, no. 1403-1-04, 8; in Ross collection [WRL], Box 3.
33 Keeran (1980) *op. cit.*, 100.
34 The AFL meeting was preceded by an August 1933 meeting in the Cass Technical High School where two Detroit congressmen explained Section 7A of the NIRA to an audience that included several auto workers; *Dodge Main News*, May 10, 1952 [in future references abbreviated to *DMN*].
35 Local 18277 Minute Book, September 24, 1933, Marquart collection [WRL], Box 3. In 1933 Chrysler spent $61,627 on labor espionage. Andrews later befriended Richard Frankensteen, president of the 'independent' Chrysler

union and sent daily reports to Corporations, Auxiliary, the spying company employed by Walter Chrysler ever since he had used its services while working for GM. They paid Andrews $40 a month for his reports and charged Chrysler $9 a day; *DMN*, May 10, 1952.

36 Ross oral history [WSU], 7–12; Zaremba oral history [WSU], 5.

37 Local 18277 Minutes, October 6, 1933.

38 *DMN*, May 10, 1952.

39 Bernstein (1969) *op. cit.*, 95.

40 John Anderson confirmed the sense of betrayal experienced by young union-minded autoworkers in 1933 when, having at first supported the building of federal local unions, it dawned upon them that the AFL would soon split the workers up into their various trade groups; Anderson and Jefferys (1983) *op. cit.*, chapter 4.

41 For many years Budd had produced a company magazine called *The Buddgette*, full of interviews with 'Buddites'; Dunn (1929) *op. cit.*, 156. The company saw the way forward to turn its paternalism into a company union. But when a strike by around 1,000 of its 4,000 workers took place to force recognition of the AFL, Budd successfully defied both Regional and National Labor Board rulings that the company should hold a proper election – a defiance which eventually helped lead to the 1935 Supreme Court where the NIRA itself was declared unconstitutional; Fine (1963) *op. cit.*, 194–202. Paradoxically, the Budd Company's Cowley plant was the first in which production workers were unionized in Britain after a key strike in 1934; Lyddon (1983) *op. cit.*, 135.

42 Shown by the October 2, 1933 cushion room firings and by the large sums spent on both Chrysler and GM on company anti-union spies between 1933 and 1937. A Dodge worker, W. Montowski, a metal finisher clock no. T369, confessed to being paid $40 a month plus expenses by Corporations Auxiliary for reporting on the activities of successively Local 18277, the Dodge AIWA locals and then UAW Local 3, from January 24, 1934 until January 26, 1937; Zaremba collection [WRL], Box 9.

43 Bernstein (1969) *op. cit.*, 39–40, cites a contemporary BLS survey of 593 company unions that found that 378 of them had been established during the NRA period. The BLS survey found: 'The great majority ... were set up entirely by management. Management conceived the idea, developed the plan, and initiated the organization.'

44 Employee Representation Plan and letter, in Zaremba collection [WRL], Box 6.

45 Zaremba collection [WRL], Box 1.

46 The plan was drafted by the future GM director of industrial relations, Merle C. Hale, following a meeting of divisional managers.

47 Dunn (1929) *op. cit.*, 152.

48 Fine (1963) *op. cit.*, 155.

49 Cited, *ibid.*, 288.

50 Harris describes Chrysler management in the late 1930s as 'ideologically antiunion and politically reactionary'. But Harris' three categories of post-

Wagner Act management industrial relations policies – 'persistent anti-unionism; realistic accommodation and adaptation; and the progressive approach' – don't quite capture the mixture of welfarism, paternalism and antiunionism that led both Chrysler and GM to establish Works Councils. Indeed, perhaps instead of a rigid line between 'antiunionism' and 'realism', a better understanding would be reached if GM and Chrysler's policy were both seen as being 'realistically antiunion' – with subsequent differences emerging from the different realities the two firms faced; Harris (1982) *op. cit.*, 29.

51 Fine (1963) *op. cit.*, 161. Fine misses the link between the Chrysler plan and an early and active shopfloor trade unionism but he does note the different impact the company union plans had on Chrysler and GM workers. He puts this down to what can be summarized as a greater sophistication on the part of GM.

52 Hyde points out that the new General Motors Cadillac plant being built on the same site and scheduled to start operations in 1985, requires 465 acres for a plant of just 3 million square feet; Hyde (1981) *op. cit.*, 23.

53 *Ibid.*, 20–5.

54 Zaremba collection [WRL], Box 1; Marquart collection [WRL], Box 3.

55 Anderson and Jefferys (1983) *op. cit.*, chapter 5.

56 Fine (1963) *op. cit.*, 157–8; Kruchko points out that the works councils GM organized at its Norwood Chevrolet and Fisher Body plants did 'provide the Norwood worker with a valuable nucleus of labor leaders'; but at Norwood the works council representatives did not eventually become the local union as occurred at Dodge Main; Kruchko (1972) *op. cit.*, 64.

57 Zaremba oral history [WSU], 8.

58 Frankensteen oral history [WSU], 5.

59 Polenberg (1980) *op. cit.*, 36.

60 Brinkley (1982) *op. cit.*, 83.

61 Cited in Denis Moniere, *Le developpement des ideologies au Quebec* (Montreal: Editions Quebec/Amerique, 1977), 257. I would like to thank Gregor Murray for this reference to the origins of Catholic trade unionism in Canada. Coughlin himself was born in and studied theology in Canada before being appointed to serve in Detroit in 1923; Brinkley (1982) *op. cit.*, 84–8.

62 Brinkley (1982) *op. cit.*, 97–102.

63 *Ibid.*, 133.

64 *Ibid.*, 287.

65 *Ibid.*, 200.

66 Zaremba oral history [WSU], 14.

67 Minutes of Employee Representatives Meeting, April 9, 1935, Zaremba collection [WRL], Box 1.

68 Marquart collection [WRL], Box 3. There were ten locals of the AIWA reported by this date. Six were in Dodge (including the trim, Local 99, the paint department and Department 76, the body-in-white), and one each for Chrysler's Kercheval plant, Packard, Hudson and the Motor Products plants.

69 Dodge Main Works Council minutes, May 2, 1935, Marquart collection [WRL], Box 3.

70 *Ibid.*, July 3, July 11, 1935.
71 *Employee Representation in the Plants of Chrysler Motors*, October 1933, in Zaremba collection [WRL], Box 6.
72 Zaremba collection [WRL], Box 6.
73 *Revised and Adopted AIWA Constitution*, March 10, 1936, Zaremba collection [WRL], Box 6. The constitution also provided that 'Any member serving full time for the organization shall be paid no more than he or she can earn at his or her occupation', reflecting both the AIWA's recruitment of women and a distinct anti-privilege sentiment. The Coughlin influence expressed itself in the clause requiring a two-thirds majority for strike action.
74 Works Council minutes, October 16, 1936, Zaremba collection [WRL], Box 1.
75 Brinkley is right to suggest 'it did not deserve the label of "a company union"'; but he is wrong to argue in chapter 4: 'but neither was the Automotive Industrial Workers Association at the center of the labor militancy that would ultimately produce the United Auto Workers'; Brinkley (1982) *op. cit.*, 200.
76 Local 18277 Minute Book, April 10, 1934, May 4, 1934, October 10, 1934; Padget was confirmed as president, while Jack Cousins, one of the cushion room workers dismissed the previous year, defeated Andrews as vice-president, and Harry Ross was elected recording secretary.
77 Fine (1963) *op. cit.*, 407.
78 Works Council minutes, March 24, April 5, September 20, 1935, April 17, 1936; Zaremba collection [WRL], Box 1.
79 Or like Walter Reuther who attended university part-time and John W. Anderson who was a full-time student under J. R. Commons in Wisconsin; see Anderson and Jefferys (1983) *op. cit.*, chapter 3.
80 This complements Ronald Schatz's findings, 'Union Pioneers: The Founders of Local Unions at General Electric and Westinghouse, 1933–1937', *Journal of American History*, no. 66 (1979), 586–602, that male union organizers 'were members of an elite stratum of the industry's work force', but expands the definition of 'elite' from craft skills to include social origins and educational and political backgrounds.
81 Friedlander (1975) *op. cit.*, 121–2.
82 Cited in Keeran (1980) *op. cit.*, 146. The CP tolerated this resolution since they didn't want to start a new fight on the matter after they had already got the constitutional proposal to ban CP members from holding office remitted to the Convention Constitutional Committee where they could bury it.
83 Marquart collection [WRL], Box 3; Howe and Widick (1949) *op. cit.*, 13.
84 Friedlander (1975) *op. cit.*, 116.
85 Wyndham Mortimer, *Organize!*, (Boston: Beacon Press, 1971), 103.
86 Ross collection [WRL], Box 3.
87 Only in a handful of other auto plants was there such a continuity of organization; one was White Motors, Cleveland, which won recognition in 1933; Mortimer (1971) *op. cit.*, 66–7. Another was Kelsey-Hayes, Detroit, where a core of at least 200 UAW members and a shop steward organization

was kept together from 1933; Cochran (1977) *op. cit.*, 114; Anderson and Jefferys (1983) *op. cit.*, chapter 4. Exactly how big the Chrysler membership was is open to some doubt. When the UAW bargaining committee met Chrysler on March 3, 1937 it claimed 20,000 UAW members at Dodge Main, *DMN, Strike Bulletin*, March 9, 1937. But Zaremba [WSU], 13, recalled that when Dodge Local 3 called the sit-down only some 800 out of the 24,000 manual workforce were actually paid-up UAW members. Given the level of participation in the sit-down, and the degree of shop steward organization already in existence by then, it is likely Zaremba's figure was those who might attend Local 3 meetings. Total membership was well over 5,000 in 1936.

4. Fair play with the management: 1936–41

1 Marquart collection [WRL], Box 3.
2 Lists in Ross collection [WRL], Box 3.
3 Leaflets and reports, *ibid.*, Box 1. How many workers actually attended these after work meetings is not known; but it was clearly enough to impress management.
4 Reported to the Automobile Manufacturers Association (that excluded Ford); cited in McPherson (1940) *op. cit.*, 98.
5 Katz (1977), *op. cit.*, 162–3.
6 Works Council Minutes, October 16, November 11, 1936, in Zaremba collection [WRL], Box 1; Anderson and Jefferys (1983), *op. cit.*, chapter 6.
7 Bernstein (1969) *op. cit.*, 553.
8 Beynon develops the idea of 'working class *factory consciousness*' in ways that apply directly to the growing anti-boss politics that developed in Dodge Main in the 1930s. This, he argues, has three aspects: (1) it provides an understanding of 'class relationships in terms of their direct manifestation in conflict between the bosses and the workers within the factory'; (2) it is 'rooted in the workplace where struggles are fought over the control of the job and the "rights" of managers and workers'; and (3) it is 'political' because it is concerned 'with exploitation and power', but 'it is a politics of the factory'; Beynon (1975) *op. cit.*, 98, 206.
9 This definition of 'legitimate' behavior gave Chrysler workers considerable influence in the shaping of what David Brody describes as the post-war 'workplace rule of law'.
10 Local 3 Business Meeting minutes, December 27, 1936, Dodge Local 3 collection [WRL], Box 3.
11 Local 3 Stewards' Meeting minutes, January 25, 1937, Local 3 collection [WRL], Box 4. All the chief stewards from one unit (like the foundry or trim) were supposed to meet and elect a 'Captain'; but this idea appears to have dropped soon after it was proposed.
12 Zaremba oral history [WSU], 28; Nalezty interview.
13 Stewards' Meeting minutes, April 5, 1937. The number of blue button stewards is difficult to estimate because their numbers varied enormously from area to area within the plant, and because their informal status has

meant documentary evidence is not as forthcoming as for the chief steward system.

14 Keeran (1980) *op. cit.*, 188.
15 Works Council Minutes, February 9, 1937.
16 Local 3 Membership Meeting minutes, January 30, 1937, Ross [WRL], Box 3.
17 Zaremba oral history [WSU], 28; Zaremba collection [WRL], Box 9. The account is written by Zaremba in 1947 on flyleaf of 'The Many and the Few'.
18 *Dodge Strike Bulletin*, March 10, March 11, 1937.
19 Zaremba collection [WRL], Box 9.
20 An indication of the numbers of UAW members at Dodge Main in 1936–37 is given by the numbers of workers making the special trip to the Local 3 hall to vote in elections. In the elections held after the merger of the AIWA into the UAW in late summer or early fall 1936, 5,739 votes were cast for the position of president. In May 1937 the vote for the three candidates for Local 3 president totalled 9,517; Local 3 Executive Board Minutes [abbreviated LEB in future], May 20, 1937, Marquart collection [WRL], Box 3.
21 *Dodge Strike Bulletin*, March 18, 1937.
22 *Ibid.*, March 12, 1937.
23 *Ibid.*, March 10, 1937.
24 *Ibid.*, March 17, 1937.
25 *Ibid.*, March 17, 19, 22, 1937.
26 The paint shop worker Alfred McNeil described Martin as 'one of the finest orators that we have ever heard'; *DMN*, March 22, 1952.
27 Stewards' meeting minutes, April 5, 1937; *Dodge News*, April 7, 1937.
28 GM–UAW Agreement, February 11, and Supplemental Agreement, March 12, 1937; Harris (1982) *op. cit.*, 28.
29 Chrysler–UAW Agreement, 6 April, Supplemental Agreement, April 14, 1937.
30 *Ibid.*, 5.
31 Anderson and Jefferys (1983) *op. cit.*, chapter 6.
32 The GM strike was a clear victory for the UAW. Anderson recalls the GM strike as the first in which he had been involved where he had actually returned to work once it was over. Previously he had always ended up fired. He and other militants were elated by the result. Anderson and Jefferys (1983) *op. cit.*, chapter 6.
33 Walter Reuther collection [WRL], GM Agreements Box. The confidence aroused by the sit-down victory at GM changed the atmosphere throughout the auto industry. Primarily this was because it was the first time that significant numbers had struck a major auto manufacturer and then returned to their jobs afterwards, cf: Anderson and Jefferys (1983) *op. cit.*, chapter 6. I am not arguing that GM workers were unaffected by this new confidence. Indeed, according to GM there were 170 sit-downs in its plants between March and June 1937; Bernstein (1969) *op. cit.*, 559. My argument is that in GM this new combativity did not become as organically linked to organizational structure via sectional bargaining as it was at Chrysler.

34 1938 GM Contract, 2.
35 Harris (1982) *op. cit.*, 29.
36 Alfred P. Sloan, *My Years with General Motors* (London: Sidgwick and Jackson, 1965), 406.
37 Cited in Bernstein (1969) *op. cit.*, 554.
38 A complicated story reworked here with Bernstein's warning in mind: 'The danger in recounting this episode is that the historian, who is expected to be coherent, will create a state of order that is the product of his imagination rather than of the real world'; Bernstein (1969) *op. cit.*, 555.
39 Shop stewards were present in GM plants. Indeed, despite a tendency to overlook their role in the Flint GM sit-down (Keeran (1980) *op. cit.*, 168, describes the stewards who attended the meeting which decided to sit-down as merely 'unionists'), stewards existed in most GM plants where there were UAW members from 1937 until at least 1946 when GM conceded the dues check-off system, and in some cases still longer; Foster oral history [WSU], 15. My argument here is that in GM stewards were neither structurally located in the GM–UAW bargaining process nor legitimized in GM workers' consciousness as a proper way of exercising restraint over management power.
40 In November 1936 the Union Party only got 892,378 votes for Lemke, and Coughlin carried out his promise of retiring from broadcasting . . . but only for a short time. Brinkley (1982) *op. cit.*, 252–61.
41 Zaremba oral history [WSU], 15.
42 Brinkley (1982) *op. cit.*, 200.
43 Strike EB Minutes, March 23, 1937, Zaremba collection [WRL], Box 9.
44 *Ibid.*
45 Business Meeting Minutes, April 25, 1937.
46 Marquart collection [WRL], Box 3. Earl Reynolds was the center slate candidate for vice-president, while Tony Probe, a former Canadian IWW member and well-known Detroit militant, came third with 12%. The left slate stood for 'A solid united local based on REAL DEMOCRACY IN THE UNION'.
47 *Program of the Unity Caucus*, Milwaukee Convention, August 1937.
48 *Martin–Frankensteen Progressive Caucus for the Preservation of the UAW and the CIO*, 1938 Convention.
49 The right-wing controlled Dodge EB warned members against attending 'unofficial' meetings, EB Minutes, July 1, 1937; and called for the exclusion of sectional shop stewards from stewards' meetings, Steward Body Minutes, May 1, 1938. Friedlander suggests Unity was also more concerned with grievances affecting ethnic workers; Friedlander (1975) *op. cit.*, 116.
50 Ross collection [WRL], Box 2.
51 Keeran (1980) *op. cit.*, 196.
52 Marquart collection [WRL], Box 3.
53 LEB Minutes, November 10, 1938.
54 *Ibid.*, December 5, 1938.
55 *Ibid.*, December 29, 1938. Frank Szymanski, a long-time Coughlinite activist in Dodge, seconded this motion.

56 Ross oral history [WSU], 26.
57 LEB Minutes, February–March 1939.
58 'Buck' Jones' songs in Ross collection [WRL], Box 3.
59 Ross collection [WRL], Box 3; Leaflet dated January 10, 1939. This was the first of many election campaigns at Dodge Main in which anti-communism was the principal campaigning issue for at least one slate.
60 Marquart collection [WRL], Box 3. The leaflet, supporting Reid for president and Szymanski for sergeant-at-arms, came out after McCann's defection to the UAW–AFL. His name for vice-president was crossed out and Joe Mehilic substituted. It presented the slate as representing the true tradition of Dodge trade unionists: 'Each of these candidates was an active member of the old AIWA and has continued to be active in the UAW. These men are proven Union Builders.'
61 LEB Minutes, November 10, September 9, 1939: one of the stewards criticized for 'indifference' about the spread of Homer Martin buttons in Department 76 in February, was Barney Hopkins, who also performed at other times a similar role to Reid's as 'honest broker'.
62 Out of 20,583 votes cast (22,000 eligible), 17,654 went to the UAW–CIO and just 837 went to the UAW–AFL. Across all thirteen Chrysler plants where the Labor Board balloted there was an 80% majority for the UAW–CIO, with 40,564 voting CIO and 4,673 voting AFL and 4,476 voting neither out of 54,000 eligible voters: *United Auto Worker: Dodge Local 3 Edition*, October 4, 1939.
63 Cochran (1977) *op. cit.*, 143, writes: 'When, clause by clause, the new constitution emerged from the convention mill, the authority of the president had been pruned, the powers of the executive board augmented, the yearly convention brought back, the rights of locals increased, and control over collective bargaining protected through a structure of intracorporation councils of delegates from the plants. The UAW came out of the Cleveland convention the most democratic union in the country.'
64 *United Auto Worker, Dodge Local 3 Edition*, October 10, 1939.
65 *Ibid.*; it reported the decisions by the Dodge steward body that no member of Local 3 should contact management without a chief steward present and that any steward who didn't report dues collected within a thirty-day period would have his button taken away.
66 *Ibid.*
67 1939 Unemployment Compensation Commission *Report*, November 3, 1939 into the eligibility of Dodge workers to claim unemployment insurance on the basis that they were locked out. This report concluded in the workers' favor; but when Chrysler appealed this decision to the Referee on August 6, 1940, he ruled that a labor dispute had taken place so the Dodge workers were not qualified to receive unemployment compensation; Zaremba collection [WRL], Box 8.
68 *UAW, Dodge Local 3 Edition*, October 18, 1939.
69 October 25, 1939.
70 Brinkley (1982) *op. cit.*, 265–6.

71 LEB Minutes, November 12, 1939.
72 Charles E. Coughlin, *The Chrysler CIO Industrial Strike* (Detroit: pamphlet, November 12, 1939); in Ross collection [WRL], Box 3.
73 Leaflet issued by the black organization, the National Association of American Workers, reported to the Local 3 executive board, LEB Minutes, November 24, 1939.
74 Chrysler Corporation–UAW Agreement, November 29, 1939; Zaremba collection [WRL], Box 6. A detailed account of the back-to-work movement is given in Meier and Rudwick (1979) *op. cit.*, 67–71.
75 LEB Minutes, November 27, 29, 1939.
76 Chrysler–UAW Contract, November 29, 1939, 14–15.
77 *DMN*, December 6, 1939.
78 Marquart oral history [WSU], 22–3. There is no way of knowing whether this incident was reported by the superintendent as a work stoppage. If the Dodge General Manager knew about it, it probably was. But if he didn't, the superintendent may well have kept quiet. The incident illustrates the problem of using strike statistics as an indicator of the true level of conflict, particularly in the early years of the UAW's existence before Chrysler created a specialist labor relations function. Chrysler later claimed there were 200 contract violations including 130 strikes in its plants between March 1937 and November 1939; 100 violations between December 1939 and December 1941; and 98 violations between January 1942 and May 1943: Chrysler Corporation, *Beyond the Facts and the Records* (Detroit: Chrysler, 1943), 7–8.
79 Interview by author with Ed Liska, Detroit, August 11, 1982.
80 Named after the strategy decided upon by Mortimer, 'Big John' Anderson (the former MESA member) and Reuther, of striking GM's skilled workers when the production workers were laid off and GM was preparing for the 1940 models; Anderson and Jefferys (1983) *op. cit.*, chapter 7.
81 Harris (1982) *op. cit.*, 29.
82 Sloan (1965) *loc. cit.*

5. World War II: sound American unionism

1 *DMN*, July 15, 1941; *Detroit Times*, January 21, 1942.
2 *DMN*, July 15, September 15, 1941.
3 *DMN*, December 18, 1941, January 1, 1942.
4 *Detroit News*, June 14, 1942. Chrysler's draughtsmen, by contrast, were able to use their bargaining strength designing the new tools and lay-outs for war production to win the recognition of their union, the Society of Designing Engineers in December 1941; Harris (1982) *op. cit.*, 163.
5 UAW, *Conference Agenda*, April 6, 1942.
6 See Local 51 Stewards' Council minutes, April 12, 1943, Local 51 collection [WRL], Box 24, where a motion was carried unanimously: 'that the Stewards' Council go on record to support the incentive plan and the EB of the Local to work out plan and present it to the membership.' As the minutes go

on to show, however, the membership did not accept the incentive plan even though it was recommended to them by the EB and the Stewards' Council.

7 Chrysler Corporation, *10 War Labor Reports*, August 27, 1943, 552, cited in Nelson Lichtenstein (1974) *op. cit.*, 357.

8 Chrysler Corporation (1943) *op. cit.*, 8.

9 *DMN*, April 15, 1943.

10 *DMN*, March 1, 1941, February 15, 1943.

11 Lichtenstein (1982) *op. cit.*, 126.

12 Nelson Lichtenstein, 'Conflict over Workers' Control: The Automobile Industry in World War II', in *Working-class America: Essays on Labor, Community and American Society*, Michael H. Frisch and Daniel J. Walleowitz (eds.) (Chicago: University of Illinois Press, 1983), 288–90.

13 Nalezty interview.

14 Lichtenstein (1974) *op. cit.*, 353–4.

15 *DMN*, March 15, 1943.

16 *DMN*, April 1, 1943.

17 *DMN*, June 1, June 15, 1943.

18 Lichtenstein (1974) *op. cit.*, 353–6.

19 Chrysler (1943) *op. cit.*, 13.

20 Lichtenstein (1982) *op. cit.*, 54.

21 *Ibid.*, 51–3.

22 *Ibid.*, 179.

23 *Ibid.*, 20. Chrysler held the dominant management view described by Harris (1982) *op. cit.*, 51–2, that the NWLB was an intrusion and should confine 'recognition of the union's institutional existence and legitimacy to an absolute minimum'.

24 *DMN*, June 15, 1943.

25 For these views see Glaberman (1980) *op. cit.*, 128, and Lichtenstein (1983) *op. cit.*, 297.

26 *DMN*, June 15, 1943.

27 *Detroit News*, September 16, December 15, 1943.

28 *Detroit Times*, January 1, 1944.

29 Certainly, what Lichtenstein describes as 'the bureaucratic imperative', Lichtenstein (1982) *op. cit.*, 178–202, was only rarely visible at Chrysler, and then it was it was not particularly intimidating.

30 Hughes oral history [WSU], 20–2.

31 *Detroit News*, February 27, 1945. Dodge Main's facilities in 1944 were allocated as follows:

	%
Production of engines for light and heavy trucks, tank transmissions and rocket shells:	68
Manufacture of parts for aircraft:	22
Manufacture of Navy bofors anti-aircraft guns:	10
	100

32 *Detroit News*, February 24, 1945.

33 *Detroit News*, February 25, 1943.
34 *Detroit Free Press*, March 2, 1945.
35 Compiled from *Detroit Free Press*, *Detroit News*, and *Detroit Times*, February 23–6, 1945.
36 *Detroit Times*, February 23, 1945.
37 *Detroit News*, February 23, 1945.
38 Business Meeting Minutes, February 23, 1945, Local 3 collection [WRL], Box 3.
39 Friedlander (1975) *op. cit.*, 127.
40 Glaberman (1980) *op. cit.*, 116–19. About 25% of the UAW's membership participated in the postal vote and while the vote was 178,824 against rescinding the pledge and 97,620 in favor, in the Detroit metropolitan area the voting was much closer: 54% against and 46% for.
41 *Detroit News*, February 25, 1945.
42 *Detroit Times*, March 3, 1945; *Detroit News*, March 2, 1945.
43 *Detroit Times*, March 5, 1945.
44 *Detroit News*, March 1, 1945, quoted one Detroit Draft Board chairman as saying, 'It was the policy of his Board to go through their 2-B (deferment classification) lists whenever a war plant strike occurred and to contact the company involved to see if the management wished to withdraw its request for deferment for employees within jurisdiction of the board ... This was now being done by these boards in the Dodge dispute.'
45 *Detroit News*, March 21, 1945.
46 *Daily Worker*, February 27, 1945.
47 *Detroit Labor News*, March 2, 1945.
48 *Detroit P.M.*, March 5, 1945.
49 Keeran (1980) *op. cit.*, 226–7, suggests the result of the CP's wartime pro-war policy was 'marginal rather than decisive' in terms of CP influence in the UAW. This view is clearly not supported by the evidence at Dodge Main.
50 Glaberman (1980) *op. cit.*, 101–3. Lichtenstein (1982) *op. cit.*, 193, also reports the imposition of Leo LaMotte as administrator of Local 490, but he fails to comment on the re-election of the previous incumbent.
51 *Detroit Times*, March 9, 1945.
52 *Detroit Times*, March 4, 1945; speech by economic consultant John W. Scoville to the Detroit Kiwani club.
53 Harris (1982) *op. cit.*, 110–11.
54 Lichtenstein (1982) *op. cit.*, 202.

6. Unionism, solidarity and militancy: 1946–1955

1 Marquart (1975) *op. cit.*, 119, 139; Howe and Widick (1949) *op. cit.*, 263–4. In the early and mid 1940s, informal factional links through the Chrysler locals had organized joint action and exerted collective pressure on the international in 1943, 1945 and 1947.
2 *Fortune*, September 1949; Stuart (1980) *op. cit.*, 50–7; Michael Moritz and

Barrett Seaman, *Going for Broke: The Chrysler Story* (New York: Doubleday, 1981), 47–52.

3 *Fortune*, September 1949, June 1958.

4 Williamson (1975) *loc. cit.*

5 Nalezty interview; Ward's Automotive Yearbook, *1969*, 79.

6 Laurence H. Seltzer, *A Financial History of the American Automobile Industry* (New Jersey: Augusta M. Kelly, 1973 [1st edn 1928]), 66.

7 *Fortune*, October 1948.

8 *Ibid.*

9 Chrysler Corporation (1973) *op. cit.*, 51.

10 See page 44. It is a crude index because it includes all manual workers employed by the 'Big Three', not merely those involved in passenger car production. This distorts the absolute value of the car output per worker figures, but although there were changes over time in car design which also affected productivity, the index does give a rough guide to changes over time and the comparative performance of the major manufacturers.

11 Company data.

12 The configuration of the Chrysler labor force differed from GM's in particular in one further significant respect: its concentration in Detroit. In July 1955, for example, 81% of its total labor force was based in Detroit plants; UAW Research Department Collection [WRL], Box 79.

13 Fox wrote of some '40 blue buttons' on the line 'a few years back'; *DMN*, June 1956.

14 The role of the dues check-off in killing the (blue button) steward system in Ford and GM from 1941 and 1946 respectively, has been often commented on as the strategic move that took the guts out of the purpose of being a sectional steward. Since Ford and GM refused to negotiate with sectional stewards, after the companies collected workers' dues there was very little point left in acting as one. Writing in 1951 Irvine (1951) *op. cit.*, 128, made a point that was more applicable to Chrysler in the longer-term. Before the check-off was introduced in the plant he was studying, each steward would have to collect between $25 and $250 a month, as the steward's constituencies varied from 15 to 211 men. 'It is obvious,' Irvine wrote, 'that he has been relieved of an almost constant burden. Yet part of that burden was to convince the rank and file of the union that it was worth their while to pay their dues.'

15 Interview by author with Edith Fox, Detroit, April 20, 1981.

16 *DMN*, December 11, 1954.

17 Liska interview.

18 Fox interview. Some skilled chief stewards representing small departments would work.

19 Interview with Robert Jensen, Administrative Assistant to Marc Stepp, UAW Chrysler vice-president, April 7, 1981: 1949 case of Dodge Main Chief Steward Jones discharged for sleeping on the job after being disciplined for the same offence *twice* previously; in Chrysler–UAW, *Digest of Umpire Decisions* (Detroit: UAW, 1980 edition), 6–15.

20 Liska interview.

21 UAW–Chrysler Contract, April 6, 1937, Clause 4.

22 UAW–Chrysler Contract, November 29, 1939, 4.

23 UAW–Chrysler Contract, May 4, 1950, 6.

24 Chrysler–UAW, *Digest*, 7–1, 7–3. Production standards were always excluded from the umpire's jurisdiction at GM and Ford.

25 *Detroit Free Press*, March 25, 1952; *Daily Worker*, April 1, 1952.

26 Chrysler–UAW, *Digest*, 2–1. *Detroit Free Press*, May 29, 1951. Chrysler–UAW, *Digest*, 2–3.

27 Liska interview.

28 *DMN*, December 10, 1949.

29 C. Denby, *Indignant Heart: Testimony of a Black American Worker* (First published 1952; London: Pluto, 1978), 124.

30 Fox interview.

31 Liska interview.

32 Nalezty interview: 'Management tried to get us to wear laundered gloves. The workers just refused to use them. Those who couldn't work without gloves just spent half an hour sitting down and then got their new gloves.'

33 Fox interview.

34 *Detroit Times*, December 21, 1949; *DMN*, January 28, 1950.

35 The 'fair' production standard was embodied in UAW policy by the IEB on April 28, 1949: 'The UAW–CIO ... insists that reduction in the unit cost of production must be made possible by improving technology and production processes, and by efficient engineering and management, and not by placing an unfair load on workers ... It is our policy to authorize strike action in any plant, large or small, big corporation or small shop, when the facts show that an employer is attempting to drive his workers to make them produce more than a fair day's work.' Reproduced in *Spotlight: Special Chrysler Bulletin*, March 1957.

36 *DMN*, April 19, May 3, 1947.

37 See Non-Communist Affidavits in Dodge Local 3 Collection [WRL]. Certain left stewards may have avoided completing these affidavits until it became an issue. Thus Edith Van Horn, the wire room chief steward who was dismissed by Chrysler on March 3, 1952 after she was named as a Communist in the House Un-American Committee hearings in Detroit, only swore a non-communist affidavit herself on March 10; Local 3 Collection, evidence to umpire.

38 *DMN*, August 9, 1947; *The Wage Earner*, March 1950.

39 The post-war resurgence of the Dodge Main right wing was due in part to the alienation of Dodge workers from the anti-strike policy of the Thomas–Addes–CP wartime UAW leadership, and in part because of the large numbers of politically very right-wing Poles who emigrated to Hamtramck as wartime displaced persons after the Russian occupation of Poland. As early as April 1945 Zaremba complained to Addes about the role of extreme right-wing Poles on a Polish American Council (opposed to the UAW's American Polish Labor Council) who, 'with the aid of the Reuther Brothers ... are causing disruption among the Polish workers'; Addes Collection [WRL], Box 107, File 17, letter dated April 5, 1945.

40 Ross collection [WRL], Box 3; Green slate election card, February 1949.

41 *Ibid.*

42 Harvard Business School, *1948 Contract Negotiations between Chrysler Corporation and the UAW* (Harvard, 1948), 17–18.

43 Ross collection [WRL], Box 3. This 'fighting' slate reflected the new national turn of the CP USA to self-isolation.

44 *DMN*, March 26, 1949, claimed it was the biggest turnout ever in a Dodge Local 3 election.

45 The alienation of Local 3 from the international union was confirmed in August 1949 when the executive board and PAC endorsed Frankensteen for mayor of Detroit against Reuther's nominee, George Edwards. It did so after learning that Frankensteen's refusal to stand down had led to Reuther sacking Don Frankensteen (Dick's brother) after thirteen years as the UAW's Chief Auditor; *DMN*, August 8, 20, 1949.

46 Stewards' Council minutes, January 24, 1950; UAW Local 3 collection [WRL], Recording Secretary's files.

47 *DMN*, February 18, 1950.

48 *Fortune*, June 1950; *Economist*, February 4, 1950.

49 *Ibid.*; *Economist*, May 13, 1950.

50 Chrysler (1973), *Facts*.

51 *Economist*, May 13, 1950.

52 *Ibid.*, June 3, 1950.

53 *Fortune*, June, 1950.

54 *DMN*, May 13, 1950.

55 A July 1950 green slate leaflet asked: 'Were you satisfied with the way the $1,500,000 of welfare checks were *dished* out during the last 100 day strike? Was there a confirmed welfare set up in our Local, or was it a political patronage depot?' Ross collection [WRL], Box 3.

56 Grudzen–Szymanski green slate leaflet; ACTU collection [WRL], Box 23.

57 *DMN*, August 5, 1950.

58 *DMN*, October 7, 1950.

59 *Detroit Times*, May 22, 1952.

60 *DMN*, June 2, 1951.

61 *DMN*, June 9, 1951.

62 *DMN*, June 23, 1951.

63 *DMN*, June 23, 1951. McNeil, a Scot, reported in the *DMN* on October 20, 1951 on a big Catholic service that took place at the Briggs (Detroit Tigers) stadium, writing: 'Religion is the answer to Communism'. He was defeated as a chief steward in the 1952 election, but was elected to the Local 3 Publicity Committee as paint shop representative, writing regular paint shop reports. He was one of the founders of the 1957 'Rank and File' caucus; see chapter 7.

64 *DMN*, June 6, 1951, reported one of the blue button stewards was fired for swearing when he was told the first one was being dismissed.

65 *DMN*, September 15, 1951.

66 Seven zig-zag springs an hour instead of five.

67 *Detroit News*, July 19, 1951.

68 *DMN*, August 11, 1951.
69 *DMN*, November 3, 1951. After the strike vote Solomon was put on the payroll at a Local 3 business meeting until such time as he would be reinstated. This, of course, never happened. In June 1953 Solomon made his peace with Reuther and was taken on the international staff; *DMN*, June 26, 1953. The two trim shop cushion builders fired were reinstated by the umpire on January 9, 1952 without pay for the period of lay-off on the argument that 'to discharge two employees and not inflict any penalty on others indicates an unbalance'; Chrysler–UAW, *Digest*, 2–4.
70 Nalezty interview.
71 *DMN*, March 29, 1952.
72 Chrysler–UAW, *Digest of Umpire Decisions*, 6–21.
73 Caute, *op. cit.*, 373.
74 Analysis of Chrysler–UAW, *Digest*, Dodge Main decisions.
75 See figures 1 and 2 (page 9) for the 1953 upturn in GM's strike frequency and especially in its unauthorized strike loss ratio.
76 Anderson and Jefferys (1983) *op. cit.*, chapter 9.
77 *Detroit Free Press*, June 20, 1953; *Detroit Times*, June 28, 1953.
78 EB statement, *DMN*, August 22, 1953.
79 *DMN*, September 5, 1953. The vote was taken on a rag-bag of thirty-one issues that suggest the growing managerial confidence induced by the 1954 recession and the McKinsey report. The first five grievances were: The Assistant Labor Relations Supervisor spying on men in latrines; transferring operations from Dodge to locations outside Michigan; management providing inaccurate information on work schedules; the use of outside contractors; and 'foremen and supervisors intimidating stewards and refusing to allow them time to take care of grievances'.
80 *DMN*, December 5, December 26, 1953.
81 *Detroit Free Press*, April 14, 1954.
82 *DMN*, May 15, 1954.
83 Grudzen, while still Local 3 President, had spoken in favor of two-yearly elections at the UAW convention. He defended himself in the *DMN*, April 18, 1953: 'First I spoke of the enormous cost to the Local Union and second, the political bitterness which is created . . . I feel that we have grown up. We are now 17 years old, and should be no different in a Local level than the entire public. It is the policy in local government to have two year elections.' The other main argument used by Reuther in support of this move was the cost of having annual elections, estimated at $90,081 for Dodge Main alone in 1952.
84 *Detroit Free Press*, July 17, 1954.
85 *Detroit Times*, July 24, July 26, 1954.
86 Letter from O. W. Franke to J. Cheal, July 30, 1954; Dodge Local 3 collection [WRL], Presidents' files.
87 *DMN*, September 14, 1957.
88 Dodge Division/Local 3 Seniority Agreement, 9–8–54; Local 3 collection [WRL], Box 5, File 107.

89 *Detroit Free Press*, September 13, 1954.
90 *DMN*, October 16, 1954.
91 Memorandum of Understanding (regarding the production dispute at the Dodge Main Plant), October 8, 1954; Dodge Local 3 collection [WRL].
92 *Ibid*. This agreement was called 'Notation of understanding or intent as to the application of the memorandum'. Johnson and Larkin were clearly not going to admit they had signed an actual *agreement* with Local 3. The stress by management on locally negotiated written *agreements* only developed from the early 1960s once the balance of forces was clearly in management's favor.
93 Memorandum, September 30, 1954; Dodge Local 3 Collection [WRL].
94 *Detroit News*, May 6, 1955.

7. A cold one: 1956–1959

1 Harris (1982) *op. cit.*, 29.
2 Frank C. Pierson, 'Recent Employer Alliances in Perspective', *Industrial Relations*, I, no. 1 (Oct. 1961), 39.
3 G. L. Mangum, 'Taming Wildcat Strikes', *Harvard Business Review*, 38, no. 2 (1960); Jack Barbash, 'Union Response to the "Hard Line"', *Industrial Relations*, I, no. 1 (Oct. 1961), 25, noted four elements in management's 'hard line': a determination to extract the maximum benefits of automation; demands for radical changes to work rules; forcing strikes; and a major public relations campaign against wage rises and 'feather-bedding'.
4 *Fortune*, June 1958; Moritz and Seaman (1981) *op. cit.*, 47, 55; Stuart (1980) *op. cit.*, 61–2.
5 *Fortune*, June 1958.
6 Hill (1981) *op. cit.*, 84.
7 Company data; *Fortune*, June 1958.
8 *DMN*, February 5, 1955, reported with surprise that seventeen time study men were now operating in Dodge Main. They were known at the time as 'crewcuts'; Liska interview.
9 *DMN*, May 7, 1955.
10 *DMN*, August 20, 1955. The restriction upon chief stewards was seen as particularly threatening because Chrysler was insisting they should not bargain during the first hour in the morning or the first hour after lunch: 'These are the hours when the foremen jockey manpower around to suit their purpose. During these two hours the boss would be supreme and no matter what the boss was doing the steward would have no right to protest.' This restriction had been in force on committeemen in GM plants for some years; Anderson and Jefferys (1983) *op. cit.*, chapter 9.
11 *DMN*, February 18, 1956.
12 Letter, Cheal to Assistant UAW Regional Director, March 10, 1956; Dodge Local 3 collection [WRL], Box 1.
13 *DMN*, April 4, 1956.
14 *DMN*, June 16, 1956.

15 Colbert letter, 'To the Men and Women of Chrysler Corporation', September 5, 1956; Dodge Local 3 collection [WRL].
16 *DMN*, October 27, November 25, 1956.
17 *DMN*, September 29, 1956, January 26, 1957.
18 *DMN*, March 16, 1957.
19 *UAW Spotlight*, Special Chrysler Bulletin, March 1957.
20 *Ibid.*
21 *Ibid.*
22 Fox and Liska interviews.
23 *DMN*, March 23, 1957.
24 Fox interview.
25 *DMN*, February 16, March 9, 1957.
26 Attendance at the week-long UAW convention was increasingly seen as a vacation by most delegates after the consolidation of Reuther's faction in power and the introduction of biennial conventions.
27 Liska interview.
28 UAW, *16th Convention Proceedings*, April 7–12, 1957, Atlantic City, New Jersey, 198.
29 *Ibid.*, 311–28.
30 *UAW-Spotlight*, March 1957, and Corporation data.
31 *UAW, 16th Convention Proceedings*, April 7–12, 1957, Atlantic City, New Jersey, 311–28.
32 Fox and Liska interviews: Anderson and Jefferys (1983) *op. cit.* The IEB won its commendation from the UAW Convention.
33 GM and Ford were also hit in this recession, but not so dramatically. Thus GM's 1958 production level of 2.12 million cars was only its lowest since 1952 and was still 30% above the average for the late 1940s; and Ford's production of 1.22 million cars in 1958 was 38% up on its average production from 1946 to 1949.
34 Stuart (1980) *op. cit.*, 65; *Fortune*, June 1958.
35 H. R. Northrup, *Industrial Relations*, vol. I, no. 1 (Oct. 1961), 9.
36 Company data.
37 *DMN*, January 18, 1958.
38 *DMN*, January 11, 1958.
39 *DMN*, March 8, 1958; in December 1957 1,649 trim department workers produced 736 cars per shift; from January 20, 1958, the remaining 1,225 workers produced 776 cars.
40 *DMN*, February 25, 1961.
41 *DMN*, February 8, 1958.
42 *DMN*, February 22, 1958.
43 File on Chrysler speed-up dispute 1958; UAW Research Department collection [WRL], Box 79.
44 *DMN*, March 15, 1958.
45 Views such as this trim shop letter no longer appeared in the 1960s or 1970s: 'Now let us say that if the company could get away with establishing standards in the Chrysler plants like those of its competitors, what then? Would they

then not point to the men and women in the unorganized shops and say to us, that these are your fellow men, all of you members of the human race, that they are working harder than you, and we therefore demand standards comparable to those of these unorganized workers? When they have completed speeding up the American workers they can begin looking around in other areas and point to the many exploited peoples elsewhere on this earth. With the conquest of space, there is no limit to what Mr. Lacy (Chrysler VP) may discover on other planets in the coming years as a basis to speed up the Chrysler workers.' *DMN*, March 15, 1958.

46 Quoted in William Serrin, *The Company and the Union* (New York: Vintage, 1974), 175.
47 Quoted approvingly in *DMN*, June 28, 1958.
48 Reuther subsequently acknowledged, *President's Report to UAW's 17th Constitutional Convention*, Atlantic City, October 9–16, 1959, 22: 'It was at Chrysler that working conditions became most difficult.'
49 Quoted in *DMN*, June 7, 1958.
50 *DMN*, June 14, 1958.
51 LEB Minutes, September 25, 1958; Local 3 collection [WRL], Executive Board meetings, Box 2.
52 *DMN*, October 4, 1958.
53 *Ibid.*
54 *DMN*, June 14, 1958. The restriction on chief stewards and plant committeemen had been seen in 1955 as a very serious threat to the shopfloor organizing role of the stewards since it was at these moments in the day that most managerial decisions about movements of labor were taken.
55 LEB minutes, June 10, 12, 1958.
56 *DMN*, November 29, 1958.
57 Northrup *op. cit.*, 13, suggests that the growth of the industrial relations function in the 1950s was partially responsible for the more conscious attempt to reshape labor relations out of the opportunity provided by the 1958 recession.
58 *DMN*, August 23, 1958.
59 LEB minutes, August 14, 1958.
60 *DMN*, July 12, 1958.
61 *DMN*, October 4, 1958.
62 *Ibid.*
63 Relief time of just twenty-four minutes per eight-hour shift had been imposed by Ford management in 1949; Brody (1981) *op. cit.*, 201.
64 UAW–Chrysler, *Production and Maintenance Contract*, September 1, 1955, 48.
65 UAW–Chrysler, *Production and Maintenance Contract*, October 1, 1958.
66 *Ibid.*
67 LEB Minutes, October 9, 1958.
68 *Ibid.*, October 15, 1958: The votes were – Yes: 3,611; No: 262; Void: 10. In late October and November 1958 Chrysler insisted on certain sections working Saturday overtime. Despite a decision by the EB not to permit this

while large numbers were laid off (EB minutes, October 23, 1958), it still persisted, leading to the local's Unemployed Committee setting up an unemployed workers' picket line in front of the plant on Saturdays in November. This created an angry protest by the Dodge stewards asking the EB to take action to stop the picketing. The stewards argued 'that something be done to organize unemployed committees in all plants of the Big Four, and then the picketing could be done on a national-wide scale', EB minutes, November 20, 1958. In the event the EB, that was attended by seventy-two 'visitors' lobbying for and against the issue of Saturday overtime, didn't vote on either position. It hoped instead that management's insistence on overtime while workers were laid off could be resolved in the continuing negotiations over what the International had by then agreed were strikeable grievances.

69 LEB minutes, December 13, 1958.
70 UAW–Chrysler Contract, November 29, 1939, 14.
71 UAW–Chrysler Memorandum, December 19, 1958, 1.
72 *Ibid.*, 2–3. While this agreement applied nationally, a special face-saving deal was drawn up for the Department 76 workers. The additional clause was to operate for the remainder of the 1959 models only, after which the twenty-four minutes a day agreement would apply. Until then, management agreed to stop the seventh and eighth floor conveyor lines for five minutes every other hour (four hours a day, providing an extra twenty minutes' relief), but in return the line speeds were increased to make up the lost production 'skips'.
73 *DMN*, February 19, 1959. This was the first time management had been able to do this.
74 *DMN*, October 10, 1959, report from the Final Assembly Unit.
75 *DMN*, February 28, August 15, 1959.
76 Nalezty interview.
77 *DMN*, June 6, 1959.
78 In non-contract years GM workers lost on average less than thirty minutes each per year from 1947 to 1965.
79 Anderson and Jefferys (1983) *op. cit.*, chapter 12. The conditions which were withdrawn at GM during the period of 'working without a contract' from June to September 1958 were largely restored afterwards.
80 Fox interview.

8. White-shirted strangers and black recruitment

1 Moritz and Seaman (1981) *op. cit.*, 62.
2 Stuart (1980) *op. cit.*, 64–7.
3 *Fortune*, November 1968; Stuart (1980) *op. cit.*, 68. Love was first appointed to the board in 1958, and was an important bridge to the Rockefeller family interests.
4 At Ford the proportion of salaried staff to total employment rose by just 1%, from 29.6% to an average of 30.6% from the late 1950s to the early 1960s; company data.

5 *Fortune*, November 1968.

6 Stuart (1980) *op. cit.*, 68–9.

7 One illustration of this was Townsend's 1964 decision to hire a New York publicity agency to come up with a fresh corporate image – the blue and white pentastar – which was taken, at a cost of $50 million, without consulting his top associates; Stuart (1980) *op. cit.*, 70–1.

8 *Fortune*, November 1968. Townsend took the chairman's job but transformed it into the chief executive.

9 *Ibid.*

10 Stuart (1980) *op. cit.*, 73–80.

11 *Ibid.*, 102.

12 Clancy interview.

13 Stuart (1980) *op. cit.*, 107–9.

14 Chrysler (1973) *op. cit.*, 12–15. In 1963 Townsend bought a controlling 64% share of Simca, France (up from the 25% stake acquired by Colbert in 1958) and he bought a 40% share of Barreiros Diesel, Spain. Between 1964 and 1967 he took over Rootes, Britain; in 1964 he set up Chrysler Peru; in 1965 he bought up the Argentinian company, Fevre y Basset, and the Columbian company Fabric Colombiana; and in 1966 he acquired the Brazilian Simca subsidiary.

15 *Fortune*, November 1968.

16 Moritz and Seaman (1981) *op. cit.*, 96–9.

17 *Ibid.*, 71.

18 *Fortune*, November 1968.

19 *Ibid.*

20 *Fortune*, April 1970.

21 *DMN*, January 16, 1960.

22 *DMN*, May 14, 1966.

23 Liska interview; *DMN*, May 21, 1960. Most of the 1957 'Rank and File' caucus activists had been laid off from January 1958 to October or November 1959, and so had not been in a position to run in the 1958 local elections. Each unit at Dodge held its own elections for unit officers and committee chairpersons, chief stewards and their alternates, one month before the local elections. The trim unit elected seven officers, eleven standing committee chairpersons and fifteen stewards and alternates on the two shifts.

24 *DMN*, June 4, 1960. 7,659 workers voted in this election, approximately 60% of the workforce. Subsequently a trend to smaller turnouts for local officers' elections developed as the relationship between local officers and the membership grew increasingly distant. This 1960 election also saw the first woman, Edith van Horn, the 1952 HUAC witch-hunt victim, elected as a Trustee to the Local 3 executive board.

25 Marquart (1975) *op. cit.*, 132.

26 *DMN*, August 27, 1960.

27 *DMN*, January 14, 1961.

28 Document dated February 23, 1961; Local 3 President's collection [WRL], Box 12, Research file.

29 *DMN*, February 25, 1961.
30 *DMN*, July 17, 1961.
31 UAW–Chrysler Agreement, November 2, 1961, *Production and Maintenance*, 49.
32 UAW–Chrysler Agreement, November 2, 1961, *Production and Maintenance*, 26. Robert Jensen, who sat on the UAW's 1961 Bargaining Committee, recalled that the union's 1961 negotiators agreed to bind the 1964 negotiators in this way so that no one would have to go direct to the membership (or the body of active stewards) and sell a deal they knew was very unpopular. As it was, the 1961 negotiators could say 'We didn't do it'; while the 1964 negotiators could say 'Our hands were tied by the 1961 negotiators'; Jensen interview. The two arguments used against reducing the steward ratio in the *Dodge Main News*, August 26, 1961, were, in order of priority: '[1] If a hundred stewards are eliminated it will mean 100 workers will be laid off. [2] It will mean workers being less represented when troubles confront them. It will weaken our Union.' When it did come to the crunch in November 1965 with management wanting to cut the number of chief stewards at Dodge Main from sixty-seven to the fifty-three specified in the national contract ratio, this was no longer an issue of principle. It was essentially about the privileges of fourteen individuals: *DMN*, December 4, 1965. Then the ratio was 1:180, with some as high as 1:419 and others as low as 1:6 (*DMN*, January 29, 1966), and the company wished to reapportion the stewards' districts to move rapidly to the contract level of 1:225. In practice, since it soon had the problems of the 'new' workforce with which to concern itself, Chrysler management never found it worthwhile to pursue a direct assault on the steward ratio, leaving equalization at the 225 level to the slow process of natural wastage as districts were amended out of existence through engineering changes. Robert Jensen estimated that the ratio of 1:225 was finally attained as late as 1980–81 as a direct result of the lay-offs caused by the 1979–82 recession. It was perhaps for this reason that Chrysler introduced in the 1982 contract negotiations a proposal to bring Chrysler's workplace representative ratio in line with GM and Ford; but symptomatic of the low significance this demand had for Chrysler after its success in removing their shopfloor bargaining role, Chrysler soon dropped it.
33 UAW–Chrysler Agreement, November 2, 1961, *Production and Maintenance*, 25.
34 *Blue–Gray News*, April 16, 1962.
35 One exception was Jordan Sims, who was elected president of Chrysler's Eldon Avenue gear and axle plant in 1973, two years after being discharged; Geschwender (1977) *op. cit.*, 200–1.
36 Clancy interview.
37 *DMN*, November 3, 1962.
38 *Leave of absence* form submitted by President Pasica to Dodge Main labor relations supervision for July 1 to July 31, 1963. In Dodge Local 3 collection [WRL], Box 4.
39 Liska interview.

40 Fox and Liska interviews.
41 *DMN*, January 12, 1963.
42 Local 3 collection [WRL], Recording Secretary Box 9; Stewards' Council minutes, February 26, 1963.
43 *Ibid.*
44 *DMN*, June 13, 1964.
45 Liska interview.
46 *DMN*, September 19, 1964.
47 *DMN*, October 24, 1964.
48 *Ibid.*
49 BLS, *Handbook of Labor Statistics 1977*, Bulletin 1966, table 89, 188, 162. The household income distribution which resulted from these significantly higher pay levels in the Detroit Metropolitan Area (SMSA) was even more favorable to Detroit because more workers in each household had these higher-paying jobs: in 1970 the median household income in Detroit was 32.5% above the median household income for the whole United States, and 44% of greater Detroit's household incomes were in the $10,000–$20,000 a year bracket compared to only 33% of households throughout the US; City of Detroit, Planning Department, Data Coordination Division, January 1982, Report No. 423.
50 Liska interview.
51 Estimate in UAW Research Department collection [WRL].
52 Company data. This rise in the level of conflict is demonstrated graphically in figures 1 and 2 (see page 9).
53 L. H. Bailer, 'The Negro Automobile Worker', *Journal of Political Economy*, Oct. 1943, 417–18; cited in K. Fujita, *Black Workers' Struggles in Detroit's Auto Industry 1935–1975* (Saratoga, CA: Century Twenty-one, 1980), 12.
54 Geschwender (1977) *op. cit.*, 34.
55 Foner (1976) *op. cit.*, 240–1.
56 Geschwender (1977) *op. cit.*, 35.
57 Meier and Rudwick (1979) *op. cit.*, 213.
58 Liska interview.
59 Geschwender (1977) *op. cit.*, 40.
60 Howe and Widick (1949) *op. cit.*, 228.
61 Geschwender (1977) *op. cit.*, 40.
62 *Ibid.*, 41.
63 Anderson and Jefferys (1983) *op. cit.*, chapter 9.
64 Geschwender (1977) *op. cit.*, 41.
65 Liska interview.
66 *DMN*, April 16, 1966; Ed Domanski was re-elected president.
67 Geschwender (1977) *op. cit.*, 42–3. Half the white male workforce were employed in the same categories.
68 *Ibid.*, 24.
69 *DMN*, June 17, 1967. The discharges exclude those of probationary employees.

70 Serrin (1974) *op. cit.*, 233.
71 Liska interview.
72 Minutes of Huber Foundry Special Meeting, October 23, 1967; in author's possession.
73 *Ibid.*
74 For an example from the Plymouth plant, see Local 51 General membership meeting minutes, December 11, 1966; Local 51 collection [WRL], Box 17, File 5.
75 Liska interview.
76 Huber Foundry special meeting minutes, *loc. cit.*
77 Liska maintained the shift took place in 1970, but this is almost certainly wrong, since he himself stated in the *Dodge Main News* in August 1968 that 56% of the chief stewards in the assembly plant were black, and the Huber foundry part of the complex had always had an even higher proportion of blacks employed there than in the assembly plant proper. Liska defeated Domanski in the April 1968 election after a campaign in which he argued for more action on the workers' complaints; *DMN*, April 24, August 3, 1968; Liska interview, 1982. Dating the transition later rather than earlier helps to justify his re-election as Local 3 president in 1970.
78 *DMN*, August 7, 1965.
79 *DMN*, September 25, 1965.

9. DRUM beats ... and is beaten: 1969–1973

1 In their book on DRUM, D. Georgakas and M. Surkin, for example, suggest the May 2, 1968 strike at Dodge Main which led to the founding of DRUM was 'the first wildcat strike to hit that factory in 14 years'; *Detroit: I do mind Dying, A Study in Urban Revolution* (New York: St. Martins, 1975), 24. Actually, four wildcat strikes occurred in the previous six months, and hundreds took place between 1954 and 1959. At a totally different level of generalization, Gordon *et al.* (1982) argue that in the late 1960s 'the character of workers' protests has changed substantially'; *op. cit.*, 220.
2 Herding (1972) *op. cit.*, 282, argues 'the worker today avoids carefully (being) caught in what may be termed "official wildcats", as management (frequently equipped with detection devices to prove participation), the International, the arbitrator, and even the local officers combine to remove any protection they owe him otherwise.'
3 The renewed restraints on shopfloor managerial authority were, however, much too short-lived to be used as evidence for the claims of Gordon *et al.* that such labor unrest was 'a principal source' of declining labor productivity in the 1970s; Gordon *et al.* (1982) *op. cit.*, 219.
4 Liska interview.
5 Geschwender (1977) *op. cit.*, 72–3.
6 *DMN*, August 12, 1967.
7 *Ibid.*
8 Geschwender (1977) *op. cit.*, 83.

9 Serrin (1974) *op. cit.*, 176.
10 Notice to all members, September 28, 1967; Local 3 collection [WRL], Box 9.
11 Fox interview.
12 *Ibid.*; Geschwender (1977) *op. cit.*, 85.
13 The detailed account of the May 2 wildcat that follows is necessary to show how DRUM originated within a standard labor relations situation. Geschwender's failure to locate DRUM within the wider shopfloor history of Dodge Main explains his poor understanding of its weaknesses: he writes 'it is somewhat unclear exactly how the walkout developed' and goes on 'For some unexplained reason their discontent reached a peak on May 2 and they decided to walk off the job'; Geschwender (1977) *op. cit.*, 88–9.
14 *DMN*, January 27, 1968.
15 Ed Liska, *Daily Dispute Diary* [in future references, *DDD*], Special walkout meeting, May 3, 1968. This record was kept by recording secretary Liska who took over as Local 3 president in July. It consists of verbatim reports of meetings of the local EB, of the whole plant leadership, of the members, and with management, and discussions with pickets and telephone calls from May 2 to May 26, 1968; in possession of author at time of writing, but to be deposited in Liska collection [WRL].
16 *DDD*, Special EB, May 15; Meeting with management, May 16.
17 *DDD*, May 16, 1968.
18 *DDD*, May 6, 20, 26, 1968.
19 *DDD*, May 26, 1968.
20 *DDD*, May 6, 1968.
21 *DDD*, May 26, 1968.
22 *Ibid.*
23 *DDD*, May 20, 1968.
24 *DDD*, May 14, 1968.
25 *DDD*, May 3, 1968.
26 *Ibid.*
27 *DDD*, May 5, 1968.
28 *Ibid.*
29 *DDD*, May 6, 1968.
30 *DDD*, May 13, 1968.
31 *DDD*, May 14, 1968.
32 Geschwender (1977) *op. cit.*, 88.
33 Author's estimate.
34 *DDD*, May 14, 1968.
35 *DDD*, May 26, 1968. The ballot, as laid down in the contract, was allowed for strike action on certain outstanding grievances but not directly against specific penalties. This was not appreciated by many workers other than those seeped in UAW rules. The plant leadership knew of the constitutional restrictions, but hoped that tempers would heal and that an arrangement could eventually be worked out with management. The wider political context, however, ensured that tempers didn't heal, and management was not prepared to accommodate the Local 3 leadership to the point of reinstat-

ing General Baker (the other six fired strikers were rehired in November). Many members therefore believed the EB was guilty of connivance in his firing.

36 Letter from Domanski to Fraser, June 5, 1968; Local 3 collection [WRL], Box 9.

37 *DDD*, various days. General Baker was a leader of the League of Revolutionary Black Workers from its inception in 1969 until its demise in 1972–73. Around 1976–77 he was hired at the Ford River Rouge, and in 1982 was a plant committeeman in the Ford foundry.

38 LEB minutes, May 23, 1968; Local 3 collection [WRL], Box 3.

39 *Drum*, vol. 1, no. 1.

40 *DDD*, various days; Geschwender (1977) *op. cit.*, 89; Liska interview.

41 *Drum*, vol. 1, no. 1.

42 *DMN*, June 15, 1968.

43 Geschwender (1977) *op. cit.*, 93; *DMN*, August 3, 1968; LEB Minutes, July 11, 1968.

44 Dodge Main was renamed the Hamtramck Assembly Plant to effect a change of image. *DDD*, various days.

45 LEB minutes, July 25, 1968; Liska interview.

46 *DDD*, May 26, 1968. Production standard grievances were the only ones on which a legal strike could take place during the course of a contract, and that would only be legal if all the stages of procedure had been fully exhausted.

47 LEB minutes, October 24, 1968.

48 Election results; Local 3 collection [WRL], Box 9.

49 Geschwender (1977) *op. cit.*, 104–9. DRUM made this charge each time it was beaten in elections. Liska denied there was any illegitimate ballot activity on his part in either this election or in his even more controversial re-election as president in 1970. But he recognized that there might have been larger numbers of Hamtramck-based (i.e. Polish) retirees voting in these elections because of the greater interest they provoked than previously – and the issue of white retirees outvoting the majority of blacks who worked in the plant was one of Drum's charges; Liska interview.

50 *Ibid.*, 94–5.

51 *Drum*, vol. 1, no. 9.

52 In 1969, a new 'integrationist' policy was consciously introduced into the plant by the new personnel manager, Dick Clancy. The recruitment of black foremen, general foremen and superintendents was accelerated, and existing supervisors were either 'educated' on the race issue or transferred. Clancy was a former FBI employee who had joined Chrysler's personnel department in the late 1950s, serving as personnel manager at the Chrysler Kercheval plant for many years before being transferred to the 'hot seat' at Dodge Main; Clancy interview.

53 League of Revolutionary Black Workers, *March on Cobo Hall*, October–November 1969, leaflet for a special UAW Convention.

54 *Drum*, vol. 1, no. 9. The October 1969 League program included the demand for the withdrawal of American troops from Vietnam.

55 Liska, *Diary*, February 25, 1969. In author's possession at time of writing.

56 *Ibid.*
57 Liska interview.
58 Forge escaped by running out of the plant. After one steward took Tom Young to the hospital, 'Young made a telephone call to Personnel Manager Leonard Nawrocki, demanding that steward Fowler be fired for not helping him when Forge was attacking him with the knife'; Liska, *Diary*, February 12, 1969.
59 *Assembly grievance book*, grievance A70-602-360, November 14, 1970. In possession of author. To be deposited in Liska Collection [WRL].
60 *Ibid.*, grievance A71-735-582, November 16, 1971.
61 Cited in Geschwender (1977) *op. cit.*, 104–5.
62 Meetings were not held if a quorum of members was not reached. Liska interview.
63 The UNC was established at the 1968 UAW convention by a core of radical skilled workers around Pete Kelly (GM) and Art Fox (Edith Fox's husband, a skilled worker at Ford's Rouge plant) arising out of the discontent of skilled workers with the 1967 contract. The UNC attempted to mobilize production workers, but, being predominantly white – even though Jordan Sims was a cochairman after 1970 – it made very little headway and was a small propaganda caucus by 1973.
64 *Drum*, vol. 3, no. 5.
65 *DMN*, May 16, 1970, prints Reuther's reply to Liska's letter of thanks: 'Dear Ed, We were pleased to be able to extend a helping hand of friendship and solidarity. The results proved there is no substitute for teamwork and solidarity when there is a problem to be settled.' This characteristic statement of Reuther practice was written just two days before he was killed in an aeroplane crash flying out to the monument he had built to himself, the UAW's residential training resort at Black Lake. Liska says of the effect of 'one week in Black Lake' on a black militant who was sent there from the local in the early 1970s: 'It turned him round. Just one week up there'; Liska interview.
66 *Drum*, vol. 3, no. 5.
67 Geschwender (1977) *op. cit.*, 120–2.
68 *Fortune*, May 1, 1969.
69 Iacocca refers to 'prejudice' in 'men in positions of great power and prestige in the auto industry' with reference to a Jew being appointed to the Chrysler board; Lee Iacocca with William Novak, *Iacocca: An Autobiography* (London: Sidgwick & Jackson, 1985), 15.
70 Clancy interview.
71 Liska and Fox interviews; Ernie Allen, 'Dying from the Inside: The Decline of the League of Revolutionary Black Workers', in *They should have served that Cup of Coffee: Seven Radicals Remember the 60s*, ed. Dick Cluster (Boston: South End, 1979), 77.
72 Fujita (1980) *op. cit.*, 62.
73 Liska interview.
74 Letter dated October 17, 1969 from Dick Clancy to Ed Liska in Local 3 Collection [WRL], Box 20.

75 Clancy interview; Liska interview. Liska maintained he never accepted the repeated invitations to discuss problems informally with Clancy, but believed that those who followed him didn't share the same scruples.
76 *DMN*, November 7, 1970.
77 *DMN*, September 26, 1970.
78 Liska interview.
79 *DMN*, July 24, 1971.
80 Georgakas and Surkin (1975) *op. cit.*, 161–3.
81 Liska, *Assembly grievance book, 1970–1972* of monthly meetings with labor relations supervisors. In possession of author, to be deposited in Liska Collection [WRL]. Grievance A71-835-695, December 13, 1971.
82 *Ibid.*, A71-445-363, November 16, 1971.
83 *Ibid.*, A71-348-307, October 27, 1971.
84 *Ibid.*, A71-315-248, September 2, 1971.
85 *Ibid.*, A71-693-779, February 3, 1972.
86 *Ibid.*, A70-1417-996, June 1971.
87 *Ibid.*, A70-1374-899, June 1971.
88 *Ibid.*, A71-263-210, November 14, 1971.
89 Moritz and Seaman (1981) *op. cit.*, 104.
90 The explanation below of why DRUM stopped running its own slate, in terms of its isolation and decline, contrasts with Geschwender's, whose book implies a stronger organizational base for the League of Revolutionary Workers inside the plants than was actually achieved. Geschwender admits: 'there is also some evidence that the revolutionary union movements in the plants were becoming weaker' with reference to events in 1969, but nowhere does he seriously estimate its real influence in 1968–69, or what impact the managerial and UAW counter-strategies had between 1969 and 1972. For Geschwender, DRUM's 1972 decision not to run was a problem for which he has to suck sophisticated possible explanations out of thin air. He argues, 'It is not entirely clear why this policy shift was made', and then suggests two possible reasons: 'It may be the case that the League cadre did not wish to risk the possible negative consequences of further election defeats. It is also possible that they were concerned with the seductive nature of reformist activity'; Geschwender (1977) *op. cit.*, 122.
91 Allen (1979) estimates the League's 1970 Detroit-wide membership as about 60; *op. cit.*, 88.
92 Fox was elected trim department committeewoman in 1970, 1972 and 1974, and got through to the run-off elections for recording secretary in 1970 and vice-president in 1972, attracting over 1,000 votes on both occasions.
93 *DMN*, June 10, 1972.
94 *DRUM*, vol. 1, no. 22.
95 *DMN*, December 7, 1968.
96 Liska interview. He had refused to condemn a major wildcat at the Chrysler Sterling Heights stamping plant in 1969.
97 *DMN*, August 25, 1973.
98 Clancy interview.
99 *DMN*, April 21, May 19, 1973. The contrast with the local officers' first

reactions to the May 1968 wildcat could not be more marked. Five years earlier president-elect Liska's *Dodge Main News* column had begun: 'Writing this article is very difficult and with great reluctance because as one of the Local Officers, it is my duty and oath of office to tell the members that illegal activities can and do end up with severe penalties . . .' *ibid.*, May 25, 1968.

100 Chrysler employment totalled 153,421 hourly and salaried staff; company data. The three wildcats were at the Jefferson Assembly plant where the seizure of a cage used for transporting car engines by two black workers protesting against harassment by a foreman was successful, leading to the foreman's removal; at the Drop Forge, where a week's strike led to fifteen strikers being dismissed; and at the Mack Avenue plant where the wildcat was also defeated.

101 Clancy interview.

102 The credibility of the UAW was also enhanced in the 1973 UAW–Chrysler contract, which included a 'voluntary overtime provision' by which workers were required to notify management on a Monday that they wished to forego all overtime that week – and if they did not, then they would be obliged to work nine hours a day for six days.

103 Letter from J. Hagel, Labor Relations Manager to Local 3 President, Ed Liska, June 1, 1972 concerning 'employees being absent for alleged union business'; Local 3 collection [WRL], Box 9.

104 Clancy interview.

10. Crisis, closure and concessions: 1974–1982

1 Three I'm aware of are Stuart (1980), Moritz and Seamen (1981), Iacocca (1985), and this argument has been made in dozens of newspaper and magazine articles, including a review article by Jerry Flint, 'Everybody Sacrificed, Everybody Profited', *New York Times*, July 7, 1985. Flint was reviewing a fourth book on the fall and rise of Chrysler by Robert Reich and John Donahue, *New Deals: The Chrysler Revival and the American System* (New York: Times Books, 1985), which argues the key to Chrysler's recovery was neither management *per se* nor the Federal government loan guarantee, but the sacrifices made by labor, creditors, and suppliers.

2 Sabel (1982) *op. cit.*, 194–231.

3 Gordon *et al.* (1982) *op. cit.*, 220.

4 Geschwender (1977) *op. cit.*, 190–3; implicit in Gordon *et al.* (1982) *op. cit.*, 219–20.

5 Millard Berry *et al.*, *Wildcat, Dodge Truck, June 1974* (Detroit: 32 pp. pamphlet, 1974), 2.

6 Terkel (1975) *op. cit.*, 226–31.

7 'We still have a civilized relationship' was the reply by Reuther's successor, Leonard Woodcock, in 1970 when asked whether the bitterness of calling a strike against GM might make new negotiations more difficult. Quoted in Serrin (1974) *op. cit.*, 69.

8 Serrin (1974) *op. cit.*, 332–3.

9 *DMN*, February 9, 1974.
10 *DMN*, May 11, 25, 1974.
11 *DMN*, July 13, 1974.
12 *DMN*, September 28, 1974.
13 *DMN*, October 12, 1974.
14 *DMN*, August 8, 1976. The attendance at the picnic, 24,000, nearly half the population of Hamtramck, at a time when Hamtramck Assembly only employed around 6,000 workers – largely from outside Hamtramck – gives an idea of the impact Dodge Main still had in the locality.
15 *DMN*, August 16, 1975.
16 *DMN*, February 15, 1975.
17 Clancy interview. This was the 1964 contract level of one chief steward to every 225 workers for a plant employing 8,000. Robert Jensen suggested that throughout the whole of Chrysler the 1964 ratio was only finally achieved in the 1979 recession. Dodge Main was therefore 'ahead' of other Chrysler plants in accepting the reduced numbers of chief stewards as early as 1975.
18 The seniority agreements that entitled laid off workers to 'claim' jobs in departments and plants other than their own if there were lower seniority workers on those jobs and they wished to make the move.
19 Fraser spelt out the calculations the international made about dealing with black militancy: 'You've got to be prepared to take issues away from them, not allow issues to arise upon which they can exploit the situation. Unless you do that they're going to grow and grow.' Quoted in Victor G. Reuther, *The Brothers Reuther and the Story of the UAW* (Boston; Houghton Mifflin, 1976), 306.
20 Serrin (1974) *op. cit.*, 148.
21 *Ibid.*, 150–1.
22 Reuther (1976) *op. cit.*, 188, 471.
23 Clancy interview.
24 *Ibid.*
25

TABLE A

Hourly paid employment at Chrysler, Ford and GM, 1974–78

	Chrysler		Ford		General Motors	
Year	Hourly employment (000s)	Change over previous year (%)	Hourly employment (000s)	Change over previous year (%)	Hourly employment (000s)	Change over previous year (%)
1974	97.3	−13.5	152	−5.9	380	−15
1975	75.3	−22.6	132	−13.2	351.8	−7.4
1976	97.1	+28.9	145.4	+10.2	402.6	+14.4
1977	99.9	+2.9	160.2	+10.2	440.2	+9.4
1978	95.9	−4	171.9	+7.3	466.4	+5.9

Source: Company data.

26 *DMN*, January 22, 1977. Some 430 separate demands were lodged and answered from the six divisions within Hamtramck Assembly, and 52 for the whole plant. Some demands contained multiple clauses; others were

repitions. Fewer than 25 could be loosely categorized as indicating an assertion of positive, struggled-for restraints over management.

27 *Ibid.*

28 *Ibid.*

29 Moritz and Seaman (1981) *op. cit.*, 165, 124.

30 See *Mid-American Outlook*, Fall 1978, 4.

31 *Ward's Automotive Yearbook, 1980*, 47, 152.

32 Riccardo was one of Townsend's 'young Turks' who had followed Townsend to Chrysler in 1959 and then, rising one rank every year over the next eight, had joined the board in 1967 – a position that usually took thirty years to reach at GM; Moritz and Seaman (1981) *op. cit.*, 127.

33 *Fortune*, June 19, 1978.

34 Cafiero, a former industrial engineer at Briggs Body when Chrysler took it over in 1953, was a sharp operator who had impressed Townsend and been catapulted up Chrysler's top management; Stuart (1980) *op. cit.*, 81–3.

35 Townsend quoted in Moritz and Seaman (1981) *op. cit.*, 126.

36 Iacocca (1985) *op. cit.*, 155.

37 *Fortune*, June 19, 1978.

38 Moritz and Seaman (1981) *op. cit.*, 233.

39 Iacocca (1985) *op. cit.*, 153–4.

40 Quoted in Moritz and Seaman (1981) *op. cit.*, 297–301.

41 Iacocca (1985) *op. cit.*, 154–5.

42 Quoted in Moritz and Seaman (1981) *op. cit.*, 190.

43 Stuart (1980) *op. cit.*, 75.

44 Moritz and Seaman (1981) *op. cit.*, 185–92.

45 *Time*, March 21, 1983. The figures are net income after taxation. For 1974 and 1975 they are taken from *Moody's Industrial Manual, 1979*, 369.

46 *Fortune*, June 19, 1978; Iacocca (1985) *op. cit.*, 143–5.

47 Riccardo had tried to get a replacement for Cafiero from GM before he approached Iacocca; Stuart (1980) *op. cit.*, 134; Iacocca (1985) *op. cit.*, 122–3.

48 *Time*, March 21, 1983; Iacocca (1985) *op. cit.*, 157.

49 *Time*, March 21, 1983; Iacocca (1985) *op. cit.*, 152–6; Moritz and Seaman (1981) *op. cit.*, 224, 282.

50 Moritz and Seaman (1981) *op. cit.*, 238–41.

51 Clancy interview. He believed there were 'no efficiencies we could have got in the short term to keep that plant open'. Liska challenges this view. He argues that Dodge Main was still capable of producing half a million cars in 1973 and could still have been retained as a major assembly plant if the investment put into the Jefferson and Belvidere plants in the late 1970s had been put instead into Dodge Main; Liska interview.

52 Fourteen other plants were closed over the next two years, including four major ones in the Detroit area: Eight Mile/Outer Drive Stamping, Mack Avenue Stamping, Huber Avenue Foundry and the Warren Recreational Vehicle Assembly plant.

53 *Labor Notes*, June 22, 1979.

54 Fox interview.

55 *Ibid.*
56 Clancy interview.
57 *Ibid.*
58 Fox interview.
59 *Ibid.*
60 Dave McCullough, 'Chrysler: Capitalizing on the Crisis', *Changes*, 1, no. 9 (October 1979), 12.
61 Clancy interview.
62 *Ibid.*
63 *Solidarity*, July 1978, 3–4.
64 R. Cohen, 'The Employment Consequences of Structural Change in the Auto Industry', Massachusetts Institute of Technology Research Paper (Boston: MIT, June 1981). The extra costs involved in continuing this industrial relocation during the 1979–82 recession, and the adoption of the Japanese *kanban* system of reducing costs by maintaining very low inventories – and ensuring steady supplies by locating the components plants close to the assembly plants – effectively brought a halt to the relocation process in 1981 and 1982; S. Jefferys, 'Recession, Innovation and Industrial Relations: The US Car Industry in Crisis', *Employee Relations*, V, no. 3 (1983), 7.
65 McCullough (1979) *op. cit.*, 8–15, argued that Chrysler was not nearly so close to bankruptcy as it pretended, that it was going for government aid because it was cheaper than the alternatives and would encourage UAW concessions, and that if the plea for a government bail-out had failed, the banks would have made more credit available in order to protect their earlier investment. But while verification of such a 'conspiracy' theory of management behavior would require access to what are totally closed company records, it is unlikely such a tactical approach can be squared with the open hostility to 'federal intrusion' in big business so often manifested by Chrysler and the Detroit managerial ethos in the past. It is also more probable that Riccardo's hurried announcement of his early retirement was the result of bitterness at the prospect of a federal-imposed solution. Iacocca is uncharacteristically reticent about the reasons for Riccardo's early retirement; while Reich and Donahue argue his resignation was a kind of symbolic sacrifice necessary before Congress would help; Iacocca (1985) *op. cit.*, 145; Flint (1985) *loc. cit.*
66 UAW, *Chrysler Newsgram*, November 1979.
67 Jensen interview. Jensen stated that the demand for a union-director was only included by the UAW in 1976 as an afterthought when it noticed that Chrysler UK had accepted a union-nominated director as the price for its bail-out by the British government in 1975.
68 UAW, *Chrysler Newsgram*, November 1979.
69 UAW, *To all UAW Members at Chrysler-US*, January 8, 1980.
70 Wages in Canada were already significantly below their American counterparts as a result of their being paid the same nominal hourly rate while the Canadian dollar was actually worth only about nine-tenths of the American.

71 Iacocca (1985) *op. cit.*, 175.
72 *Ibid.*, 175–6; interview by author with plant worker, June 1982.
73 Iacocca (1985) *op. cit.*, 234.
74 *Detroit Free Press*, August 9, 1982.
75 *New York Times*, October 27, 1982.
76 Moritz and Seaman (1981) *op. cit.*, 329–33.
77 Douglas Fraser, letter to Lee A. Iacocca, December 2, 1980 circulated to all UAW–Chrysler locals.
78 Statement by UAW International Chrysler Council, December 22, 1980.
79 Iacocca (1985) *op. cit.*, 232–3.
80 UAW–Chrysler, *Additional provisions pertaining to US and Canadian employees*, January 14, 1981.
81 *Ibid.*, 6.
82 *Ibid.*, 14.
83 Clancy interview. He remarked a big change in UAW officers' attitudes from the 1960s to the 1970s.
84 Quoted in Moritz and Seaman (1981) *op. cit.*, 34.
85 Interview by author in Solidarity House, Summer 1982.
86 Stephen Wood. 'Technological Change and the Cooperitive Labor Strategy' (Cambridge, MA: Harvard Center for European Studies, 1985), 32–3 (mimeographed).
87 C. Kerr, 'Industrial Conflict and its Mediation', *American Journal of Sociology*, LX, no. 3 (November 1954), 231.

11. Power and exceptionalism

1 Hyman (1975) argues: 'The objective characteristics of capital, and the policies adopted by managers, create pressures and constraints which set limits to the possibilities of trade union action. But their determining effect depends *also* on the extent to which prevailing patterns of relationships are treated as inevitable by trade unionists themselves'; *op. cit.*, 118.
2 Harris (1982) *op. cit.*, 198.
3 *Fortune*, August 12, 1979: 1978 net sales of these companies were: GM, $634.2 billion; Ford, $42.8 billion; IBM, $21.1 billion; Sears & Roebuck, $18.0 billion; Chrysler, $16.3 billion; IT&T, $15.3 billion.
4 See Seymour Martin Lipset's review of the debate, 'Why no Socialism in the United States?', *Sources of Contemporary Radicalism*, ed. Seweryn Bialer (Boulder: Westview, 1977). Davis takes a different approach. He argues that while Western European labor was 'incorporated' through reformism, US labor was similarly 'incorporated', but through the 'negativities of its internal stratification, its privatization in consumption, and its disorganization viz-a-viz political and trade union bureaucracies'. He believes the key difference between America and other advanced industrial societies is 'the absence of the level of working class self-organization and consciousness represented in every other capitalist country by the prevalence of labourist, social-democratic, or Communist parties...', Davis (1980) *op. cit.*, 7–8, 4. However, these political parties do not all represent a similar degree of 'class

self-organization and consciousness', as a comparison of working class British Labour Party activists with, for example, French Communists shows. In many respects the former would have more in common with American working class Democrats. A 1971 assessment of the Democratic Party is a little crude, but close to the mark: 'The Democratic Party is dominated by labor in every respect but one – the actual politicians are not of the labor movement, and they get its backing on the cheap'; Paul Booth, 'Theses on Contemporary US Labor Unionism', *Radical America*, 5, no. 1 (Jan.–Feb. 1971), 2.

P. K. Edwards has recently revitalized the debate by shifting its terms of reference. He argues that US management's greater power resources over labor's dovetailed with a historic opposition to unionism to create the major divergences in industrial relations patterns between Britain and the United States; Edwards (1983a) *op. cit.*, 16–30; and P. K. Edwards, 'The Political Economy of Industrial Conflict: Britain and the United States', Industrial Relations Research Unit Research Paper (Coventry: University of Warwick, 1983), 19 (mimeographed).

5 A comparative examination by the author of the development of shopfloor industrial relations at the Austin/BMC/British Leyland/Austin Rover plant at Longbridge, Birmingham from 1935 to 1985 and at the Pressed Steel/Rootes/Chrysler/Talbot Linwood plant from 1942 to 1981 (forthcoming).

6 For example, Jeremy Brecher's history begins: 'This book is the story of repeated, massive and often violent revolts by ordinary people in America'; (1972) *op. cit.*, 10.

7 The most obvious differences are the absence of multi-union bargaining units in the US, the determination of US pay and conditions primarily through centralized company- or industry-wide long-term contract bargaining, and the comparative lack of involvement of shopfloor union representatives in bargaining; J. David Edelstein and Malcolm Warner, *Comparative Union Democracy: Organization and Opposition in British and American Unions* (New Brunswick, NJ: Transaction, 1979), 18–20. An earlier list of differences drawn up by Jack Steiber stressed (1) the involvement of the international union in US plant agreements, (2) the vertical organization of US unions, (3) the greater coverage of detail and the provision of arbitration in US contracts, (4) the fixed duration of US contracts, and (5) several lesser differences including the existence of the Taft–Hartley Act; Steiber (1968) *op. cit.*, 235–7.

8 Edwards (1983a) *op. cit.*, 3.

9 H. A. Turner, Garfield Clack and Geoffrey Roberts, *Labour Relations in the Motor Industry* (London: Allen and Unwin, 1967), 193.

10 Steven Tolliday, 'Government, Employers and Shopfloor Organization in the British Motor Industry, 1939–69', Research Paper (Cambridge: King's College Research Centre, September 1982), 3–5, 18–23; Research by author in progress at Longbridge and at Linwood.

11 In the early 1970s, a study of management and labor conflict in British industry found '100 per cent unionism continued to be one of the liveliest issues in workplace industrial relations'; H. A. Turner, G. Roberts and D. Roberts, *Management Characteristics and Labour Conflict: A Study of*

Managerial Organization, Attitudes and Industrial Relations (Cambridge: Cambridge University Press, 1977), 23.

12 Turner, Clack and Roberts (1967) *op. cit.*, 279; Beynon (1975) *op. cit.*, 147; Friedman and Meredeen (1980) *op. cit.*, 62.

13 Turner, Clack and Roberts (1967) *op. cit.*, 207.

14 Peter J. S. Dunnett, *The Decline of the British Motor Industry* (London: Croom Helm, 1980), 34, 96–8.

15 Central Policy Review Staff, *The Future of the British Car Industry* (London: HMSO, 1975), 102.

16 Beynon (1975) *op. cit.*, 160.

17 Central Policy Review Staff (1975) *op. cit.*, 102. Measured day work was brought in on the new Marina car at BL's Cowley complex early in 1971, and by September 1974 some 94% of BL's hourly rated employees were on day work. But as the Ryder report admitted, management had paid a high price for the change: 'BL accepts that in order to secure acceptance of the measured day work system, they had to agree to manning levels which were often excessive'; H. L. Ryder, *British Leyland: The Next Decade* (London: HMSO, 1975), 34–5.

18 Central Policy Review Staff (1975) *op. cit.*, 65–70.

19 Overall numbers employed in UK motor vehicle manufacture (including commercial vehicles and components) fell from 457,200 in September 1979 to 290,600 in March 1983; Department of Employment, *Employment Gazette* (London: HMSO, various issues); British Leyland's employment fell from 192,000 in 1978 to 105,000 in 1982; and Talbot (formerly Chrysler UK), from 25,240 in December 1978 to 13,257 in December 1981; *Coventry Economic Monitor*, 1982.

20 *New Statesman*, December 7, 1979, January 2, 9, October 30, November 6, 1981; Robert Taylor, 'Where Edwardes drove BL', *Management Today*, June 1982.

21 Paul Willman and Graham Winch, *Innovation and Management Control: Labour Relations at BL Cars* (Cambridge: Cambridge University Press, 1985), 129–48; Tom Forester, 'The New Model Halewood', *New Society*, Feb. 14, 1980; Patrick Wintour, 'Ford and the Mysteries of the Orient', *New Statesman*, Nov. 28, 1980; Steve Jefferys, 'The Washing-up War', *New Society*, April 21, 1983; D. Arnott, 'How Vauxhall shifted gear', *Management Today*, July 1983; Interview by author with Norman Hasslam, Employee Relations Director, Austin Rover, August 13, 1985.

22 See Brody (1981) *op. cit.*, 206; and Lichtenstein (1980) *op. cit.*, 348. My argument endorses the view argued by Lyddon (1983), that unionization in Britain experienced 'painfully slow' post-war growth; *op. cit.*, 136.

23 Several interviews with Linwood workers, various dates, 1980–82; Linwood trade union archive, Mitchell Library, Glasgow.

24 The Dodge Main evidence does not support the Steven Tolliday and Jonathan Zeitlin thesis that the introduction of formal 'just cause' grievance procedures in the US in the 1940s had 'a profoundly subversive effect on shop floor discipline'; S. Tolliday and J. Zeitlin, 'Shop Floor Bargaining, Contract

Unionism, and Job Control: An Anglo–American Comparison'. In Nelson Lichtenstein and Steve Meyer (eds), *The American Automobile Industry: A Social History* (Chicago: University of Illinois, forthcoming 1986). Indeed the present study comes to the opposite conclusion: that the earlier imposition of a formal collective bargaining system in the US served to limit the exercise of shopfloor restraints over management rather than to extend them.

25 Stuart (1980) *op. cit.*, 106; Dunnett (1980) *op. cit.*, 39.

26 Edwards (1983a) *op. cit.*, tables 1 and 3. The figures can only be tentatively compared since both US and UK statistics understate the number of very short and small strikes, and it cannot be assumed that they do so either equally or consistently:

TABLE B

Trends in strike indices, United States and United Kingdom, 1931–79

Period	Frequency strikes per million employees		% strikes lasting under one week	
	US	UK	US	UK
1931–36	60.1		37.8	
1931–39		37.8		68.8
1937–41	106		38.0	
1940–45		81.5		88.4
1942–45	99.6		70.5	
1946–49	90.1	87.5	38.6	—
1950–59	84.6	98.5	44.8	91.7
1960–69	67.5	106	45.3	85.5
1970–79	75.7(a)	115	38.6(a)	67.4

(a) 1970–78

27 Child (1969) *op. cit.*, 111; Bernstein (1960) *op. cit.*, 166–7.

28 Turner, Clack and Roberts (1967) *op. cit.*, 10.

29 Littler (1982) *op. cit.*, 115, 163; G. Turner, *The Leyland Papers* (London: Pan, 1973) 204–5; J. G. Norman, 'The Crippling of Chrysler', *Management Today*, Feb. 1981; Rex Winsburg, 'The Labours of British Leyland', *Management Today*, Oct. 1969.

30 Edwards, P. K. (1983a) *op. cit.*, 35.

Sources

The sources available for this study present another reason to describe it as an historical reconstruction rather than 'history'. For while the archives of Dodge Local 3, now at Wayne State University's Walter Reuther Library, were a very rich source for the researcher, financial stringency at Chrysler Corporation had closed management's archives. The same crisis brought, however, a useful bonus: following the interest aroused by the biggest-ever federal bailout, Chrysler's management structure and business policy came under scrutiny in two studies by American auto industry journalists: *Bailout* by R. Stuart, and the more substantial *Going for Broke: The Chrysler Story* by Michael Moritz and Barrett Seaman. Lee Iacocca's autobiography with William Novak, *Iacocca*, complements these accounts and, together with the relevant archive material in the Reuther Library, coverage of Chrysler affairs in *Fortune* and the *Economist*, and the studies of the period by Irving Bernstein, Sidney Fine, Nelson Lichtenstein and Howell Harris, allowed the reconstruction of Chrysler management's organization structure, politics and business policy given in the study.

The focus of the study on the frontier of managerial shopfloor authority led to a major concern with strikes as a measurable indicator of conflict. It was greatly assisted here by two series of strike statistics made available to the author by Chrysler Corporation and by General Motors. These ran from 1940 to 1980 and recorded the hours lost in both authorized and unauthorized strikes that were reported to their respective corporate labor relations departments. Combined with yearly average employment figures, fairly sensitive strike frequency and loss ratio statistics could be developed, providing an important empirical basis for comparisons between the levels of open industrial conflict between the two companies. Ford made data from 1978 available but claimed, implausibly, that similar data were not kept prior to that date.

The reconstruction of management labor-relations policy and the availability of these indexes of labor conflict were the starting point for a detailed examination of the relationship between this policy and the changing level of conflict. This required extensive use of the Dodge Local 3 collection referred to above. The material researched included the very valuable and almost complete run of the *Dodge Main News*. This local newsheet began as the *Dodge Bulletin* during the 1937 strike and appeared on a twice-monthly basis from then until the plant was closed. The collection also included a complete set of local and local executive board minutes dating from the attempt to build an American Federation of Labor (AFL) local in the plant in 1933, and a set of minutes of stewards' meetings from 1937 to 1940. The correspondence files of the Local 3 president and recording secretary and the local's grievance files from 1950 until 1972 were also used, as were the miscellaneous Local 3 boxes that included material on the 1930s and on DRUM. The only restriction here was the library's ten-year closed access rule, so it was not as possible to obtain detailed observations for the period since 1972 as it was for the period before. Important additional archive material was also made available to me by Ed Liska, Local 3 president from 1968 to 1972: a nearly complete set of early DRUM bulletins, a daily diary he kept of the events around the May 1968 DRUM strike, and his personal files of notes on assembly grievances from 1969 to 1972.

Other important UAW collections consulted at the Walter Reuther Library were the following: Chrysler Department, Research Department, Local 51, Local 7, Local 889 and the Association of Catholic Trade Unionists. Individual collections that were very useful included: Walter Reuther, Richard Frankensteen, John Zaremba, Harry Ross, George Addes, Emil Mazey, Arthur Hughes, Frank Marquart and Bernard Hoffman. Together, these archival sources provided a mass of material that was then placed in context through contemporary, mainly Detroit-based newspaper accounts of the events, through reading many of the oral histories taped twenty years ago for Wayne State University's labor archive library, and through conducting additional oral interviews myself. The most useful oral histories were those of John Zaremba, Harry Ross, Frank Marquart, Richard Frankensteen and Arthur Hughes. Others consulted included: Kenneth Bannon, Jack Beni, Joseph Ferris, Bert Foster, Martin Jenson, Norman Matthews, Lew Michener, Patrick O'Malley, Nat Ganley and Carl Haessler.

The biggest problem for the present research into the labor process and shopfloor organization with these interviews – by Jack Skeel – is that the questions he asked were primarily aimed at soliciting replies about the *international* UAW. The result is that the word 'steward', for example, appears only once or twice, and he treated the sinews of shopfloor organization as unproblematic. This omission was partly rectified in a small number of additional interviews conducted by the author in 1981 and 1982: with former Dodge Main workers Gertrude Nalezty, Edie Fox, Ed Liska and Robert Jenson, and with former Dodge Main personnel manager Dick Clancy. These interviews were in turn assisted greatly by the earlier research conducted by the author on a joint oral history with John W. Anderson, a Detroit autoworker from 1927 to 1966. This study, covering in depth the life of a rank-and-file autoworker who was based in the GM Fleetwood Cadillac plant for thirty years from 1936, helped considerably in exploring the central themes of the present research: How and why was Chrysler different? And what does this difference tell us about the processes which shaped the wider American working class?

A contemporary assessment of industrial-relations developments in the auto industry was provided in a series of interviews with corporate executives conducted in June 1982: at General Motors with Fred Haubold, International Labor Relations Director, John Maciarz, Public Relations Executive; at Ford with Ernie Savoie, Labor Relations Director, and Jack Barnes, Economic Analysis Director; and at Chrysler with Dick Clancy, Labor Relations Executive, and Bob Heath, Public Relations Executive.

Bibliography

Allen, E. 'Dying from the Inside: The Decline of the League of Revolutionary Black Workers'. In D. Cluster (ed.) *They should have served that Cup of Coffee: Seven Radicals remember the 60s.*

Anderson, J. W. and Jefferys, S. 'Enlisted in the Suitcase Brigade: The Life of an Autoworker who Stayed in the Shop'. Unpublished MS, 1983.

Armstrong, P. J., Goodman, J. F. B. and Hyman, J. D. *Ideology and Shopfloor Industrial Relations.* London: Croom Helm, 1981.

Arnott, D. 'How Vauxhall shifted gear'. *Management Today*, July 1983.

Aronowitz, S. *False Promises: The Shaping of American Working Class Consciousness.* New York: McGraw Hill, 1973.

Babson, S., Alpern, R., Elsila, D. and Revitte, J. *Working Detroit: The Making of a Union Town.* New York: Adama, 1984.

Bain, G., and Price, R. *Profiles of Union Growth: A Comparative Statistical Portrait of eight Countries.* Oxford: Blackwell, 1980.

Baldamus, W. *Efficiency and Effort: An Analysis of Industrial Administration.* London: Tavistock, 1961.

Barbash, J. 'Union Response to the "Hard Line"'. *Industrial Relations*, vol. I, October 1961.

Batstone, E., Boraston, I. and Frenkel, S. *Shop Stewards in Action: The Organization of Workplace Conflict and Accommodation.* Oxford: Blackwell, 1977.

Bernstein, I. *The Lean Years: A History of the American Worker, 1920–1933.* Boston: Houghton Mifflin, 1960.

Bernstein, I. *Turbulent Years: A History of the American Worker, 1933–1941.* Boston: Houghton Mifflin, 1969.

Berry, M., *et al. Wildcat, Dodge Truck, June 1974.* Detroit: 32 page pamphlet, 1974.

Beynon, H. *Working for Ford.* Wakefield: EP Publishing, 1975.

Booth, P. 'Theses on Contemporary US Labor Unionism'. *Radical America*, vol. 5, no. 1, Jan.–Feb. 1971.

Braverman, H. *Labor and Monopoly Capital: The Degradation of Work in the Twentieth Century.* New York: Monthly Review, 1974.

Brecher, J. *Strike!* Greenwich, CT: Fawcett, 1972.

Brinkley, A. *Voices of Protest: Huey Long, Father Coughlin, and the Great Depression*. New York: Alfred A. Knopf, 1982.

Brody, D. *Workers in Industrial America: Essays on the 20th Century Struggle*. New York: Oxford University Press, 1981.

Brown, W. *Piecework Bargaining*. London: Heinemann, 1973.

Brown, W., Ebsworth, R. and Terry, M. 'Factors shaping Shop Steward Organization in Britain'. *British Journal of Industrial Relations*, vol. XVI, no. 2, 1978.

Burawoy, M. *Manufacturing Consent: Changes in the Labor Process under Monopoly Capitalism*. Chicago: University Press, 1979.

Burawoy, M. 'Between the Labor Process and the State: The changing face of Factory Regimes under Advanced Capitalism'. *American Sociological Review*, vol. 48, Oct. 1983.

Bureau of Labor Statistics. *Handbook of Labor Statistics 1977*. Bulletin 1966.

Bureau of Labor Statistics. *Collective Bargaining in the Motor Vehicle and Equipment Industry*. Report 148, October 1959. Report 574, Sept. 1979.

Campbell, A. 'A Classification of Presidential Elections'. In J. M. Clubb and H. W. Allen (eds) *Electoral Change and Stability in American Political History*. New York: Free Press, 1971.

Caute, D. *The Great Fear: The Anti-Communist Purge under Truman and Eisenhower*. London: Secker & Warburg, 1978.

Central Policy Review Staff. *The Future of the British Car Industry*. London: HMSO, 1975.

Chandler, A. D. *Giant Enterprise*. New York: Harcourt, Brace & World, 1964.

Chandler, A. D. *Strategy and Structure*. New York: Doubleday, 1966.

Child, J. *British Managerial Thought*. London: Allen & Unwin, 1969.

Child, J. 'Managerial Strategies, Labour Process and New Technology'. Work Organization Research Centre Occasional Paper. Birmingham: Aston University, 1983 (mimeographed).

Chrysler Corporation. *Beyond the Facts and the Records: War Labor Board Panel admittedly ignores the Evidence and Rewards Union Irresponsibility*. Detroit: Chrysler, 1943.

Chrysler Corporation. *Financial and General Fact Book*. Detroit: Chrysler, 1973.

Cochran, B. *Labor and Communism: The Conflict that Shaped American Unions*. Princeton: Princeton University Press, 1977.

Cohen, R. 'The Employment Consequences of Structural Change in the Auto Industry'. Massachusetts Institute of Technology Research Paper. Boston: MIT, June 1981.

Coughlin, C. E. *The Chrysler CIO Industrial Strike*. Detroit: pamphlet, Nov. 12, 1939.

Davies, D. F. 'The Price of Conspicuous Production: The Detroit Elite and the Automobile Industry, 1900–1933'. *Journal of Social History*, Fall 1982.

Davis, M. 'The Barren Marriage of American Labour and the Democratic Party'. *New Left Review*, vol. 124, Nov.–Dec. 1980.

Denby, C. *Indignant Heart: Testimony of a Black American Worker*. London: Pluto, 1978.

Detroit Free Press. *Blacks in Detroit*. Detroit Free Press reprint, December 1980.

Dunn, R. W. *Labor and Automobiles*. New York: International Publishers, 1929.

Dunnett, P. J. S. *The Decline of the British Motor Industry*. London: Croom Helm, 1980.

Edelstein, J. D. and Warner, M. *Comparative Union Democracy: Organization and Opposition in British and American Unions*. New Brunswick, NJ: Transaction, 1979.

Edwards, P. K. *Strikes in the United States, 1881–1974*. Oxford: Blackwell, 1981.

Edwards, P. K. 'The Exceptionalism of the American Labour Movement: The Neglected Role of Workplace Struggle'. SSRC Industrial Relations Research Unit paper. Coventry: University of Warwick, 1983a.

Edwards, P. K. 'The Political Economy of Industrial Conflict: Britain and the United States'. Industrial Relations Research Unit Research Paper. Coventry: University of Warwick, 1983b.

Fine, S. *The Automobile under the Blue Eagle*. Ann Arbor: University of Michigan, 1963.

Fine, S. *Sit-down: The GM Strike of 1936–1937*. Ann Arbor: University of Michigan, 1969.

Flanders, A. *Management and Unions: The Theory and Reform of Industrial Relations*. London: Faber and Faber, 1975.

Flint, J. 'Everybody Sacrificed, Everybody Profited'. *New York Times*, July 7, 1985.

Foner, P. S. *Organized Labor and the Black Worker, 1619–1973*. New York: International Publishers, 1976.

Forester, T. 'The New Model Halewood'. *New Society*, Feb. 14, 1980.

Fox, A. 'Industrial Sociology and Industrial Relations'. Royal Commission on Trade Unions and Employers Associations, Research Paper 3. London: HMSO, 1966.

Friedlander, P. *The Emergence of a UAW Local, 1936–1939: A Study in Class and Culture*. Pittsburg: University of Pittsburg Press, 1975.

Friedman, A. L. *Industry and Labour: Class Struggle at Work and Monopoly Capitalism*. London: Macmillan, 1977.

Friedman, H. and Meredeen, S. *The Dynamics of Industrial Conflict: Lessons from Ford*. London: Croom Helm, 1980.

Fujita, K. *Black Workers' Struggles in Detroit's Auto Industry, 1935–1975*. Saratoga, CA: Century Twenty-One, 1980.

Georgakas, D. and Surkin, M. *Detroit: I do mind Dying. A Study in Urban Revolution*. New York: St. Martin's, 1975.

Geschwender, J. A. *Class, Race, and Worker Insurgency: The League of Revolutionary Black Workers*. New York: Cambridge University Press, 1977.

Glaberman, M. *Wartime Strikes: The Struggle against the No-strike Pledge in the UAW during World War II*. Detroit: Bewick, 1980.

Goodrich, C. L. *The Frontier of Control*, 1st edn 1920. London: Pluto, 1975.

Gordon, D., Edwards, R. and Reich, M. *Segmented Work, Divided Workers: The Historical Transformation of Labor in the United States*. New York: Cambridge University Press, 1982.

Gouldner, A. W. *Wildcat Strike*. Yellow Springs, OH: Antioch, 1954.

Green, J. R. *The World of the Worker: Labor in Twentieth Century America*. New York: Hill & Wang, 1980.

Greer, E. *Big Steel: Black Politics and Corporate Power in Gary, Indiana*. New York: Monthly Review, 1979.

Guerin, D. *100 Years of Labor in the USA*. London: Ink Links, 1979.

Harris, H. J. *The Right to Manage: Industrial Relations Policies of American Business in the 1940s*. Madison: University of Wisconsin, 1982.

Harvard Business School. *1948 Conflict Negotiations between Chrysler Corporation and the UAW*. Harvard: Harvard Business School, 1948.

Herding, R. *Job Council and Union Structure*. Rotterdam: Rotterdam University Press, 1972.

Hill, S. *Competition and Control at Work*. London: Heinemann, 1981.

Howe, I. and Widick, B. J. *The UAW and Walter Reuther*. New York: Random, 1949.

Humphrey, J. *Capitalist Control and Workers' Struggles in the Brazilian Auto Industry*. Princeton, NJ: Princeton University Press, 1982.

Hyde, C. K. *History of the Dodge Brothers Motor Car Company Plant 1910–1980*. Detroit: Wayne State University, 1981 (mimeographed).

Hyman, R. *Industrial Relations: A Marxist Introduction*. London: Macmillan, 1975.

Hyman, R. and Fryer, R. H. 'Trade Unions: Sociology and Political Economy'. In T. Clements and L. Clarke (eds) *Trade Unions under Capitalism*. London: Fontana, 1977.

Iacocca, L., with Novak, W. *Iacocca: An Autobiography*. London: Sidgwick & Jackson, 1985.

Irvine, H. 'The UAW–CIO Shop Steward. A Consideration of his Role as a Force for Democracy'. M.A. thesis, University of Buffalo, Feb. 1951.

Jefferys, S. 'Recession, Innovation and Industrial Relations: The US Car Industry in Crisis'. *Employee Relations*, vol. V, no. 3, 1983a.

Jefferys, S. 'The Washing-up War'. *New Society*, April 21, 1983b.

Katz, H. *The Decline of the Competition in the Automobile Industry, 1920–1940*. New York: Arno, 1977.

Keeran, R. *The Communist Party and the Auto Workers' Unions*. Bloomington: Indiana University Press, 1980.

Kerr, C. 'Industrial Conflict and its Mediation'. *American Journal of Sociology*, vol. LX, no. 3, Nov. 1954.

Kruchko, J. G. *The Birth of a Union Local: The History of UAW Local 674, Norwood, Ohio, 1933–1940*. New York: Cornell University School of Industrial and Labor Relations, 1972.

Kuhn, J. W. *Bargaining in Grievance Settlement: The Power at Industrial Work Groups*. New York: Columbia University Press, 1961.

Lasch, C. *The Agony of the American Left: One Hundred Years of Radicalism.* London: Penguin, 1973.

Lazonick, W. 'Industrial Relations and Technical Change: The Case of the Self-acting Mule'. *Cambridge Journal of Economics*, no. 3, 1979.

Lens, S. *Radicalism in America.* New York: Cromwell, 1969.

Lichtenstein, N. *Industrial Unionism under the No Strike Pledge: A Study of the CIO during the Second World War.* Ph.D. Thesis, University of California, Berkeley, 1974.

Lichtenstein, N. 'Auto Worker Militancy and the Structure of Factory Life, 1937–1955'. *Journal of American History*, Sept. 1980.

Lichtenstein, N. *Labor's War at Home: The CIO in World War II.* New York: Cambridge University Press, 1982.

Lichtenstein, N. 'Conflict over Workers' Control: the Automobile Industry in World War II'. In Michael H. Frisch and Daniel J. Walleowitz (eds) *Working-class America: Essays on Labor, Community and American Society.* Chicago: University of Illinois Press, 1983.

Lipset, S. M. 'Why no Socialism in the United States?' In Seweryn Bialer (ed.) *Sources of Contemporary Radicalism.* Boulder: Westview, 1977.

Littler, C. R. *The Development of the Labour Process in Capitalist Societies.* London: Heinemann, 1982.

Lubell, S. 'Revolt of the City'. In J. M. Clubb and H. W. Allen (eds) *Electoral Change and Stability in American Political History.* New York: Free Press, 1971.

Lyddon, D. 'Workplace Organization in the British Car Industry. A Critique of Jonathan Zeitlin'. *History Workshop*, no. 15, spring 1983.

Lynd, S. 'Workers' Control in a Time of Diminished Workers' Rights'. *Radical America*, vol. 10, no. 5, Sept.–Oct. 1976.

McCullough, D. 'Chrysler: Capitalizing on the Crisis'. *Changes*, vol. 1, no. 9, Oct. 1979, p. 12.

MacDonald, R. M. *Collective Bargaining in the Automobile Industry: A Study of Wage Structures and Competitive Relations.* New Haven: Yale University Press, 1963.

McPherson, W. *Labor Relations in the Automobile Industry.* Washington DC: Brookings Institute, 1940.

Maitland, I. *The Causes of Industrial Disorder: A Comparison of a British and a German Factory.* London: Routledge and Kegan Paul, 1983.

Mangura, G. L. 'Taming Wildcat Strikes'. *Harvard Business Review*, vol. 38, no. 2, 1960.

Marglin, S. A. 'What do Bosses do? The Origins and Functions of Hierarchy in Capitalist Production'. In Andre Gorz (ed.) *The Division of Labour: The Labour Process and Class Struggle in Modern Capitalism.* Hassocks, Sussex: Harvester, 1978.

Marquart, F. *An Autoworker's Journal.* Pennsylvania: Pennsylvania University Press, 1975.

Mathewson, S. B. *Restriction of Output among Unorganized Workers.* New York: Viking Press, 1931.

Meier, A. and Rudwick, E. *Black Detroit and the Rise of the UAW*. New York: Oxford University Press, 1979.

Mills, D. Q. 'Reforming the United States System of Collective Bargaining'. *Monthly Labor Review*, March 1983.

Moniere, D. *Le developpement des ideologies au Quebec*. Montreal: Editions Quebec/Amerique, 1977.

Montgomery, D. 'Spontaneity and Organization: Some Comments'. *Radical America*, vol. 7, no. 6, Nov.–Dec. 1973.

Montgomery, D. 'To Study the People: The American Working Class'. *Labor History*, vol. 21, no. 4, Fall 1980.

Montgomery, D. 'The Past and Future of Workers' Control'. In J. Green (ed.) *Workers' Struggles, Past and Present: A 'Radical America' Reader*. Philadelphia: Temple University Press, 1983.

Moody, K. and Woodward, J. *Battle Line: The Coal Strike of '78*. Detroit: Sun, 1978.

Moritz, M. and Seaman, B. *Going for Broke: The Chrysler Story*. New York: Doubleday, 1981.

Mortimer, W. *Organize!* Boston: Beacon Press, 1971.

Noble, D. *America by Design: Science, Technology and the Role of Corporate Capitalism*. New York: Alfred A. Kempf, 1977.

Norman, J. G. 'The Crippling of Chrysler'. *Management Today*, Feb. 1981.

Norsworthy, J. R. and Zabala, C. A. 'Worker Attitude, Worker Performance, and Productivity'. *Industrial and Labor Relations*, 1985. Washington DC: Bureau of the Census, Sept. 1983 (mimeographed).

Northrup, H. R. *Industrial Relations*, vol. I, no. 1, Oct. 1961.

Ozanne, R. *A Century of Labor–Management Relations at McCormick and International Harvester*, Madison: University of Wisconsin, 1967.

Pierson, F. C. 'Recent Employer Alliances in Perspective'. *Industrial Relations*, vol. I, no. 1, Oct. 1961.

Polenberg, R. *One Nation Divisible: Class, Race and Ethnicity in the United States since 1938*. New York: Viking, 1980.

Preis, A. *Labor's Giant Step: Twenty Years of the CIO*. New York: Pathfinder, 1972.

Price, R. *Masters, Unions and Men: Work Control in Building and the Rise of Labour, 1830–1914*. Cambridge: Cambridge University Press, 1980.

Reich, R. and Donahue, J. *New Deals: The Chrysler Revival and the American System*. New York: Times Books, 1985.

Reuther, V. G. *The Brothers Reuther and the Story of the UAW*. Boston: Houghton Mifflin, 1976.

Ruben, G. 'Organized Labor in 1981: A Shifting of Priorities'. *Monthly Labor Review*, Jan. 1982.

Ryder, H. L. *British Leyland: The Next Decade*. London: HMSO, 1975.

Sabel, C. F. *Work and Politics: The Division of Labor in Industry*. New York: Cambridge University Press, 1982.

Sayles, L. R., and Srauss, G. *The Local Union*. New York: Harcourt, Brace, 1967.

Schatz, R. 'Union Pioneers: The Founders of Local Unions at General Electric and Westinghouse, 1933–1937'. *Journal of American History*, no. 66, 1979.

Schatz, R. 'American Electrical Workers: Work, Struggle, Aspirations, 1930–1950'. Ph.D. Thesis, University of Pittsburgh, 1977.

Seltzer, L. H. *A Financial History of the American Automobile Industry*. New Jersey: Augusta M. Kelly, 1973.

Serrin, W. *The Company and the Union*. New York: Vintage, 1974.

Slichter, S. H. *Union Policies and Industrial Management*. Washington DC: Brookings Institute, 1941.

Slichter, S. H., Healy, J. E. and Livernash, E. R. *The Impact of Collective Bargaining on Management*. Washington DC: Brookings Institute, 1960.

Sloan, A. P. *My Years with General Motors*. London: Sidgwick & Jackson, 1965.

Steiber, J. *Governing the UAW*. New York: Wiley and Sons, 1962.

Steiber, J. 'Unauthorized Strikes under the American and British Industrial Relations Systems'. *British Journal of Industrial Relations*, vol. 6, no. 2, July 1968.

Stuart, R. *Bailout*. South Bend, IN: And Books, 1980.

Swados, H. 'The UAW – Over the Top or Over the Hill?'. *Dissent*, vol. X, no. 4, Autumn 1963.

Taylor, R. 'Where Edwardes drove BL'. *Management Today*, June 1982.

Terkel, S. *Working*. New York: Avon, 1975.

Thurley, K. and Wood, S. *Industrial Relations and Management Strategy*. London: Cambridge University Press, 1983.

Tolliday, S. 'Government, Employers and Shopfloor Organization in the British Motor Industry, 1939–69'. Research Paper. Cambridge: King's College Research Centre, Sept. 1982.

Tolliday, S. and Zeitlin, J. 'Shop Floor Bargaining, Contract Unionism, and Job Control: An Anglo-American Comparison'. In N. Lichtenstein and S. Meyer (eds) *The American Automobile Industry: A Social History*. Chicago: University of Illinois, 1986.

Turner, G. *The Leyland Papers*. London: Pan, 1973.

Turner, H. A., Clack, G. and Roberts, G. *Labour Relations in the Motor Industry*. London: Allen & Unwin, 1967.

Turner, H. A., Roberts, G. and Roberts, D. *Management Characteristics and Labour Conflict: A Study of Managerial Organization, Attitudes and Industrial Relations*. Cambridge: Cambridge University Press, 1977.

Walker, C. R. and Guest, R. H. *The Man on the Assembly Line*. Cambridge, MA: Harvard University Press, 1952.

Widick, B. J. 'Black Workers: Double Discontent'. In B. J. Widick (ed.) *Auto Work and its Discontents*. Baltimore: Johns Hopkins University Press, 1976.

Williamson, O. E. *Markets and Hierarchies: Analysis and Antitrust Legislation*. New York: Free Press, 1975.

Willman, P. and Winch, G. *Innovation and Management Control: Labour Relations at BL Cars*. Cambridge: Cambridge University Press, 1985.

Winsburg, R. 'The Labours of British Leyland'. *Management Today*, Oct. 1969.

Wintour, P. 'Ford and the Mysteries of the Orient'. *New Statesman*, Nov. 28, 1980.

Wood, S. *The Degradation of Work? Skill, Deskilling and the Labour Process*. London: Hutchinson, 1982.

Wood, S. 'Technological Change and the Cooperitive Labor Strategy'. Mimeographed. Cambridge, MA: Harvard Center for European Studies, 1985.

Zabala, C. A. 'Collective Bargaining at UAW Local 645, General Motors Assembly Division, Van Nuys, California, 1976–1982'. Ph.D. Thesis, University of California, Los Angeles, 1983.

Zeitlin, J. 'Workplace Organization in the British Car Industry: A Review'. *History Workshop*, vol. 10, Autumn 1980.

Index